PULLING THE RIGHT THREADS

Pulling the Right Threads

THE ETHNOGRAPHIC LIFE AND
LEGACY OF JANE C. GOODALE

Edited by
LAURA ZIMMER-TAMAKOSHI AND
JEANETTE DICKERSON-PUTMAN

UNIVERSITY OF ILLINOIS PRESS
URBANA AND CHICAGO

Library of Congress Cataloging-in-Publication Data
Pulling the right threads : the ethnographic life and legacy
of Jane C. Goodale / edited by Laura Zimmer-Tamakoshi and
Jeanette Dickerson-Putman.
p. cm.

"This volume grew out of two special sessions in honor of
Jane C. Goodale . . . at the annual meetings of the American
Anthropological Association (1998) and the Association for
Social Anthropology in Oceania (2003)"—Ack.

Includes bibliographical references and index.
ISBN-13: 978-0-252-03267-7 (cloth : alk. paper)
ISBN-10: 0-252-03267-5 (cloth : alk. paper)
ISBN-13: 978-0-252-07484-4 (pbk. : alk. paper)
ISBN-10: 0-252-07484-x (pbk. : alk. paper)
1. Goodale, Jane C. (Jane Carter), 1926–
2. Women ethnologists—United States—Biography.
3. Women ethnologists—Papua New Guinea—Biography.
4. Feminist anthropology.
5. Tiwi (Australian people)
6. Kaulong (Papua New Guinean people)
I. Zimmer-Tamakoshi, Laura, 1944–
II. Dickerson-Putman, Jeanette.
GN21.G66P85   2008
305.80092—dc22 [B]   2007023283

Contents

Acknowledgments

This volume grew out of two special sessions in honor of Jane C. Goodale. The sessions were organized by Laura Zimmer-Tamakoshi and Jeanette Dickerson-Putman and were given at the annual meetings of the American Anthropological Association (1998) and the Association for Social Anthropology in Oceania (2003). Fred Myers served as discussant at the AAA session. With the exception of Jane Fajans, the contributors to this volume presented earlier versions of their chapters in one or both special sessions. The coorganizers invited a variety of Jane's former students and colleagues to participate in these seminal sessions. Unfortunately, not all of these individuals were able to participate, and Bob Rubinstein, who gave a paper at the 1998 session, was unable to contribute a chapter for this volume. Individuals who contributed to these sessions in various ways but did not write papers include Ann Chowning, the late Freddy de Laguna, Ward Goodenough, and Phil Kilbride. Jeanette and Laura would like to thank all the participants for the parts they played in honoring Jane's legacy. In addition, they especially would like to thank their husbands, Duncan Putman and Ryojin Tamakoshi, for their patience and support.

LAURA ZIMMER-TAMAKOSHI

Introduction

Theoretically stimulating and often cited, an early piece on Tiwi marriage contracts (1962) and her groundbreaking *Tiwi Wives* (1971) earned Jane Goodale the immediate respect and ongoing interest of other scholars (Estioko-Griffin and Griffin 1981; Keesing 1975; Lepowsky 1993; Meggitt 1968; Slocum 1975; Yengoyan 1968). While Marcus and Fischer (1986) characterize such grounded works as ethnographic realism, reflexivity is a core element in Jane's views and teachings on the ethnographic enterprise. As striking as Jane's considerable body of writings on her research in Australia and Papua New Guinea (PNG) have been her generous commitment of time and ideas to students and colleagues and her evident empathy for the people she studies. The writers in this volume recognize and build on these seminal aspects of Jane's work. They investigate the ways Jane has helped shape ethnographic and theoretical contributions in such fields as gender studies, the anthropology of aging, Pacific ethnography, and applied and development anthropology. They honor Jane's teaching and involvement in the development of the anthropology program at Bryn Mawr College, the Philadelphia Anthropological Society (PAS), and the Association for Social Anthropology in Oceania (ASAO); in addition, they reflect upon Jane's experimental, engaged, and moral ethnographic stance and her place in the history and future of anthropology.

Jane's New England–bred diffidence prevents her from the self-promotion that earmarks trendsetters who "reinvent anthropology" by lumping other anthropologists under contrasting and unsavory labels. Yet it is obvious from the chapters in this book that for over half a century Jane

I

has been a vibrant and generative presence in an evolving and contentious field. It should also be obvious that Jane's teaching of ethnographic methods and her empirically grounded, holistic, morally sensitive, and collaborative ethnography are equally suited for twenty-first-century anthropology. "Pulling the right thread"—Jane's metaphor for solving ethnographic puzzles (and, one might add, picking students and colleagues)—is as apt a metaphor for anthropological praxis as more masculine metaphors of "following anthropological trails" and "routes." Although it is true that our informants are everywhere and that we must trail after them in complex global fields, they often conceive of their societies and cultural identities as being singular, of a piece however variegated or internally contested. Examples include a Pacific "*sea* of islands"; a Papua New Guinea "*parliament* of a thousand tribes"; the Melanesian "*way*." By *pulling the right threads*[1] themselves, the contributors[2] to this volume share the richness of the ethnographic and anthropological tapestries Jane helped reveal and—in the case of "ASAO" and "Bryn Mawr anthropology"—helped to fashion.

The Field Is Everywhere

One piece of advice Jane gave to all of us is that "the field is everywhere." At my off-to-Papua-New-Guinea-for-the-first-time party—hosted by Jeanette and Duncan Putman on a cold day in late January 1982—Jane reiterated this advice, telling me that if I hadn't already done so, I should start keeping a field journal at once. I worried aloud that sometimes there might be nothing special to write about. Both Jane and Freddy de Laguna cried out, "Write anyway!" Recording as much as one can on a daily basis (and well before entering one's official field site), one preserves details and context that upon reflection make greater sense and often produce surprising threads to pull. The prescience of Jane's advice was not long in manifesting itself.

Reviewing my field notes for February 2, 1982, I am reminded that on the flight from Los Angeles to Honolulu "I sat next to a very large Hawaiian man, married with three children. I was crunched into the window seat of the Pan Am 747" and wanted only to lose myself in tears and missing my own family. The man lectured me on the unlikelihood of my research bringing about "changes beneficial to indigenous peoples" and the "immorality of Americans doing research in Papua New Guinea rather than Hawaii or Micronesia where they might rectify injustices brought about by their own kind." A week later, after a stopover in Australia and another night flight, I landed in the dark at Jackson Airport in

Port Moresby. My immediate concerns were being picked up at the airport and making duty calls to government officers and resident academics before beginning fieldwork on migration and rural-urban exchange in Morobe Province. In Lae, the capital of Morobe Province, I continued to meet with important people, including leaders of the Pindiu people I hoped to do research with. Most meetings were perfunctory and encouraging. I had received official permission to do the research months before leaving the States. But someone in the government was now throwing up roadblocks and stalling my progress. My journal entries for the next several months reveal my descent into a world in which anthropology was decidedly on trial and Papua New Guinean nationalists and their expatriate advisers were the judges. I have yet to share this saga in a publication, but, thanks to Jane, it is in my notes. With the perspectives and knowledge I have gained in the years since—on the politics of culture in the Pacific, on nationalism and sexuality, and with Hawaiian sovereignty activists on teaching the "new Pacific"—I may one day write that saga. For now, reflecting on old notes, I wish I'd written down my Hawaiian airplane partner's name. I wonder how his life turned out. Does he have grandchildren, as I do? Is he as radical now as he claimed to be? Would he be surprised—or even care—that after I was unfairly ousted from Morobe, I worked in other parts of Papua New Guinea and, later, worked with Papua New Guinean academics at the University of Papua New Guinea (UPNG), teaching students how to do ethnography in their own country and abroad? And would his reactions to me have been different if I had been male and not female? I believe so, for as I discuss in my chapter, gender played a role in all my field experiences even though my research was never about women only.

While seemingly simplistic, "the field is everywhere" is a nuanced expression. A primary meaning, evident in my interaction with the Hawaiian activist, is that the cultures we study, however unique each may be, are systems within systems, systems whose boundaries are permeable and not easily defined because people move about and interact with other people and because people and cultures change over time. When Jane first visited the Tiwi in 1954, they were not isolated from the rest of Australia. Tiwi living at Snake Bay Settlement were under the supervision of F. H. Grimster, his assistant supervisor, and a schoolteacher (Goodale 1971: xvi). Nevertheless, in 1954, the Tiwi (and Jane) enjoyed the freedom of living on two naturally abundant islands where they went off to the bush to hunt and gather in much the same way as their ancestors had and continued to enact traditional Tiwi rites of passage. By 1962 (the time of Jane's second field trip), most of the resident Snake Bay Tiwi were attending school or—along with aborigines from other tribes—were employed at a local full-scale forestry project (Goodale 1971: xx). Representing Tiwi culture and social organization as "a consistently fluid, flexible, and structurally changeable entity," Jane incorporated egocentric and diachronic sociocentric analyses in *Tiwi Wives*, using her own and other's data from a time span of about fifty years, from 1914 to 1962 (1971: xxiv).

In chapter 10, Eric Venbrux expands his field to discover the cause and cultural ramifications of a 1913 epidemic that killed 200 (out of a total of 650–700) Melville and Bathurst islanders. The first non-Tiwi to investigate the epidemic, Australian medical officer H. K. Fry, concluded that a low number of infant deaths supported the native diagnosis of magic as opposed to measles. Thirty years later, in 1954, Jane observed Tiwi men discussing "the fact that the people of the islands were now few because the white people had brought other tribesmen into their land who sang magic songs of poison that caused the tribe to dwindle" (1971: 224). Over the course of many field trips, Jane maintained an interest in the impact of the epidemic on Tiwi society and Tiwi ceremony. Spurred by Jane's call for further investigation into the cause of the epidemic (Goodale 1971: 225), Venbrux examines early- and later-twentieth-century Tiwi discussions and cultural production in relation to the epidemic by situating them—as they were in reality—in intercultural spaces in which Tiwi interact with other Australian Aborigines and white people at historical moments. Viewed this way, in time and intercultural space, Tiwi religion and worldview are shown in the processes of both accommodation and resistance to the wider world.

The concept of a larger, complex field of cultures and societies is evident in most of the chapters in this book. Multisited fieldwork of the sort carried out by Pam Rosi (studying PNG artists at the National Arts School in Port Moresby, at a settlement on the town "dump," and during art exhibitions in the United States) or Mimi Kahn (interacting with Tahitians in places as far apart as French Polynesia and tattoo parlors in Seattle) is becoming a commonplace anthropological experience. Noting that 40 percent of Jane's doctoral students did their dissertations on places and cultures outside of Oceania, Joy Bilharz's chapter raises a second nuance to the notion that the field is everywhere: an anthropological understanding of the world that is multiauthored and multisited. While Jane never did research with the Allegany Seneca, her work in the Pacific and her knowledge of similar cultures enabled her to relate to Bilharz's data on many levels and find comparative interest in Seneca social organization (matrilineal descent) and the fact that although Seneca women (once the traditional providers and distributors of food staples) were disenfranchised in 1848, they continue to exercise considerable informal political power by dominating committees (and associated rehabilitation funds) concerned with traditional female domains such as education and health.

In his chapter, Mike Lieber elaborates on this larger field and collaboration, what he sees as the core of Jane's success as researcher, colleague, and educator. Jane's affinity for collaboration is grounded in awareness that there are different angles to be explored in any cultural setting (e.g., Tiwi society from Tiwi women's point of view) as well as rich fields of comparative research and puzzles to be solved within particular regions of the world or among similar societies. Writing about the Kaulong of West New Britain in "Pig's Teeth and Skull Cycles" (Goodale 1985: 228), Jane situates the Kaulong within the larger field of Melanesian studies, contending that each [Melanesian] "society" is linked to other Melanesian societies through exchange and ritual activities so that "Melanesia is, truly, and indigenously, a plural society of considerable structural complexity."

Widening the field, Lieber illustrates how his work in Kapingamarangi, a Polynesian atoll in Micronesia, and Jane's work with the Kaulong and Tiwi benefited from their ongoing dialogue. Both Lieber and Jane were founders of the Association for Social Anthropology in Oceania (ASAO). Both helped develop its multiyear evolving-discussion format of ethnographic comparison and "face-to-face engagement" among a group of researchers focusing on a single ethnographic topic, such as adoption in Oceania. Jane's students and colleagues alike have benefited from ASAO's collaborative process and Jane's inherent generosity and openness. Eric Venbrux notes how Jane graciously evolved from being a mentor to a young colleague to being his informant in his search for answers to the Tiwi epidemic puzzle. Nowhere, however, is the impact of Jane's emphasis on collaboration and collegiality more evident than among her former students. Jane encouraged students to learn from one another and to consider one another (and herself) future colleagues. Each of us can recite our own chain of connections.

Around the time of my first fieldwork, mine included Ali Pomponio, Mimi Kahn, and Bob Rubinstein. All three had returned from the field and were working on their Ph.D. dissertations at Bryn Mawr College, and each gave helpful advice on maintaining my health and sanity in the field as well as the names of useful contacts in Port Moresby. In turn, I was useful to Jeanette Dickerson and Pam Rosi. Jeanette and I practiced Tok Pisin once a week for a year before I left for Papua New Guinea in 1982. Jeanette arrived in the highlands more than a year later and, along with my Gende "parents," I showed up at the Lutheran Guest House in time to cheer her up during her first experience of homesickness and culture shock.

Over the years, the chains have lengthened and intertwined in intricate patterns of collaboration and support. Because Jane also encouraged those of us who hoped to work in Oceania to attend ASAO meetings well before any of us went to the field, we early on developed a sense of the ASAO process and a fair degree of comfort with other ASAO members. In the introduction to her chapter, Jane Fajans remarks how her participation in the ASAO community gave her confidence and solidified her desire to go to Melanesia. All of us who work in Oceania could say the same. At my first ASAO meeting in 1978, however, when I was a first-year graduate student and many of those present were students or former students of Jane's, I was privy to the sour comment made by one long-term member who was discomfited by our enthusiastic presence and branded us the "Bryn Mawr Mafia." That this expression is now a term of endearment is a testament to Jane, Mike Lieber, David and Dorothy Counts, Mac Marshall, and numerous other committed ASAO members who over the years have welcomed students into the ranks and to the fact that many of these students have gone on to hold ASAO leadership positions themselves and encouraged their own students to participate in the ASAO experience.

Jane's relationship with her students yields a third understanding of the dictum, "the field is everywhere," and that is that the classroom is part of the larger field or ethnographic enterprise. Not only did Jane illustrate lectures with cultural specifics and colorful slides of Tiwi or Kaulong ceremonies, but she also brought her own interpretive puzzles and ethical issues into the classroom for discussion. Demystifying ethnography, Jane gave us the tools we needed to begin thinking and acting like anthropologists. We, in turn, gave her more to think about as she wrestled with her material. Jane freely acknowledged these intellectual exchanges with current and former students, both in general—"the students at Bryn Mawr College" (Goodale 1996b: ix)—and by name, as in her article on Kaulong siblings as spouses—"Judith Huntsman, Robert Rubinstein, DeVerne Smith and Annette Weiner" (Goodale 1983/1979: 304). Teachers often admit that teaching is a learning experience, but at Bryn Mawr, Jane institutionalized the process. In her chapter, Joy Bilharz remembers the lively discussions held among faculty and students during Pig Lunch, an institution introduced by Jane and her first graduate student Judith Huntsman.

As Jeanette makes clear in her retrospective, Jane's emphasis on making field methodology a regular part of students' education derives from her own lack of such experience on the eve of her first fieldwork in 1954. Working with Bryn Mawr College colleague Phil Kilbride, Jane guided hundreds of undergraduates and graduates through intensive methods training (see Mimi Kahn's chapter). In 1990, Phil and Jane were coeditors along with former undergraduate Elizabeth R. Ameisen (and in collaboration with Carolyn G. Friedman) of *Encounters With American Ethnic Cultures*, a collection based on original field studies carried out by Bryn Mawr students as part of an undergraduate methods seminar.

Several of Jane's non–Bryn Mawr colleagues—including Bill Davenport from the University of Pennsylvania and Mike Lieber (University of Illinois at Chicago)—chose to teach at Bryn Mawr for a semester or two as a way of learning Jane's "secret" to producing so many outstanding undergraduate and graduate students in anthropology. Mike characterizes Jane's relationship with her students as evolving from a master–apprentice relationship in the beginning to a partnership by the time dissertations are being written. Jane's engagement with her students' fieldwork is often personal, with letters to the field and sometimes visits, as when she visited Mimi Kahn in French Polynesia, Debbie Rose in Australia, and me in Port Moresby when I was teaching at the University of Papua New Guinea. Her most intensely interactive field partnership was with anthropologist Ann Chowning as they carried out tandem field studies of nearby peoples in West New Britain, visiting one another's "villages" and discussing and arguing data and interpretations, some of which is captured in Jane's *The Two-Party Line* (1996b).

However far or near, Jane's advice and example are with us in the field, as are the advice and examples of others in our far-flung field of anthropological inquiry. A fourth nuance to Jane's sense of the field is that whatever boundaries exist between informants and fieldworker, most are permeable. Permeability makes participant observation and the acquisition of an insider's perspective possible. It allows for friendships to grow. And the subjects of our ethnographic gaze achieve ethnographic understandings of their own: of us as cultured beings and of the difficulties, complexities, and awkward fit of their own culture as they observe it through our first fumbling efforts. In his chapter, Bill Donner relates how, as one of the older bachelors on Sikaiana, he was the subject of good-natured ridicule for his then-unmarried state as well as an accepted part of a "very personal, public community" characterized by "constant interaction, participation in, and knowledge about one another's life." Being privy to men's and women's reflections upon their marital and extramarital affairs afforded Donner a comfortable grasp of how sexuality is integrated into relations between men and women on Sikaiana.

His understanding deepened over the course of several field trips as he continued playing the roles of unmarried Sikaiana bachelor and foreign ethnographer. Donner had become an integral, albeit somewhat odd or foreign, part of the field he studied. Families, too, often are part of our field studies. Mimi Kahn recounts many "human interactions" she and her husband and daughter had in Huahine, including being drawn into a dance competition on the island of Taha'a. How interactive and gratifying the field can be for both sides of the ethnographic equation is evident in a poem written by Debbie Rose's daughter, Chantal Jackson (2003). A now-grown Chantal remembers dancing, as a child, in the company of her mother and Australian Aboriginal women as they "made boys into men." Remembering that ceremony, Chantal writes how she was set free by the women to be "one who decides and acts" like an adult as the boys' "childhood fell away."

It is not always so easy. Jane has often noted that she felt more akin to the Tiwi than the Kaulong. In Jeanette Dickerson's retrospective of Jane's life and work, Jane comments that it was "easy to establish rapport with the Tiwi because they shared a set of core values based around the importance of reciprocal relationships within the family and because they were quick to reach out and establish relationships as individuals." One of Jane's closest relationships was with Happy: "'I first went off to the bush with her. I knew she was fond of me and I was fond of her.'" Jane found her research with the Kaulong of Papua New Guinea more challenging and often alienating. "'The Kaulong cultural ethos of what is right to do was diametrically opposite from what the Tiwi ethos is. The Kaulong are competitive where the Tiwi are cooperative. . . . It was a constant battle with my own culture. . . . One of the biggest shocks of the Kaulong was this whole credit economy.'" Being a New England Yankee, this was foreign to her.

Learning from People, Not Voices

Regardless of the challenges the Kaulong posed, Jane achieved many penetrating analyses of Kaulong society and cultural beliefs. One especially difficult fact of Kaulong life for Jane was their keen sense of privacy and the separation of married from nonmarried persons, with couples (and their children) spending much of their time away from the hamlets and villages in their gardens and garden houses. Forced to reside in a settlement often deserted during the day by all but the occasional child or two, Jane remembers searching for her informants in their garden homes, often several miles distant. By night the settlement housed her single male assistants and occasionally other single men or married families. Rarely, except for government-enforced workdays (Mondays), the settlement would fill up for important events. The very thing that made her Kaulong fieldwork difficult, however, became a source of important insights.

In a paper published in 1980, Jane used her Kaulong data to effectively challenge social science models attributing women's inequality to universal cultural models equating women with nature (inferior) and men with culture (superior) as well as a private–public dichotomy in which men dominate the public sphere of life. The Kaulong did not place women as a category on the periphery with men at the center. Rather, the Kaulong model was one in which *culture* was symbolically associated with "human" activities in the "clearing" (subsistence gardening, clearing the forest for new hamlets and gardens, trade, pig raising, and establishing peaceful relationships) and *nature* was associated with "nonhuman" activities in the "forest" (sexual reproduction, associating with spirits and wild pigs while hunting and foraging in the forest, and aggressive relationships). Men and women were to be found equally in these different spheres. Within the Kaulong household, there was little necessary sexual division of labor. Both men and women could raise and exchange pigs and ambitious bachelors could rely on mothers and sisters to help them raise pigs for distribution.

A primary reason for Kaulong marriage was reproduction. Given the Kaulong belief in the lethal effects of sex for men, men were wary of marriage, putting it off as long as they could, in some cases forever. In her paper on "Siblings as Spouses" (1983/1979: 277–79), Jane states that the "Kaulong are not as concerned with maintaining a cultural distinction between men and women as they are in distinguishing between the sexually active and the celibate" and that the Kaulong see a conceptual similarity between the "sexual intimacy defining the spouse relationship (required to reproduce persons important to the hamlet through time) and between the economic, emotional, nurturant intimacy defining the brother–sister relationship (also necessary to maintaining the hamlet resources and identity through time)." Thirty years after the bulk of her actual fieldwork with the Kaulong, Jane integrated these and other insights in a comprehensive description and interpretation in *To Sing With Pigs Is Human* (1995).

A part of Jane's success is her understanding that culture and the creation of meaning is a human process, achieved by people pursuing specific goals and discovered—usually through many blunders—by all-too-human anthropologists. Observing and interacting with people—and not disembodied "male" or "female" voices—anthropologists learn just enough details, distinctions, and complexities to make finding patterns or threads difficult but not—if the anthropologist keeps at it—impossible. Jane's ethnographic process among the Kaulong was grounded in this kind of inductive research and "in the field" conversations and correspondence with nearby anthropologist and friend Ann Chowning. This experiential process—at once inductive and comparative—is captured in Jane's *The Two-Party Line* (1996b). Working in separate language groups, Jane and Ann could not assume that the Kaulong and Sengseng cultures were similar in any way until demonstrated. Jane admits that she and Ann fruitfully used this comparative back-and-forth method to inspire their Kaulong and Sengseng assistants to compete to teach the anthropologists various aspects of their cultures (1996b: 181). Comparison allowed them to formulate hypotheses that could then be tested almost at once. In a later field trip, when she worked with the more acculturated Kaulong living in Angelek, Jane would discover, through comparisons of a different kind, that "curiosity about the *other* is learned behavior." In contrast to Umbi, the Kaulong living at Angelek had experienced earlier and more extensive contact with Europeans and Asians and were constantly asking Jane questions about her culture at the same time she was asking them about theirs (1996b: 189–90).

In "Pulling the Right Thread" (this volume), Michele Dominy examines Jane's practice and teaching of anthropology and her allegiance to ethnographic realism and the need to balance theoretical assertions with ethnographic cases and details. Looking back over notes she had written during a required undergraduate majors course taken with "Miss Goodale" back in the fall of 1972, Dominy was "surprised to discover in Jane's instructions for taking the final exam [the source of] the same guidelines" that Dominy gives to her own students some thirty years later. According to Dominy, Jane's legacy to her students and to anthropology can be summed up in five words: depth, breadth, integration, comparison, and theory. Jane's instructions to "balance theoretical assertions with ethnographic cases [is a] relationship we now call 'praxis.'" Dominy also refers to the use of Frederica de Laguna's "Style Sheet for Taking Notes in Anthropology." Notes are recorded on one side of a page while metacommentary is recorded on the other, a process now called "dialectical notebooks" and necessary to respecting the multiple authorships of fieldwork practice. Putting Jane's praxis into practice, Dominy recalls how her course notes, while mainly factual, also include marginal notes on Jane's classroom asides. Dominy notes that Jane's advice and assertions "belie the presumed straightforwardness of the realist idiom and its ally 'ethnographic typification'" and are strongly inductive and empirical in motivation. Rather than simplify matters, Jane advised her students to find exceptions and to remember that despite structural similarities, underlying reasons may vary. Honoring complexity and individuality, Jane calls on us to find the thread that holds an intricate system or pattern together.

A commitment to learning from individuals and honoring complexity is evident in the papers in this volume. In his chapter, Bill Donner continually links his statements on Sikaiana gender relations to the actions of many different people, individuals who sat down and talked with him about their past affairs or the veracity of particular songs regarding the past love affairs and conquests of others and sung at ceremonial song festivals. On every page, Bill grounds his generalizations in specifics: "Most people, including women, told me . . ."; "Sometimes, young men . . ."; "Many parents . . ."; "Some Sikaiana . . ."; and "One elderly woman. . . ." Like Dominy and Fajans in their chapters, Donner recognizes Jane's greatest inspiration to her students to be her stress on the importance of "a holistic and sympathetic study of other cultures," integrative analyses and symbolic interpretations based upon ethnographic descriptions that are rich in detail, and a commitment to solving the puzzles or pulling the right thread even if one's research simply leads to even more questions to perplex us. Bill recalls how Jane "stressed that anthropology was for the curious, and that intellectual progress was not so much in finding answers, but in asking better questions." It is also essential to recognize individual "agency," a contemporary concept that Jane taught but rarely referred to as such. In Jane's conception of things, people are individual agents of cultural transmission and emergence, not types or all-inclusive voices representing entire social categories.

A Reflexive and Moral Anthropology

How challenging today's ethnographic fieldwork can be and how difficult it is to generalize about the lives and interactions of real people became evident when I returned to Papua New Guinea in 1986 (and for years after) to teach at UPNG and extend my village studies to include urban settlements and sites of potential economic development for the Gende people. In Port Moresby, the Gende were everywhere—on the faculty, in my classroom, cleaning the library, in the grocery store, at the airport, and in my guest room when they were in town and needed a place to stay—and it was impossible to see them as simply informants. When Pam Rosi (this volume) stayed with me during her first fieldwork, she and I were part of an expatriate and local elite social set that gave and attended lavish parties and dinners. Drinks in hand at a faculty club Halloween party, we laughed along with everyone else at a Papua New Guinean colleague dressed up as a cartoon character—Roots—while the real grass roots bussed tables or stood outside the gates observing our peculiar rites. Although we also spent much of our time with people of more humble means and were by no means snobs, class differences were obvious in town and we sometimes found ourselves in awkward situations. Self-consciousness was a given. Dancing at the club was decidedly different than dressing up in traditional attire and dancing at village festivals. Our hosts in the village and university, however, expected both behaviors. Were we to go barefoot and act like *meri bilong ples* (village women) in town (as one young Australian woman did), both sides of the class divide would have mocked us. As it was, participating in both contexts and being open to discussion about the inevitable inequalities resulted in rich social interactions and ethnographic knowledge. Sometimes, however, the resulting interactions were upsetting, as when a drunken expatriate and, on another occasion, a local politician attempted to assault me be-cause—from a conservative (or opportunistic) male perspective—danc-ing at discos demonstrates a looseness often attributed to *ol meri bilong taun* (townswomen). None of this escaped the attention of my long-term field population living back in the Gende homeland in Madang Province. During a visit to Yandera village—two airplane rides and a twenty-mile hike away from Port Moresby—my Gende family advised that I should quit teaching at that "immoral university" and help develop the village. They also suggested, only half seriously, that if I married one of those rich, urban elites, I could bring them a big bride-price!

What draws us to Jane—her most appealing characteristic and the basis of her ethnographic prowess—is her moral engagement with every person she interacts with. She fully understands the ethical dilemmas and multiple spaces anthropologists face in an extended field. For Jane, competent ethnography and teaching require a reflexive and moral em-pathy for both individuals and their cultures. The Tiwi and Kaulong are as complex as us. They are not steps in some evolutionary chain that leads to us. Rather, they can tell us things about contemporary cul-tural process. At the 1998 AAA session we organized in honor of Jane, our discussant Fred Myers noted that Jane paid serious attention to the Tiwi and Kaulong, an ethical stance that Bob Rubinstein—also a partici-pant—described as pragmatic, positional, expansive, and moral. Being an anthropologist requires cultural empathy and respect for individuals, differences, seeming chaos, and other ways. As everyone who knows her discovers, Jane is impatient with arrogance. She can go anywhere and with anyone, secure in her own humanity, never patronizing or elitist. In the classroom, she nurtured her students by listening and teaching without domination or special claims of authority. She often insisted that graduate students call her "Jane." In her chapter, Joy Bilharz writes that Jane's humanity is extended to giving something back and always asking herself, Have I gotten it right? Jane's respect for others also shows in her commitment to her students—Bryn Mawr Mafia and non-Mafia alike. As all of us can attest, she supported us through thick and thin, through traumatic separations from loved ones and difficulties in the field. When my permission to do research in Morobe Province was abruptly rescinded in 1982, it was as much Jane's reputation as a fair-minded, decent human being and ethnographer that encouraged others to help me stay in Papua New Guinea and to relocate to Madang Province. Believing in me, Jane cashed her chips in and made the necessary phone calls to key persons. After that, it was up to me. With that kind of support, you can't quit, no matter how ready you are to throw in the towel. Besides, Jane said, just think of all you have already learned about politics and culture in Papua New Guinea!

Two of the 1998 session participants focused in particular on Jane's reflexive and moral empathy. In his paper, Bob Rubinstein attributed Jane's moral stance as influencing his work on the anthropology of aging by setting up a morally "valued space in which individuals are accorded pragmatic wholeness and in which there is the notion that everything makes sense." Assuming cultural systems are rational imbues them and the individuals who create them with moral authority. Ethnographers are faced with the task of teasing apart the many layers and textures of this moral space, of recognizing "native sensibility in creating hybridity and in choosing to accept or reject external phenomena." Rubinstein believes that Jane's thoughts in this area occurred before current ideas on "resistance," "master stories," and the like. When, more than twenty years ago, Rubinstein began fieldwork with older informants in Philadelphia, there was little research to draw upon other than quantitative, psychological studies that never questioned long-held assumptions about the needs and feelings of the elderly. Taking the lead from Jane, Bob's initial focus was pragmatic. After hours spent discussing and following his informants' daily activities, Bob discovered the men were "managing and reflecting on their routines and how these related to their sense of self in a culture that did not value them." Beyond even a pragmatic function, the men's routines were acts of "self-presentation, self-identity, and narrativization of the self to establish, maintain, and communicate the self to others and to oneself." More interesting than a simple study of social roles, focusing on the experiential positioning of older men and women over the course of their lives opened up personal cultures and lives rich in experience and meaning, as well as the psychological, symbolic, and cultural mechanisms that organize narrative accounts of self. As Jane taught us, there is honor and symbolism in everyday acts and their entailments. In Bob's words, "Each informant has a moral stance, a value, and something to teach me" (Rubinstein 1998).

In her chapter, Debbie Rose recalls Jane's methods course, claiming that it was the most engaging and continuously relevant of all her anthropology course work. Especially important was Jane's belief that in good anthropology, methods and ethics are enmeshed. Drawing on Gregory Bateson's *Naven* (1958/1936) and *Steps to an Ecology of the Mind* (1972), Jane taught that anthropology's central method is "learning to learn." Good fieldwork requires opening ourselves to other people's epistemologies, a whole-person experience that is both cognitive and emotional and experiential. Essential to this deuterolearning, which leads us to contextualize boundaries of discipline and of categories as well as boundaries of a normative or rational self, is an *engaged attention*. In Debbie's view, "an ethical encounter demands of anthropologists that we engage attentively [*both*] with our [research]/teachers *and* with that which engages . . . [their attention.]" Reflecting on her research, Debbie writes of how the Yarralin people of Australia see humans as having at least two animating spirits: one that keeps returning from life to life, and another that returns to the country to become a nurturing presence. When Jessie, Debbie's Yarralin friend, dies, she joins the other "dead bodies" in her country, becoming part of a nourishing ecology of the place. Noting that colonization has meant the obliteration of languages and the destruction of environments and whole clans or tribes, Debbie writes that her friend and others experience *double death*. The first death is ordinary death; the second is the impossibility for Jessie's spirit to overcome the ecological violence rendered in her country.

Debbie imagines a third death for the people we study; namely, obliteration brought about by anthropologists' silences about such matters. Holding one's self open to learning how others learn is risky because you do not know where it will lead. Yet by making yourself available to others, you learn what needs saying or doing or believing in. In her chapter, Pam Rosi describes her conflicts about whether helping Papua New Guinea artists to display their works of art in the United States sets up unrealistic expectations for the artists and their families. Shall she let them drift, virtually unrecognized by their own government? Or should she intervene? I struggle with similar issues as in just how much to reveal when I write about gender violence in Papua New Guinea. Risking men's ire and the possibility of violent payback, I choose to write about the subject for women and girls who cannot so readily escape their dangerous social environment. Such moral dilemmas teach us about the realities of life for the people we study. Having Jane as a role model, we can neither ignore ethics nor shy away from any but ardent and exacting engagement.

Jane Goodale and Late-Twentieth- and Twenty-First-Century Anthropology

In the last decades of the twentieth century, some anthropologists writhed in crises of confidence regarding the proper subjects of anthropology, anthropological methods, and anthropological representations. Responding to challenges from Third World intellectuals, newly politicized minorities, and social protest movements over who was doing what to whom and who was being left out, self-appointed arbiters of Western anthropology called for a new or *reinvented anthropology*. Ignoring many solid, change-oriented, and innovative ethnographies of their contemporaries and earlier generations of anthropologists, anthropology's critics selectively focused on the worst misunderstandings and misrepresentations of *others'* cultures, implying that all anthropology—except their own—was seriously flawed. In his introduction to *Reinventing Anthropology* (1972), Dell Hymes depicted anthropology as a discipline that specializes in the study of others who increasingly reject it. Commenting favorably—but only briefly—on a proliferation of detailed ethnographies that represented cultures "in their own terms," he dismissed the methodological relativism that underpins such studies as an inadequate ethnographic stance for systematic inquiries into the complexities of modern life. Hymes argued the necessity to include institutional anthropology and the emerging world community in the larger picture or context of whatever group or society we are studying. In Hymes's view, anthropologists could more fruitfully study culture(s) if they took a historical perspective and viewed cultures in terms of both tradition and emergent cultural practices. An anthropology that might survive outside challenge would be one that is self-critical as well as critical, dialectical, and activist. According to Hymes, anthropologists should strive for a more political and ethical discipline, a discipline that advances our empirical knowledge at the same time as it advances the welfare of humanity; a discipline that seeks mutuality in formulating what others already know and pays serious attention to questions of who benefits from the knowledge we collect and represent for world consumption. A professor at the University of Pennsylvania and frequenter of the Philadelphia Anthropological Society meetings, Hymes should have been aware of the more "historical" research and publications of many of the attendees, including Jane and her early graduate students (Judith Huntsman, Carol Hoffer, Annette Weiner, Fred Myers, and DeVerne Smith[3]) who attended PAS meetings back in the sixties and early seventies. Even before the publication of *Tiwi Wives* (1971), Jane was researching and writing about the 1964 and 1968 national elections and local politics leading up to Papua New Guinea independence in 1975 (Chowning and Goodale 1965; Chowning et al. 1971) and ritual change among the Tiwi (Goodale 1970). In representing anthropology as stuck in the past and unconcerned with change, inequality, and the politics of culture, Hymes ignored his contemporaries and anthropological classics such as Margaret Mead's *New Lives for Old* (1956), Richard Salisbury's *From Stone to Steel* (1962), Peter Lawrence's *Road Belong Cargo* (1964) and Hortense Powdermaker's *Stranger and Friend* (1966), all of which are standard fare in courses on theory and methodology, economic anthropology, and Melanesia.

In 1986, a collection of essays arising out of a 1984 seminar at the School of American Research and edited by anthropologists James Clifford and George Marcus was even more critical of Western ethnography, arguing that all ethnographies are rhetorical performances and at best represent partial truths in their portrayals of non-Western peoples. In his introduction to *Writing Culture*, Clifford observed that "the usual portrait of anthropological fieldwork" is of the anthropologist engaged in participant observation and not seated at a typewriter creating texts. According to Clifford, this misrepresentation obscures writing's centrality to what anthropologists do both in the field and after, ethnography involving more than "keeping good field notes, making accurate maps, 'writing up' results" (Clifford and Marcus 1986: 2).

Clifford and the other essayists in *Writing Culture* "see culture as composed of seriously contested codes and representations; they assume that the poetic and the political are inseparable, that science is in, not above, historical and linguistic processes" and that "the writing of cultural descriptions is properly experimental and ethical." According to Clifford, focusing on text making and rhetoric highlights the "constructed, artificial nature of cultural accounts" and "undermines overly transparent modes of authority" drawing "attention to the historical predicament of ethnography, the fact that it is always caught up in the invention, not the representation, of cultures" (1986: 1–2). Going beyond simple literary analysis, most of the essays in *Writing Culture* call for the exploration of contexts of power, resistance, institutional constraint, and innovation. It is important to specify discourses in ethnography: "who speaks? who writes? when and where? with or to whom? under what institutional and historical constraints?" (1986: 13). Clifford validates a subgenre of ethnographic writing that was prevalent in the 1960s and 1970s—self-reflexive accounts of fieldwork such as David Maybury-Lewis's *The Savage and the Innocent* (1965), Jean Brigg's *Never in Anger* (1970), and Jean-Paul Dumont's *The Headman and I* (1978)—that placed the ethnographer at center stage, "a character in fiction" who can speak of previously "irrelevant" topics such as their feelings of "violence and desire, confusions" and "struggles and economic transactions with informants" (14). Dialogical and polyvocal modes of textual production that include myriad voices recast and bring into question a traditional monophonic authority typical of "a science that has claimed to *represent* cultures" (15; emphasis in original).

Reflecting upon the omission of voices, Clifford remarked that now that feminists have begun correcting the exclusion of women's experiences from the ethnographic record, it is more obvious that "men's experience (as gendered subjects, not cultural types—'Dinka' or 'Trobrianders') is itself largely unstudied" (19). In an effort to excuse the absence of essays written by female anthropologists or from primarily feminist standpoints, Clifford argued that when organizing the advanced seminar, he and George Marcus were confronted by "what seemed to us an obvious—important and regrettable—fact. Feminists had not contributed much to the theoretical analysis of ethnographies as texts" (19–20). He added that while some female anthropologists had made textual innovations in their ethnographies, they had not done so on *feminist* grounds.

In 1995, the other shoe dropped when the book *Women Writing Culture* (Behar and Gordon 1995)—with twenty-three essays as opposed to *Writing Culture*'s eleven—definitively demonstrated female anthropologists' long history of innovative and theoretically significant ethnographic writing and their multivocal and often practical perspectives on the important issues of their times. In her introduction, Behar chides Clifford for "an interesting slip" when he used Margaret Mead to represent the "usual portrait of anthropological fieldwork": Mead photographed playing with children as opposed to writing (8). In her essay, Nancy Lutkehaus points out that throughout her career Mead published more than 1,300 books, biographies, articles, and reviews. The prolific Mead also wrote social criticism for popular magazines and appeared frequently on television talk shows (186–88).

Clifford's biggest slip was portraying men's writing as more "theo-

retical" than women's. Behar and Deborah Gordon—a former student of
Clifford's and early critic (Gordon 1988) of Clifford and Marcus's book—
planned their own volume as both a feminist response to *Writing Culture*
and "another history of the story of anthropology and another vision of
anthropology waiting to be built out of our creative writing about the past
and the present" (Behar and Gordon 1995: xi). *Women Writing Culture*
is more inclusive in its "democratizing politics, its attentions to race
and ethnicity as well as culture, its engendered self-consciousness, its
awareness of the academy as a knowledge factory, its dreams" (6). Many
of the volume's essays expose what Gordon argued was "an important
problem with 'experimental ethnographic authority'"; namely, that its
masculine subjectivity and men's "ineffective management" of their ne-
gotiations with feminism relegated feminism to a position of servitude,
women anthropologists being expected to discover "my dear, are women
among the Bongo Bongo so different [than men]?"

Sally Cole's essay on Ruth Landes is exemplary of how anthropology's
gendered hierarchy worked to marginalize Landes's writings, preventing
generations of young women scholars from reading her innovative and
important works on race, gender, and culture. Cole's analysis of Landes's
The City of Women (1947) shows a woman who rejected the assertion of
textual authority through the customary ethnographic naturalism and the
removal of Bahian culture from its social, political, and economic contexts. Landes's insistence "on situating herself as a Jew and a woman in
her writing" (Cole 1995: 168) and inserting her subject into history, writing about "women ritual specialists who, through *candomblé*, help give
meaning to the lives of women living in poverty in black Bahia" (169).
Although most of her contemporaries saw the women-centered spirit-
possession religion as syncretic or as an African survival, Landes showed
candomblé to be vital expressions of poor black women's authority and
sexual power and the emergence of "Afro-Brazilian" identities. While in
Bahia, Landes had an affair with Edison Carneiro, a black folklorist and
scholar of *candomblé*. With Carneiro as escort, Landes was able to escape
"the constraints of life as a white woman and to begin intensive participant observation in the *candomblé* temples of the black neighborhoods
of Bahia" (171). Cole argues that Landes's marginalization in American
anthropology was brought about by Melville Herskovits's critical review
(1948) of *The City of Women* in which he based his criticism on "three
perceived problems: Landes's theoretical focus on race and not culture
. . .; her gender-conscious and sexualized analysis of *candomblé*; and her
field methods and conduct" (176). Herskovits and other male contemporaries were not the only anthropologists to marginalize Landes in the

academy and anthropological canon. In her important 1978 article on "Women's Status in Egalitarian Society," feminist pioneer Eleanor Leacock "devalued the work of a pioneer from a previous generation when she took Landes's" *Ojibwa Woman* (1938) "out of historical context to use as cannon fodder in an academic debate with her primarily male Marxist colleagues" (Cole 1995: 180).

In the midst of all the arguably necessary chest- and breast-beating of the late twentieth century, Jane Goodale and her students were confidently doing and teaching quality ethnography. Without fanfare, they and others in ASAO and the larger anthropological community were supporting indigenous anthropology with scholarships and collaboration, becoming more activist, writing more reflexive ethnographies, and always seeking the right interpretations—or threads—of other's cultural practices. Following in Jane's footsteps, many of her students contributed to the astounding growth of the anthropology of gender from the 1970s on, always remembering—as I detail in my chapter—that it's never about men or women only and that gender and sex are not the same things. In her experimental ethnography, *Tiwi Wives,* Jane used the female ego to describe Tiwi society. Seen this way, one of the more interesting observations is that Tiwi history is gendered in that within the same historic time frame, women will cycle through four generations (twenty years each) while men will cycle through only two (forty years each). Tiwi men's and women's economic and political interdependence were demonstrated over and over as Jane deftly recorded the changing responsibilities and rights of Tiwi women as they progressed through the life cycle from birth to death. Far from being men's pawns, Jane found Tiwi women to be "directly and importantly" involved in most Tiwi ceremonies (Goodale 1971: xxii). As Tiwi women aged, they might become *taramaguti,* or first wives, with authority over their daughters and their husbands' other wives and the potential for influencing men's marriage options as well as their own future marriages to younger, more pliable husbands (228–29). Jane's students made important findings of their own when they too looked at cultural definitions of aging, gender, and the life cycle. Challenging theoretical assumptions about the universality of female–male contrasts and the contrast being a universal metaphoric transformation of the nature–culture contrast, Carol MacCormack argued that "ideas about nature and culture are not value free" and that linking "nature with wildness and with femaleness" is in keeping with much of our Judeo-Christian and industrial traditions (MacCormack 1980: 6) but not the traditions of the Sherbro people she studied in West Africa. Among the Sherbro, protosocial children are to initiated adults as nature is to culture (11). Ignoring such findings and their challenges to Lévi-Straussian universal structures and universal female subordination as atheoretical or not feminist enough is poor scholarship. Yet neither Clifford and Marcus (1986) nor Behar and Gordon (1995) or their respective authors chose to recognize the theoretical contributions of Jane or the other writers in MacCormack and Marilyn Strathern's *Nature, Culture and Gender* (1980), a work explicitly focused on testing the assumptions of our own intellectual traditions as well as gaining insights into "what other 'cultures' imagine they are all about" (MacCormack and Strathern 1980: viii).

Other areas in which Jane and her students have been ahead of the curve are their appreciation for aesthetics and the ways local artists are expressing new identities in their art, their investigations into the role of entrepreneurs in a globalizing world, and their analyses of the relationships between the politics of culture and ecology, kinship, and sexuality. Boundaries between us and them are collapsed when we learn that as early as the 1960s, objects of Western manufacture were replacing native Tiwi craft as proper payment for the makers of the ceremonial Pukamani poles (Goodale 1971: 308). Poles originally valued at $10 or $12 are now worth thousands of dollars in the international art market. The first anthropologist to do extensive research into the role of contemporary art and architecture in Papua New Guinea, Pamela Rosi compares the unacknowledged status of PNG artists with the fame and national value accorded Australian Aboriginal art in *Exploring World Art*, which she co-edited with Eric Venbrux and Robert Welsch (Venbrux, Rosi, and Welsch 2006).[4] In his article in *Exploring World Art*, anthropologist Paul Stoller trails the different pathways African art takes as it enters the global art market at the prestigious Tribal Antiquities: The New York International Show. At the 2001 show, Stoller observed the intersection of two universes of meaning as "tribal" antiquities dealers showcased rare West African masks and statuary while African art traders lured potential buyers away with "better prices" for "very similar pieces" (Stoller 2006: 88).

Stoller's article exemplifies the holism and empirically grounded ethnographic research that reveal contemporary social worlds and global interconnectedness and are typical of the writings of Jane Goodale and her students. In a 1993 collaborative essay on love and marriage in Port Moresby, Pam Rosi and I examined the influences of Christianity, higher education, and other elements of popular Western culture in young Papua New Guineans' romantic conceptions and ideas. We found that educated men and women agreed with the untraditional notion that "love was the most important tie between men and women and that it should lead to marriage" (Rosi and Zimmer-Tamakoshi 1993: 183), but educated males were more conservative in their views on women's participation in the urban workplace and national life. Rejecting ideas that their jobs or political interests should take second place to homemaking or men's interests, many elite women were marrying across racial and international boundaries and finding support for their resistance in local and international women's groups. In an analysis of Melanesian big men and development, and their larger-than-life presence in the anthropological imagination (1997d), I described the rise and fall of a self-proclaimed "last Big Man." In spite of years of effort manipulating both old and new exchange systems in an attempt to save his society from capitalist development's indifference to local traditions of family, reputation, and leadership, the "last Big Man" could not prevent his society from being ravaged by inequality. Losing his life in a fight with a returned migrant angered over the loss of land rights to more prosperous clan members, the "last Big Man" died as a result of the incongruities between Gende exchange ethics and Western-style capitalism. At the time of his death, the big man was working for his oldest child, a former Air Niugini hostess, and her Australian husband. Having failed at "helping her people" by setting up a coffee-buying business in Yandera village, the enterprising daughter relocated to land leased from the government and just outside Gende territory. Avoiding traditional exchange entanglements (as she had with her nontraditional marriage), the daughter (and her husband) built a lucrative commercial enterprise, selling fresh vegetables, flowers, and farm-raised trout to urban markets throughout Papua New Guinea. Her individual success and disregard for the Gende ethic that "everyone, or no one, is a winner" has aroused the ire of many Gende.

The contest over Western and Gende ethics continues at Kurumbukare, the site of a proposed mine that may generate untold wealth for local landowners. While most Gende and their neighbors are renegotiating their relations with one another and with ancestral spirits guarding the sparsely populated rainforest and virtual no-man's-land, others—including the "last Big Man's" daughter—are trying to prove more singular rights to large tracts of the contested land (Zimmer-Tamakoshi 2001a). Called upon as an outside "expert" to decipher local customs or receiving e-mails from the "last Big Man's" daughter asking me to support more exclusive land claims, I find myself in a very serious playing field of contested meanings. Grounding my writings in detailed empirical research is both a personal and moral necessity. What is key to proper representation of these opposing interests is cultural analysis, analysis not only of the politics or economics of cultural "traditions" but also of the *living* relationships between people and place.

None of Jane's students is better than Debbie Rose in capturing the essence of indigenous land and environmental issues. In *Country of the Heart* (2002), Debbie, eco-photographer Sharon D'Amico, and five Mak Mak women—Nancy Daiyi; her daughters Kathy Deveraux, Margaret Daiyi, and Linda Ford; and April Bright—represent the ecology and sacred geography of the Mak Mak clan's homeland in a multilayered textual and visual format. Mixing her descriptions of place and history with Mak Mak women's words and cultural understandings and with hundreds of D'Amico's photos of contemporary Mak Mak and their homeland in northern Australia, Debbie produced a landmark work demonstrating her commitment to justice for the people and environmental justice for the country. Making her work available to a global community of concerned environmentalists and all who appreciate the mutuality of indigenous owners of the land caring best for the land that in turn supports them, Debbie authorized a Japanese edition in 2003 of her 1996 *Nourishing Terrains: Australian Aboriginal Views of Landscape and Wilderness.* In her article in this volume, Debbie describes Jane's experiential approach to fieldwork. Following in Jane's footsteps and exceeding "the boundaries of disciplines and categories [and] normative or rational self" and producing multilayered texts, Debbie helps readers experience the deuterolearning that allows anthropologists to learn how to learn like the people they are studying.

In Jane's distinguished lecture at the 1994 ASAO meetings (included, along with a postscript, as the conclusion of this collection), Jane recalled former students' dismay—back in the '70s—at the attacks on anthropology and their questions of whether ethnography is "real" or merely a mix of inventions and partial truths. Jane told her students to forget what others were saying, "that for at least as long as I lived, ethnography was not obsolete or dead" (Goodale 1994b). In her talk, Jane reviewed aspects of her own training in anthropology, remarking on what stood the test of time and what needed improving in the years that followed. For Jane, the essentials of good ethnography continue to include holistic training in the four (now five) fields of anthropology, a dedication to the accumulation of facts and the encouragement to speculate when there are no readily observable facts, and asking questions that allow one to eventually "pull the right thread" and solve the ethnographic puzzle. For Jane, ethnography has always been an experimental arm of the science of anthropology. What have improved are the questions we ask. We look at a society through female as well as male eyes. We remember that individuals act in many different capacities—as brothers and husbands, sisters and wives—and that they move through cycles of changing responsibilities and opportunities as they age and participate in key cultural events. We not only recognize that informants know more than we do about their own culture (so when in doubt, ask!), we also realize that participant observation is a two-way mirror, that we may or may not be a cultural match, and that our informants are our contemporaries and as capable as we at reflecting upon difference and changing opportunities. History and repetitive fieldwork continue to yield important insights, as do comparison and critical discussions with our colleagues and students.

Throughout Jane's 1994 distinguished lecture, she challenged anthropologists who are in the habit of throwing out the baby—ethnography—with the bathwater by suggesting they use "an evolutionary model of theoretical change rather than a catastrophic one." While critical works are necessary in refining and maintaining high standards in any discipline, Jane bemoaned the tendency among some anthropologists to overlook the many solid ethnographies and complex studies by past and living anthropologists in favor of creating disciplinary chaos. In the infancy of the twenty-first century and post-9/11, anthropological grandstanding seems to be on the ebb. In recent issues of *Anthropology News*, the official newspaper of the American Anthropological Association, anthropologists demonstrate a growing concern for ethics and the politics of responsible ethnographic representation as well as access to ethnographic knowledge, increasing globalization, and the question of where the field really is. In an article on public anthropology, David Napier warns that "the central problem with advocacy is . . . that the chances of positive outcomes for our subjects may actually *decrease* as an advocate's visibility *increases* (2004: 7; emphasis in original). In the same issue, Floyd Rudmin observes that some of the torture at Abu Ghraib Prison required cultural expertise that was probably derived from the ethnographic works of social scientists. Rudmin reminds us that our professional code of ethics demands that our research and activities benefit those we study and should do them no harm; instead of remaining silent, we "should be vociferous in prohibiting such abuses of science" (2004: 9). As anthropology rushes toward "shared anthropology," designers of anthropological Web sites should consider such ethical dilemmas in terms of how much and what kinds of data are made "open access" to indiscriminate, global audiences. Although restricting access to members and aimed at supporting a "global community of scholars, teachers, and students in the field," AAA's new *AnthroSource* may be as liable to abuse as it is appealing to librarians to acquire *AnthroSource* for their institutions—and not just individual members—in ads in *Anthropology News* (e.g., February 2005) and elsewhere.

With so much good, innovative, and morally concerned ethnography already available, as is evident in the references in this collection and in anthropology more generally, it was with a certain bemusement that I read in a recent issue of the *American Anthropologist* of a need for a neo-Boasian anthropology (Bashkow, Bunzl, Handler, Orta, and Rosenblatt 2004). In their introduction to a special issue of the journal, dedicated to the subject of "Theory for the Twenty-First Century," the authors state that contemporary critics of anthropology have been "too quick to reject, in wholesale fashion, the anthropological past—too indiscriminate in their characterization of all anthropological epistemologies as positivistic, all anthropological politics as complicit in imperialism" (Bashkow et al. 433). The authors' efforts to remember the best of Boasian thinking and methodology are commendable. Their attempts to birth a neo-Boasian anthropology, however, such as the intersection of "Foucauldian genealogy, Boasian historicism, and the epistemic rethinking of the discipline's Self/Other binary" (Bunzl 2004: 435) or by retheorizing and extending "Boasians' open concept of cultural boundaries" that are cultural distinctions that are "irreducibly plural, perspectival, and permeable" versus barriers to outside influence or historical change (Bashkow 2004: 443) are less commendable. Less commendable because, like the critics they revile, the authors focus too much on the distant anthropological past and give short shrift to generations of anthropologists who have been doing everything the authors say we ought to be doing. Most American anthropologists are familiar with Boas's writings, having read—as students and again as teachers of the discipline—at least some of *Race, Language, and Culture* (Boas 1940), including Boas's 1896 classic "The Limitations of the Comparative Method of Anthropology" (Boas 1940/1896). Suggesting an alternative to the Malinowskian fieldwork tradition of heroized journeys into Otherness, Bunzl calls for the "recuperation of Boasian fieldwork" methods and perspectives such as taking for granted the historical specificity of cultural or ethnic phenomena and devoting our attention to others not because they were Others but because they contribute to the plenitude of humanity (Bunzl 2004: 439). Like other critics, the authors fail to mention who among us are allegedly taking "heroized journeys into Otherness" or failing to "engage with what is worthiest in the genealogy of our ideas" (Bashkow 2004: 444).

This collection in honor of Jane Goodale was conceived around the same time as was the special issue of the *American Anthropologist* on the need for a neo-Boasian anthropology in the twenty-first century. Jeanette and I organized a session in honor of Jane at the 1998 American Anthropological Association meetings in Philadelphia. Matti Bunzl and Richard

Handler presented their panel on "The Pasts, Presents, and Futures of Boasian Anthropology" at the 1999 annual meeting of AAA in Chicago. While the special issue on Boasian anthropology will be informative for young scholars unfamiliar with the works of Boas and his students, this volume looks at the accomplishments of living anthropologists who ground their ethnographic methods, teaching, and writing within a continuum of experimentation and learning, building—over time—a solid anthropology that is responsive to critique and the concerns of those we study. Jane's legacy has been to teach her students to stand lightly on the shoulders of giants. She has taught us that it is not necessary to reinvent anthropology. Rather, we must keep searching for the right threads and never be afraid to recognize our own or others' fallibility and to move on to a more promising thread. In keeping with AAA's 2005 annual meeting theme—Bringing the Past into the Present—this collection reminds us that we must bring the *near past* into the present as well as the more distant past.

Notes

1. I would like to thank Michele Dominy for allowing me to use the title for her chapter as part of the title of this collection. Jane's oft-repeated expression—"pulling the right thread"—seems especially apt, when pluralized, for capturing the essence of Jane's ethnographic legacy and our attempts to write about it.

2. With the exception of Jane Fajans, the contributors to this volume presented earlier versions of their chapters in one or both special sessions organized by the editors of this volume and given at the American Anthropological Association meeting in Philadelphia in 1998 and the Association for Social Anthropology in Oceania meeting in Vancouver in 2003. The participants at the two sessions were chosen to represent and speak on major aspects of Jane's legacy.

3. Carol Hoffer and Annette Weiner are both deceased. Fred Myers was the discussant for our 1998 AAA session in Philadelphia. Other commitments prevented him from participating in this volume. Judith Huntsman teaches anthropology in New Zealand. DeVerne Smith works in Micronesia.

4. Fred Myers also has an article in *Exploring World Art* (Myers 2006).

1. *An Ethnographic Life*

I was fortunate enough to spend three days with Jane in her tranquil Ipswich home during the summer of 1998. During these magical days I tape-recorded and later transcribed our discussions about Jane's life. What follows can best be described as a collography (Davison 1996: 17) or a text that is derived from a collaboration between Jane and I. The text adheres to Jane's oral narrative and retains *her* emphasis on and perspectives of her accomplishments as a fieldworker, teacher, and mentor from her point of view.

Jane is exceedingly proud of her New England heritage. Her forebears have been in New England since the 1630s and one branch of the family was even involved in the Salem witch trials. One of Jane's Massachusetts ancestresses, Lucy Goodale Thurston, answered an ad in the Boston newspaper that was placed by a group of young theological students who had just graduated from Yale. King Kamehameha of Hawaii had invited the students to come and missionize in Hawaii but only if they were married beforehand. Lucy married one of the students and in 1882 published a wonderful book about those early missionary days entitled *Life and Times of Mrs. Lucy C. Thurston, Wife of Rev. Asa Thurston, Pioneer Missionary to the Sandwich Islands*. Although Jane never met this woman, she feels somehow that she has a genetic predilection to go to far and unknown places. Another possible role model for Jane was her uncle, Eddie Goodale, who left Harvard in 1929, after his freshman year, to drive a dog team with Admiral Byrd to the South Pole.

Although Jane is not sure if either of these relatives directly affected her choice of an ethnographic life, she has always had a spirit of adven-

27

ture, a ken for science, a desire to see new places, and a deep curiosity to understand how things work. The knowledge of poker playing, passed on to Jane by her paternal grandfather, Joseph Lincoln Goodale, M.D., would also prove crucial in different ways to her later South Pacific ethnographic research among the Tiwi and Kaulong.

Jane was born in 1926 in Boston to Susan Bainbridge Sturgis and Robert Lincoln Goodale. She has an older sister Susan B., a younger brother, Robert L. Jr., and a younger sister, Mary B. Certainly, the fact that both Jane's father and paternal grandfather were physicians contributed to her strong attraction to science and the process of discovery. As a young girl, Jane, inspired by the works of Asa Johnson, wanted to go to the Gobi Desert and hunt dinosaur eggs. As a teenager, Jane loved to play the game "Missing the Arrows Come Softly Two by Two." This was a game in which the listener had to infer an underlying reality from a set of clues. When she got older, her paternal grandfather introduced her to detective stories. Being both a chemist and physician, he particularly liked mysteries with poisonous concoctions as the weapon. Jane grew to love the inductive and deductive reasoning required to solve the puzzles put forward in these stories.

Her father's medical practice in Boston kept the family in Boston for nine months of the year. Glorious summers were spent in the Ipswich area where the Goodales had a family home. Jane, as both a child and adult, has very fond memories of sailing, exploring the saltwater marshes and beach dunes around her home, and climbing the beautiful White and Green mountains. It was during these summers that Jane's father shared his affinity with nature and Jane developed both a love for and a bond with this local environment.

Jane does not have especially fond memories of her early grade school years in Cambridge. In fact, her distaste for formal learning was so strong that as a young woman she could not possibly have envisioned herself as a teacher. Jane feels that her anxiety about her early education was undoubtedly related to her undiagnosed dyslexia. She said that "my teachers had no appreciation of my creative spelling and grammar, and, most unjustly, of my ideas" (Dickerson-Putman 1998). Later, at the all-girls Oldfields School in Maryland, Jane encountered a nurturing environment that emphasized the discovery of each child's talent. This school was founded in 1867 by one of Jane's maternal relatives. Jane utilized her growing skills in inductive reasoning and problem solving to complete her high school course work at Oldfields. She developed a particularly close relationship with one of her teachers. As Jane recalls, "Miss Anderson nurtured my ideas, creativity and writing and helped me to discover my lifelong love of history, physics, geometry and music" (Dickerson-Putman 1998). The time that she spent at Oldfields not only gave Jane firsthand experience with the value of mentoring but also prepared her for her admittance to Radcliffe.

Jane entered Radcliffe as a commuter student in the fall of 1944. When she began her undergraduate education, Jane was hoping to apply her interest in science to a career in either medicine or geography. In her sophomore year, a classmate and childhood friend suggested that they enroll in an anthropology course so that "they could find out what those strange people in the Peabody Museum were doing" (Dickerson-Putman 1998). Before she majored in anthropology, however, her parents had to be reassured by George Valliant, a prominent archaeologist of the time, that while Jane would never be rich, she would be able to make a living as an anthropologist.

Jane and her friend became two of the five anthropology majors in their class; in those early Radcliffe years, they took anthropology courses with Ernest Hooten and Carleton Coon. The Radcliffe/Harvard department offered its students a holistic exposure to the subfields of anthropology. Jane remembers that "quite often Archaeology, Physical Anthropology and Ethnology went together in the same course, taught by the same professor and intended to give us data pertinent to the questions of who the people were and how they adapted during a specific period" (1994b: 9). She especially remembers the day that Patrick Putman visited Coon's class and gave the Radcliffe women a demonstration of how Ituri pygmy women beat the bush during an elephant hunt: "Patrick Putman led us as we participated in an elephant hunt down the halls of Radcliffe. Picture, if you will, Coon the trumpeting elephant, being chased by forty pygmy women screaming in culturally correct accent and volume to where Patrick Putman lay in wait with his spears hidden under his very long beard" (Dickerson-Putman 1998). Other Radcliffe/Harvard faculty in residence during the 1940s included Joe Brew, A. B. Kidder, Douglas Oliver, and Clyde Kluckhohn. Jane especially remembers Gregory Bateson sitting cross-legged on the desk lecturing about the sexual meanings in Naven ceremonies.

During her undergraduate years, Jane and Robert Dyson cofounded the Harvard/Radcliffe Anthropology Club and Jane served as its first president. The club published a newsletter called *A.P.E.* (archaeology, physical anthropology, and ethnography). Jane's growing interest in anthropology was encouraged when Alfred L. Kroeber came to speak to the club. When one of the students asked him why he became an anthropologist, he said, "I became an anthropologist because I can go anywhere in the world. I can sit in the shade and if someone asks me what I'm doing I can say I'm doing anthropology" (Dickerson-Putman 1998). For Jane and the other club members, Kroeber's words were a validation of their own interest in observation as a primary method.

It was Jane's mentorship with the pragmatic and grounded Carleton Coon that captivated her imagination and led her to declare her dedication to an ethnographic life. C. S. Coon, trained by E. A. Hooten and others in the holistic curriculum of anthropology at Harvard, did fieldwork and published significant works in ethnography, physical anthropology, and archaeology as well as two novels on the Rif people of the Atlas Mountains. Jane recalls that "Coon was extremely creative in writing, thinking, and speaking and was continually revising his interpretation when new empirical data arose from others' work. In teaching he often proposed a new interpretation at the beginning of class only to declare that, although discussions with students had proven it wrong, that it was a good exercise in inductive reasoning" (personal communication February 2003). For two years, Coon encouraged her to go to the original ethnographic sources and tutored her as she immersed herself in the classics of anthropology, including works by Shapira, Radcliffe-Brown, and Malinowski. Coon also taught Jane to dedicate herself to the scientific accumulation of data and facts and to free one's mind to speculate when there were no facts. This process would eventually reveal a pattern or interpretation. Jane welcomed this attitude toward anthropological education with open arms. A strategy that Jane developed in graduate school would be a model for the future analysis of her own ethnographic materials.

> I constructed humongous charts where millenniums of time met unbounded geographical space, in which I placed all my known facts that I had color-coded for numerous factors. I had fun as I walked the length of the chart and speculated on exam questions that might be asked. The very process of chart construction on many feet of shelf paper had the desired effect of ordering my mental processes as facts became detached from time and space and recombined with each new line of thought I conceived. (Goodale 1994b: 9)

When she graduated from Radcliffe in 1948, Jane was sure of two things: that she did not want to go on to graduate school and that she did not want to be a teacher. Jane recalls, "I was tired of school and public speaking did not come easily to me. In fact, I rarely asked a question in any class. I wanted a job in the Foreign Service so I turned down a job on an Indian reservation as a leader of the young women's group" (Dickerson-Putman

1998). After graduating, Jane worked as a toy tester for Woolworth's and then took a job as an assistant fly spanker for Dr. Bart J. Bok, the associate head of Harvard's Astronomy Department.

> A fly spanker was a piece of photographic plate that helped Dr. Bok to measure the brightness of variable stars in the Milky Way. I loved working with the heart of the Astronomy Department. I discovered that astronomers were even crazier than anthropologists because we go everywhere around the world but what they want to do is to get out of it. I worked there for a year and discovered that I loved that kind of environment. I wanted an academic life, so I applied to the graduate program in anthropology. (Dickerson-Putman 1998)

She was accepted as a graduate student in the Harvard Anthropology Department in 1949. As her undergraduate honors advisor, Coon suggested that Jane read a late-nineteenth-century book by Major Robinson on the Hindu Kush people. She was immediately fascinated by these isolated populations and, in fact, wrote her honors thesis on the origin, history, and ethnography of the Hindu Kush. Jane continued to pursue her interest in the cultures of the Hindu Kush area during her early graduate years. She also took Hooten's bone class, where she learned to beat the clock in his challenging bone identification quizzes. As Jane remembers, "We worked like dogs but every single moment of it was glorious as far as I was concerned" (Dickerson-Putman 1998).

Carleton Coon left Harvard for the University of Pennsylvania Museum in 1948. Jane transferred there in 1950 when Coon offered her a job as his assistant. Although the salary was minimal, she was allowed to take one free course each semester. Jane processed artifacts and identified bones from Coon's various excavations and also helped him mount a major exhibit on the history of mankind in the university museum's Hall of Man. After the exhibit was open to the public, one of Jane's jobs was to take groups of sixth-grade children through the hall. She remembers that "it was challenging and rewarding as I covered the time period ranging from Australopithecine Man to Contemporary Culture in one hour" (personal communication February 2003). It was this experience that convinced Jane that she would love to teach anthropology.

During her years at Penn, Jane took courses with A. B. Kidder, Loren Eisley, and Ward Goodenough. Jane recalls, "Through a course in the History of Anthropology given by A. I. Hallowell I learned about prior studies in kinship (Morgan, Kroeber) and in a later course on Social Organization, also with Hallowell, I came to grips with the complexities which this topic presents to fieldworkers and theorists. This topic was at that time on the cutting edge of social anthropology. In the same year I grappled with Australian kinship in a paper for Ward Goodenough for his course on Oceania" (2003: 1). She became part of a close-knit group of graduate students that included Ted Swartz, Mary Ann Stoler, and Charles and Eve Valentine. It was also at Penn that Jane began her lifelong friendship with Ann Chowning.

Jane also became active in the Philadelphia Anthropological Society (PAS). The PAS, founded sometime prior to 1915, was a thriving organization in the 1950s–1970s. Monthly meetings held at the University of Pennsylvania Museum featured presentations given by prominent local, national, and international anthropologists from all of the four subfields of the discipline. Jane remembers these meetings as a significant part of her professional life because they provided "an integrating social and intellectual force for anthropologists that also served as a basis for further collaboration in the region" (personal communication April 2002). As a graduate student in the 1950s, she served the PAS as editor of the newsletter.

Although Jane had taken a course on Pacific cultures with Ward Goodenough, "the Pacific itself did not appeal to me as a research site as much as the many unknown regions of central Asia. Unfortunately, Asia was closed" (Dickerson-Putman 1998). The course of her ethnographic life changed, however, when Coon received an invitation from Charles Mountford to join his National Geographic–funded expedition to Melville Island to study the Australian Aboriginal population that lived there. Coon was headed for Afghanistan, so he asked Jane if she would like to do her fieldwork in Australia. Jane remembers that "this opportunity initially both excited me and threw me into a panic. How does anyone understand Australian kinship and marriage rules!" (2003: 2). Jane overcame the initial fear of working with Australian marriage classes and kinship and agreed to go.

From the beginning, Mountford decided that Jane would concentrate her fieldwork on women's lives because there was practically nothing written about women except Kaberry's (1939) work in the Kimberly region of Australia. Her initial reaction to this was hardly enthusiastic. She felt that:

> As far as I knew from my studies the men did all of the exciting stuff and the women raised the children. That's all that was in the ethnography at the time. They were wives and mothers. They were never young and they never got old. They just died. As soon as they finished being mothers they disappeared. I soon discovered, however, that Tiwi women were fully engaged in the ceremonial life of their people. At no time did I con-

sider that I was studying only women's lives, but naturally I spent a fair amount of time in the company of women. (Dickerson-Putman 1998)

Jane's belief in the importance of collaboration and the sharing of knowledge were reflected in her first interactions in Australia. Although she had accepted her assignment to study the women for her dissertation research, Jane really had no formal training in field methodology. Bill Stanner, of the Australian National University (ANU), gave her a two-day crash course in field methodology when she visited the university on her way to Melville Island. As Jane recollects, "Stanner told me what to look for, how to ask questions and how to recognize and recover from culture shock" (1994b: 14). He gave her one particularly valuable piece of advice: "There will be days when you can't stand the faces of the people you are living with for one more minute. On these days you should take a day off and when you wake up the next morning, things will be fine" (Dickerson-Putman 1998).

Once she got to Melville Island in 1954, Jane received invaluable advice and support from another member of the expedition, Bill Harney. He was especially helpful to Jane in the early phase of her research because he facilitated her interaction with Tiwi women. "Bill Harney, or Bilarny as the Aboriginal people knew him, was a legendary Australian man of the bush or outback. He gave me the title of 'mate' and this gave me instant rapport with the Tiwi with whom he had had prior contact" (personal communication February 2003). Jane also found his technique of "spinning a yarn" especially helpful. "Bilarny would spin a yarn in order to get certain kinds of information. The Tiwi would spin a yarn back. They knew that he was spinning a yarn but it got them on to the kind of data that he wanted. He also gave me hints of key questions to ask the women based on his previous knowledge and information he picked up as a translator for Mountford" (Dickerson-Putman 1998).

During the early months of her first Tiwi work, it was Bill Harney who encouraged her to focus on social organization. According to Jane, "Kinship data was absolutely essential to my work because you can't understand anything about Aborigines until you figure out their relationships" (Dickerson-Putman 1998). Before she arrived on Melville Island, Jane had been told that the Tiwi were different from other Aboriginal groups. Jane attributes this difference to the fact that:

> They have not been shot at and they have not been deprived of their liberties. They have had a fairly benign relationship with missionaries and government people. Their land was never fully taken away from them. They were allowed to hunt on it so they never really lost the feeling that

they were equal to whites. In 1954 they said that the only thing that separates us from the whites is that we don't have an education. If we can read and write, we can do anything. And it is somehow that attitude that comes through. And I have been following that attitude all the way through. (Dickerson-Putman 1998)

Jane firmly believes that the cultural interpretation of ethnographic field-work requires that ethnographers not only continually reflect on their own cultural assumptions but that they find this interpretation embedded in the cross-cultural dialogue between informant and anthropologist (Goodale 1995: 18). Jane found it easy to establish rapport with the Tiwi because they shared a set of core values based around the importance of reciprocal relationships within the family and because they were quick to reach out and establish relationships as individuals. One of the individuals that Jane met during this first fieldwork was Happy. As she remembers, "I first went off to the bush with her. I knew she was fond of me and I was fond of her. I mean it was a bond there right from the beginning" (Dickerson-Putman 1998). Jane spent ten months among the Tiwi and then returned to Philadelphia to write her dissertation and take up her full-time job at the university museum.

Jane now began the process of sorting the facts and finding the metaphors, patterns, and threads that connected them. The inductive process she learned from Coon and her paternal grandfather was even more interesting now because she could play detective with her own data! What emerged from her trial-and-error experiments with her data was "the importance of relative age in marital relationships, and particularly that marriage was really an exchange of mothers-in-law rather than daughters" (personal communication February 2003).

Eventually Jane decided to use the unfolding of an individual woman's life course as the essential organizing principle for her dissertation. As she recalls:

Most of my data was [sic] on the social organization of the funeral ceremony. But in order to understand the funeral ceremony you have to understand the life of the individual that has died. So I decided to start with birth and end up with death. Since the Tiwi don't really discriminate that much between men and women I decided that it would be ethnographically sound to choose the life of either a man or a woman. Since most monographs of the time were written from a male point of view, I thought it would be more fun and original to trace a woman's life from birth to death and use this framework to describe Tiwi society. I did not fully realize the impact that this little twist of the kaleidoscope would make (Dickerson-Putman 1998).

Jane got invaluable help and advice from Ward Goodenough while she was working on her dissertation. According to Jane:

> Ward was a wonderful friend to us all. I mean he was the youngest member of the department who really made connection with the graduate students. He was very accessible and he was the only one who really helped me map out the social organization of the Tiwi. I gave Ward a freshly typed copy to read and he absolutely marked up each page with comments. I was furious because I had just finished typing it but then I realized that in one weekend he had spent a tremendous amount of time really polishing it up and when I went in to tell him I was furious, he said "I was furious at Murdock. He did the same thing to me." (Dickerson-Putman 1998)

As co-supervisor of her dissertation, Ward also felt that Jane should get more recognition within anthropology because "Jane's life history material on women led to the solution of a major problem in the formal, ritual kinship system of the Australian Aborigine" (personal communication June 1999). While working full time at the university museum, Jane completed her dissertation and received her Ph.D. in 1959.

Jane was a firm believer in extensive and repetitive fieldwork and she was able to undertake additional fieldwork with the Tiwi in 1962, 1980–81, 1986–87, 1995, 1996–97, 1999, and 2002. These long-term revisits allowed her to collect new data as well as to "check" her current linkages and interpretations on an Australian Aborigine audience. During a short visit in 1962, Jane had access to rich census data that gave her great insight into the importance of age in Tiwi kinship and marriage. These insights enabled Jane to explore the importance of the mother-in-law/son-in-law relationship and the relationship between a person and his or her maternal grandmother. Jane found that "a person's mother's mother (aged forty at a grandchild's birth) was a repository of tribal and family history whom a grandchild knew for many years" (Dickerson-Putman 1998). She also was able to observe firsthand what she felt was the appalling nature of the interaction between the government personnel and the Tiwi during the assimilation period.

During this 1962 research trip, Jane first began her formal work as an advocate for the Tiwi. She acted as a cultural broker during the inaugural meeting of the newly integrated Milikapiti Country Women's Association (CWA). As Jane recalls:

> The CWA was proposed and imposed on the women of Milikapiti. Neither the white women or the black women appeared to have a clue as to what they were to do. I suggested that they begin by exchanging cook-

ing methods and recipes. I began by emulating Julia Child and teaching all to make Polish bread using hands for measures and cooking in the earth oven. I served the tea-sized "breads" while the wife of the superintendent distributed tea in mugs first to Aboriginal women and in cups to white women. I reversed the order in serving the tea breads. (Dickerson-Putman 1998)

During her sixteen months of fieldwork in 1980–81, Jane was able to witness the formation of the Tiwi Land Council. At the request of the Tiwi, Jane utilized data from her earlier fieldwork to help the Tiwi iron out issues of individual land ownership. Jane felt that "participating in Tiwi Land Council meetings was an extraordinary opportunity for me to witness how the Tiwi learned to be consummate politicians of a new order" (2003: 8). Later in this period of fieldwork, Jane was the acting manager of the Tiwi Land Council. As acting manager, she was involved in facilitating the voice of women in the vote on alcohol on the island, and she also attended meetings with the chief minister of the Northern Territories as an elected delegate of the Tiwi.

She also played a pivotal role in helping the Tiwi understand the potential impact of a Japanese timber-cutting project. The representative for the company assured the Tiwi that trees would be replanted and the environment would be just like it was before. Jane was present and asked, "But will the trees you plant have holes that possums can live in, that the sugar-bag can build their nests of honey in and the bandicoots can live in?" (Dickerson-Putman 1998). Jane looked at the Tiwi that were present and she could tell that she had gotten them to realize that these "Whitemen" were trying to con them.

Jane was able to continue her work with the Tiwi during 1986–87 when she served as a visiting principal lecturer at the Darwin Institute of Technology. While at the Darwin Institute, she taught Introductory Social Anthropology, Aboriginal and Pacific Ethnography, and Gender Difference. Jane also developed a curriculum for a proposed Department of Applied Anthropology, which unfortunately did not materialize because of the merger of the Darwin Institute and the University of the Northern Territory.

During her most recent visits to the Tiwi in 1995, 1996–97, and 2002, Jane deposited extensive Milikapiti genealogies with the Tiwi Land Council. These genealogies will be an invaluable resource as the Tiwi continue to work out the intricacies of land ownership. While reflecting on her long-term research among the Tiwi, Jane said, "From the beginning I have found relationships relating to kinship and social organization among the Tiwi to be fascinating and central to my understanding of the dynamics of externally mandated and internally derived social changes which have challenged them as well as me over nearly fifty years. I have been principally interested in continuity and change through the exercise of choice by the Tiwi community of Milikapiti" (2003: 2). To date, Jane has published one book, *Tiwi Wives* (1971 [first edition], 1994a [second edition]), and numerous articles utilizing various threads of her Tiwi data (1960, 1962, 1970, 1982, 1987, 1996a, 1999). The Tiwi who have read *Tiwi Wives* say, "This is our history."

Jane is especially proud of an article entitled "Production and Reproduction of Key Resources Among the Tiwi of North Australia" (1982). Jane remembers that:

> [W]hen reconceptualizing my data for this article I followed an apparently random path of data recombination that astonished me. What I had done was not to reduce the complex to the simple but I found a logical path through the complexity. The pattern of reasoning was regenerative in that I was constantly led into new areas whose connectedness was only at that moment revealed. What my mind was able to do was to re-sort my headnotes, fieldnotes and published notes into some very new combinations. This successful process is one in which I often compare to finding the right thread when undoing a hem: The right thread frees the entire hem while the wrong allows only snippets of thread to come free. (1994b: 18)

In this article she argues that:

> [F]or the Tiwi, sexual division of labor in resource management is apparently related to a classification of the physical environment in terms of gender, and that the shared and complementary roles with which Tiwi men and women traditionally regulated and maintained both food resources and population can best be understood in relation to the ideological order in which the yam is the key unifying symbol linking food and people. (1982: 198)

Jane formulated this model just before leaving for her 1980–81 field trip and was thrilled to find that the Tiwi also felt that she had put the pieces of the puzzle together in a way that truly reflected their indigenous ideology. Jane is currently working on a book entitled *History of Milikapiti* that will explore the histories of two to three Tiwi families set within the context of the development of the Milikapiti settlement. Jane hopes this work will be useful for the Tiwi and that the understanding she has gained through long-term fieldwork will provide a historical description of their perspective that can inform those who work with the Tiwi in the future. When I asked Jane what she thought her impact on the Tiwi was, she said, "I'm an outsider who has become a Tiwi. I'm often compared to other white people and the Tiwi say I'm not like them. They have learned that it is possible that white people can learn to like and respect them for who they are. In fact, they are some of the finest human beings that I have ever met. And if that is all the impact that I have had, that's fine" (Dickerson-Putman 1998).

Jane's ethnographic life has also been enriched through her repetitive fieldwork in Papua New Guinea. In 1960, Ann Chowning had done some work on the island of New Britain and suggested to Jane that they organize a joint venture into unknown cultural territory there. Jane's love of adventure and her desire for some comparative research made her a willing coexplorer. She was also eager to be involved in comparative research because "it was ingrained in my training to believe that comparison was the key method to understanding what is basic to all human life, what culture means, and to how cultures change over time" (Dickerson-Putman 1998). In 1962, Jane and Ann did six weeks of reconnaissance on New Britain and returned for thirteen months in 1963–64. Their collaboration during this period is creatively documented in *The Two-Party Line: Conversations in the Field* (Goodale 1996b). Their initial objectives were to develop a holistic ethnographic description of their respective cultural groups, including data on social, economic, and religious organization, beliefs, and practices and the relationships between these institutions (Goodale 1996b: 7). Jane's lifelong interest in comparative ethnography meant that she was also eager to collect facts about the Kaulong's foraging adaptation and women's worldview to compare with her Tiwi data.

Jane has often said that she might not have become an anthropologist if this had been her first fieldwork experience. The Kaulong of Umbi had had little experience with outsiders and this, coupled with their very different worldview, made for some extremely challenging and sometimes alienating fieldwork. As Jane explains:

> Most Kaulong did not know that there were many other ways of living and that white people were different from Kaulong. Although I was struggling to learn a culture which in most peoples' minds I must have come from a culture similar to theirs and they treated me as if I knew everything except their language which they eagerly began to teach me on my first encounter. . . . They simply did not believe that the world was made up of different modes of life. (personal communication February 2003)

As in her Tiwi research, Jane was always reflective about the ways in which her personality and role shaped the Kaulong ethnographic experience.

The Kaulong cultural ethos of what is right to do was diametrically opposite from what the Tiwi ethos is. The Kaulong are competitive where
the Tiwi are cooperative. With the Tiwi there was no battle with my
own culture because in many ways I'm much more like the Tiwi than I
am a Kaulong. It was a constant battle with my own culture to begin to
understand the Kaulong. One of the biggest shocks of the Kaulong was
this whole credit economy which being a Yankee was totally foreign to
me. I mean Yankees ideologically don't have debts and Kaulong culture
is built on credit and debt. They can't just share because it's always a
matter of economic calculation. (Dickerson-Putman 1998)

When Jane returned to New Britain in 1967–68 and 1974 she conducted
fieldwork from the village of Angelek. She deliberately chose this village
because it had had contact with other cultures since German occupation.
While keenly interested in comparing life in the two villages, Jane's research in Angelek also explored cultural ideas about gender and marriage,
what it means to be a human being, and rituals surrounding death and
big man leadership. Jane says of her Kaulong research, "The total immer-
sion that I had in their culture because there wasn't anything else to do
meant that in my repetitive trips there, within a relatively short period of
time of twelve years, I feel that they allowed me to get deeper into their
culture than I've ever been able to do with the Tiwi. With the Kaulong
it was essentially one ethnographic presence within twelve years. I had
two communities so that also gave me change and contrast" (Dickerson-Putman 1998). The 1980s shift in American anthropology from an
interest in social structure to personhood is very visible in her 1995 book
entitled *To Sing With Pigs Is Human: Concepts of Person in Papua New
Guinea* and all of the other publications that Jane based on her Kaulong
fieldwork (Goodale 1980, 1983, 1985). As a body of work, Jane's Oceanic
research and publications have contributed to the anthropological study
of gender, age, personhood, long-term change, applied anthropology, and
ethnographic methodology and description.

It is truly difficult to draw a boundary between Jane's ethnographic
experiences and research accomplishments and her style and legacy as
a mentor and classroom teacher. After receiving her doctorate in 1959,
she taught at Bryn Mawr College and the next year at Barnard and the
University of Pennsylvania. She was eventually offered jobs at each of
these three schools, but took the job at Bryn Mawr in 1960, where she
remained until her retirement in 1996.

My role in the department was almost at once head of anthropology in
a joint Anthropology/Sociology Department replacing Freddy de Laguna
who was on leave. On her return we both taught a yearlong multi-field

Introduction to Anthropology. In more advanced courses I taught Physical and Evolutionary Anthropology, Kinship and Social Organization (for thirty-six years), and Archaeology. For thirty-six years I also taught the required Senior Seminar, which evolved over the years from a preparation for comprehensive examinations to experimental courses such as the Anthropology of Women (later Gender) and Anthropology through Fiction. Over the thirty-six years that I taught at Bryn Mawr College, the numbers of students grew from two graduate students to over twenty and the number of undergraduate majors grew from ten to over fifty. These students were trained by four full-time professors and sometimes one or more part-timers. (personal communication February 2003)

Jane worked together with Freddy de Laguna to establish both the stand-alone Department of Anthropology and the undergraduate and graduate programs at Bryn Mawr College. As Jane reflects, "Freddy was a wonderful boss and role model and the knowledge she shared about how to handle people was invaluable when I became chair" (Dickerson-Putman 1998). Phil Kilbride, another colleague of Jane's at Bryn Mawr College, remembers:

When I first came to Bryn Mawr in 1969, Freddy and Jane were, even by then, widely respected colleagues. It was only a few years before Jane would publish her seminal work *Tiwi Wives*, which would put her at the top of her profession. In those early years, Dalton Hall was a flurry of excitement signaled by the fact that every one of our dozen or so senior majors went on to graduate school and we in the department were pushing ahead with strong programs of ethnographic research ourselves. Jane was crucial in establishing the strong tradition for ethnographic research that we as a college have become known for. Many of these students are now considered household names in their various fields of study! Nevertheless, Bryn Mawr College provided a minimum of institutional support for anthropology. In the early years, for example, there was one phone in Jane's office. Whenever I had a call she would ring a bell out in the hallway and she would point to me or the other member of the department who lived at the other end of the corridor. As a role model and colleague Jane was a dedicated scholar who brought to the table her New England virtues of hard work, honesty, trustworthiness, and individualism. She would never, under any circumstances, compromise what she considered to be the department's best interest and would never say a negative thing in public about a colleague for fear of damaging the department which she loved. (personal communication February 2003)

One of the most important reasons Jane joined Bryn Mawr was because she and Freddy de Laguna shared a strong belief in the importance and necessity of solid, repetitive fieldwork and the need to broadly train students in all of the subfields of anthropology. They were also especially concerned to produce the best-trained female students so that they could be competitive in the academic marketplace. In the 1990s, when the graduate program at Bryn Mawr came under threat, Jane received a supportive phone call that she will never forget: "A high-level representative of the Wenner Gren Foundation called me and said that Bryn Mawr students and their research proposals were always top drawer because our department never went with fads. We emphasized good, solid ethnographic research that showed breadth, depth, imagination, and a high level of technical skill" (Dickerson-Putman 1998).

Jane recognized the necessity for ethnographic training and she drew invaluable lessons from her own ethnographic experiences when, in the early 1980s, she and her colleague Phil Kilbride developed a yearlong field methods senior seminar that was required of all seniors majoring in anthropology. As Jane remembers:

> When Phil and I first developed the course we required students to do a full year of ethnographic work on American ethnic groups in the Philadelphia area and later any group such as street graffiti artists, cross-dressers, undertakers, and motorcycle gangs. The course involved preparing a research grant, finding a field location, and getting started with fieldwork in the first semester with continued fieldwork and preparation of a seventy-plus-page thesis in the second semester. The overall goal for the course was to provide a structure in which students can cultivate their own sense of discovery. Many undergraduates consider this the most useful course of all of their undergraduate training. (Dickerson-Putman 1998)

Although Jane had not taken a formal field methods course with Coon, Jane feels that his perspective has importantly influenced the way she approaches the process of fieldwork and ethnographic analysis.

> It is clear that I believe in and teach the primacy of the inductive method, considering deduction a device to prove what induction has already revealed to you. Fieldwork is what anthropology is all about. First you must collect data as holistically as you can. You should not have a narrow focus but instead try to the best of your ability to learn the world as they see it. This includes social relationships and relationships with nature. Write it all down and sort and re-sort notes into categories because you never know when some data will trigger an insight. Never stop trying to integrate the facts and make some sense of it. You must immerse yourself in the culture and internalize the culture, not just write it down. (Dickerson-Putman 1998)

Jane encouraged her students to learn more about the ethnographic process of description and comparison and the value of long-term research through participation in the Association for Social Anthropology in Oceania (ASAO). Jane attended one of the first meetings, which was held in Santa Cruz, California. The first paper she presented at ASAO would later become her 1980 chapter entitled "Gender, Sexuality and Marriage: A Kaulong Model of Nature and Culture." From her perspective, ASAO played a crucial role in the later success of her Oceania undergraduates and graduates because "we were a small department and we made it a success through our own networks with our own colleagues. The ASAO essentially trained all of the people that went to the Pacific as well as we did" (Dickerson-Putman 1998). Jane has served as a contributor, officer, and board member of the organization and was made an honorary fellow in 1994. Many of her Pacific students followed her role model by presenting papers, organizing sessions, and acting in ASAO leadership positions.

Throughout her years at Bryn Mawr, Jane continued as a vital force in the monthly meetings of the PAS and she also served as secretary and later president of the organization. Jane strongly encouraged her students to attend the monthly meetings as well. She remembers that "for those of us in smaller institutions, the PAS was a significant part of our professional lives and most of us made it so for our students as well" (personal communication April 2002).

Jane also emulated Coon in her belief that the student–professor relationship should be one of sharing, collaboration, and mentorship. When I asked Jane to think about her contribution to anthropology, she said:

> First I think that I made a contribution to anthropology by showing that men and women view the world differently. Also I think it's a whole host of good students who are going out there and going further than I did. If I passed anything on it's this idea that one needs to mentor people and it comes back one-hundredfold. I got paid back for all of the effort I put in because my students became my colleagues. I tried to give them the tools to go further. And I think that's what my mentors did for me. They never held me back from going in any direction. The administration at Bryn Mawr never understood how we achieved such success with so few faculty and so little support inside the college. It was a total collaboration. The secret of course is that we mentored every student, both our own and those of other faculty. It is also true that every student that passed through contributed to the education of the students coming afterwards and we used all of our networks on the outside to nurture our students on the inside. (Dickerson-Putman 1998)

In her role as mentor to Bryn Mawr students, Jane has directed eighteen M.A.'s and eighteen Ph.D. dissertations (twelve of which were based on

Oceanic research). She was also an outside examiner on nine Ph.D.'s (eight of which were based on ethnographic research on Australian Aboriginal communities).

Jane's graduate seminars at Bryn Mawr College were forums for active collaboration. Depending on your cohort, you were part of Jane's team and together you worked on creating linkages and defining metaphors in either her Tiwi and/or Kaulong data. Jane feels that student collaboration and intellectual exchange helped her to discover some of the symbolic interconnections she has shared in her ethnographic publications. For example, Jane remembers that the inspiration for the creative symbolic analyses reflected in her later publications came through her discussion with Bryn Mawr students about the metaphoric nature of Lévi-Strauss's perspective (personal communication February 2003). Jane has also collaborated with her students in various publications through the years (1980, 1987, 1996a; Kilbride, Goodale, and Ameisen 1990).

Jane's students learned through her example and not through her criticism. Her feminist practice of learning and teaching avoided domination and imperious claims of authority (Myers 1998). She relished the time she spent in cultivating individual students, and through these interactions Jane came to understand which field situation would be best for both the student and the local population. No matter where she placed her students, Jane always believed that "a certain amount of sympathetic empathy must exist in order to carry out an ethnographic study. Cultural empathy has, I believe, little to do with similarity of cultural background—but rather with the ability to connect on some level of human understanding" (1994b: 16). Jane's fieldwork style and her commitment to the cultural groups she worked with has also helped to pave the way for students and colleagues who did not formally train with her. The collaboration, nurturance, confidence, and unselfish mentorship Jane offered to her students formed the basis for the development of the "Bryn Mawr Mafia," an enduring social group that was first identified at an ASAO meeting in the late 1970s.

Encouraged by Coon's mentorship and support, Jane embraced the craft of ethnography and made it a central component of her life. As the following contributions show, Jane's students continue her legacy both through their own mentorship of students and through their contributions to the life and relevancy of contemporary ethnography.

2. *Pulling the Right Thread*

At Bryn Mawr College in the fall of 1972, Miss Goodale's Anthropology 203 course for majors, Primitive Society, was structured, she told us, as a four-ringed circus. She offered us a syllabus that juxtaposed (1) readings of canonical ethnographies (Evans-Pritchard's *The Nuer*, Raymond Firth's *We the Tikopia*, Edmund Leach's *Political Systems of Highland Burma*, and James West's *Plainville USA*) with (2) selected reprints from Nelson Graburn's *Readings in Kinship and Social Structure* (beginning with Lewis Henry Morgan and ending with David Schneider) with (3) an innovative workbook in field methods by Pierre Maranda (that began with census and mapping exercises and ended with network analyses of primary groups) and finally with (4) lectures that began by differentiating social structure from social organization and ended with alliance theory and gift exchange via Marcel Mauss, Claude Lévi-Strauss, and Richard Salisbury. Bound firmly by classic monographs, fieldwork principles, kinship and social organization theory, and the specificity of Jane Goodale's own data on Tiwi and Kaulong and those of her graduate student Judith Huntsman on Tokelau, the course was in its content and structure an expression of ethnographic realism.

At the end of my course notes, I was surprised to discover in Jane's instructions for taking the final exam the same guidelines I now more than thirty years later give to my undergraduate students. Implicitly, these instructions retain an allegiance to the realist idiom, instructing students to balance theoretical assertions with ethnographic cases (a relationship we now call "praxis") and to approach the whole exam as if it was a single question by not repeating examples. Boldly circled in blue fountain pen in my notebook are: "depth," "breadth," and "INTEGRA-TION." Similarly, our research papers were to emphasize "comparison" and "theory." In these five words rests Jane's legacy to her students and to her discipline.

Although I know that the Primitive Society course has been renamed to reflect a different anthropological moment, I am sure that certain learning conventions to which we were tethered at Bryn Mawr persist, as they do at Bard College where I teach. My introductory students read Frederica de Laguna's "Style Sheet for Taking Notes in Anthropology." They take notes on one side of the page, they record page numbers, they separate their own metacommentary from the author's words in a process we now call "dialectical notebooks," and assiduously follow in-noting conventions and the *American Ethnologist* style sheet. I explain to them that these skills are necessary for fieldworkers as well as classroom learners. Moreover, while they persistently ask me for photocopied course packs, I steadily maintain (despite the technological revolution in Reserve Web, which provides anytime online access to the full text of assigned course readings, searchable by course, instructor, and keywords) that taking detailed notes by reading articles on reserve is part of their training in ethnography. The conventions embody, as did Jane's course and the ethos of anthropology at Bryn Mawr, the detail, rigor, and responsibility involved in respecting the multiple authorships of fieldwork practice. The referential and the expressive—Sapir's linguistic distinctions that Freddy taught us in Cultural Theory in the fall of 1973—are fused.

While mainly factual, my course notes every so often marginally notate Jane's asides—advice and assertions that actually belie the presumed straightforwardness of the realist idiom and its ally "ethnographic typification." These notes are strongly inductive and empirical in motivation, such as:

"Find questions, not answers."
Ask, "For what question is this observation an answer?"
Remember: "Everything found in a society has a reason for being there."
In collecting genealogies, say, "Tell me about your ancestors . . ." and then shut up.
In examining residence, ask, "Why make a choice?" Find exceptions and ask, "Under what conditions does one not make a choice?"
"Despite structural similarities, underlying reasons may vary."
"Never, in anthropology, ask a question that can be answered 'yes' or 'no'; don't assume; don't ask leading questions."

If the facts in my notebooks are creditable to the astoundingly complex and patterned cognitive and kinship worlds that Jane's informants inhabited, the asides honor the complexity of fieldwork as a kind of cultural practice in which Jane was instructing us. Former Bryn Mawr undergraduate Sherry Ortner retains this essence as a minimum definition of ethnography: "The attempt to understand another life world using the self as much of it as possible as an instrument of knowing" (Ortner 1995: 173).

In titling this paper, I used Jane's gendered metaphor for practicing anthropology. Ethnographic explanation is, she writes, "similar to the pleasure one feels when, in unraveling a skirt hem, the right thread is cut and pulled . . . there is only one thread that allows a smooth and complete undoing in one pull" (Goodale 1995: xiii). Jane has sought patterns in culture that allow for no "loose ends" or "snipped threads." Her thread is singular. Systems and their patterns defined the anthropology that Jane would have encountered at Radcliffe College with Carleton Coon and at the University of Pennsylvania with Irving Hallowell and Ward Goodenough in the moment of "post–[Second World War] exuberance" recently characterized by Clifford Geertz in an essay on the development of his life and career. Drawing on the legacy of Clyde Kluckhohn, Edward Sapir, and Ruth Benedict, he writes, "A phoneme, a practice, a role, an attitude, a habit, a trait, an idea, a custom was, as the slogan had it, 'a point in a pattern'; it was systems we were after, forms, structures, shapes, contexts—the social geometry of sense" (Geertz 2002: 5). Geertz's geometry is Goodale's thread.

This is the anthropology I miss. For those of us problem solvers who think like social scientists, Jane's ethnographic method was very satisfying. It was documentary, investigative, logical, doable, measurable, and comparative. Its focus on the activities of everyday life, the inductive gathering of empirical data (see Rosi, this volume), and the puzzle-solving in finding the pattern in those data seemed at the time straightforward or at least manageable (see Venbrux, this volume). The tools were maps and censuses, kinship charts and calorie counts, steno pads and pencils, sneakers and large-pocketed skirts. The goal was description, analysis, interpretation, comparison, and explanation. By the time I began graduate study at Cornell University in 1975, this ethnographic realism was on the wane. For the first ten years of my professional life, Michelle Rosaldo's and Sherry Ortner's interpretive version of feminist anthropology and symbolic anthropology defined the discipline for me. To be sure, Meyer Fortes's distinction between "domestic" and "public," Claude Lévi-Strauss's distinction between "nature" and "culture," Talcott Parson's dynamic transformation of the stratigraphic to the cybernetic model, Victor Turner's extended case method, and Clifford Geertz's textual interpretive model of culture dominated the discipline I practiced.

By 1986, an even more dramatic literary turn forced anthropology down another road with the publication of James Clifford and George Marcus's *Writing Culture*, the fascinating complexities of historical ethnography in Marshall Sahlins's Hawaiian work on the death of James Cook, and the pleasantly dislocating and unsettling dominance of postmodernism and reflexivity. A decade later, a fused economic, discursive, and historical turn—forged by John and Jean Comaroff and Michael Taussig, among others—brought us multisited ethnography, discourse's erasure of culture, and global transnational flows of capital and people in a fractured digital world. Keeping up with anthropology's new worlds has meant keeping up not only with changes in method and modes of analysis, but also with a new vocabulary and new ways of writing and talking in a shifting academic culture of unrelentingly blurred disciplinary boundaries. Where in this newest version of anthropology is Jane Goodale's pedagogical and ethnographic legacy?

Through almost five decades, from descriptive realism in the 1950s to a still-emerging postmodernist and poststructuralist critical ethnography, the essence of her method has sustained anthropology. Essential are participant observation as an experiential dialogic process through the inductive method, comparison, exhaustive completeness, and aiming for "culturally constructed concepts of humanness and the social order." Committed to gender analysis, but rejecting the "feminist" modifier as anthropologist, Jane trained several generations of women undergraduates, including Harriet Whitehead, Sherry Ortner, Jane Atkinson, Jane Fajans, and Martha Kaplan, whose work embodies her ethnographic principles while spinning off in varied theoretically innovative directions. Here I reconcile the seeming singularity of Jane's thread with a multiperspectival transcultural anthropology where, as the late Annette Weiner explained to Bard senior Amanda Tumulty, who interviewed her in 1994 for a thesis on fieldwork and feminist theory, "Anthropology is always saying but let's pull the rug out from under that a little bit" in our refusal "to reach narrow, easy conclusions" (Tumulty 1994: 142). What are the consequences for anthropology of imagining the analytic potential of a thread that becomes at times twisted, frayed, tangled, or knotted?

To avoid reification, my students and I, in Introduction to Anthropology, follow Roger Keesing's lead in "Theories of Culture Revisited" by challenging ourselves to avoid using "culture" as a noun throughout the semester; turning it into an adjective instead, we speak of "the cultural."

Keesing's "cultural" engages the production of cultural forms, their ideological force, and cultural multiplicities in terms of subjectivities and fluid boundaries. A parallel exercise might be to turn Jane's conception, practice, production, and writing of ethnography into an adjective as well. We have many examples of this shaping the discipline from Bryn Mawr–trained anthropologists: Sherry Ortner's "ethnographic stance" and "ethnographic refusal"; Annette Weiner's reassertion of the "ethnographic enterprise"; Fred Myers's "locating ethnographic practice"; Jane Fajans's "ethnographic necessity . . . [as] the mother of theoretical invention" (1997: 9); and Martha Kaplan's ethnographic readings of political-religious histories and the colonial state, in which the archive has become a field site, and now this volume's "ethnographic legacy."

Like ethnographic realism, ethnographic typification with its search for patterns also has been unfashionable since the mid-1980s. In "Writing Against Culture," Abu-Lughod celebrates writing ethnographies of the particular (1991: 149) as both a play on and against the title of Clifford and Marcus's influential volume and as an argument against culture as an essential tool for making the other, for essentializing difference (1991: 143). By doing so, she does not dismantle institutions such as patrilineality or polygyny or patrilateral parallel-cousin marriage; rather, she uses them as chapter headings in her experimental ethnography *Writing Women's Worlds* (1993) as she examines how women, for example, "live the institution of polygyny" (1991: 153). Nor does she dismiss the salience of systems, as evidenced in her focus on the ways in which "gender as a system of difference" intersects with other systems of difference. Even configurations of global power as patterned remain intact. Abu-Lughod, like many anthropologists who are invested in exploring the politics of representation, is writing about writing—ethnographic typification is, after all, a rhetorical device. Even so, her main point returns us firmly to fieldwork: "I propose that we experiment with narrative ethnographies of the particular in a continuing tradition of fieldwork-based writing" (1991: 153). Abu-Lughod wants us not to neglect or tidy up the loose threads and snipped ends, but to acknowledge and integrate them into the messiness of narrative. If we return to Jane's documented asides in my notebooks, they suggest field methods that are fully sensitive to Abu-Lughod's urgings—to pay attention to contradictions, "conflicts of interest, and doubts and arguments" (1991: 153). Jane's metaphor for ethnography may allow for the possibility of the frayed thread or an acknowledgment of the ways in which thread is systematically plied—twisted, bent, multiplied.

On the surface this seems not so different from the direction Jane Goodale set in *Tiwi Wives*, published in 1971, the year I began undergraduate college and the year she coauthored "The Contaminating Woman" with Ann Chowning for the American Anthropological Association meetings. Although Jane has described her centering of the Tiwi female ego as merely a "cute little twist of the kaleidoscope" (1994b: 10), it turned out to be of fundamental importance in establishing feminist anthropology and ultimately in decentering and recentering the discipline. Similarly the counterpoint between ego-centered and sociocentered networks and genealogies, and the dynamic aspect that the integration of the life cycle brought to a strongly kinship-centered analysis, undercut any notion of the fixity of culture and its typification. As Jane acknowledges in her introduction to *Tiwi Wives*, she delayed publication until she could go back to Snake Bay to fill in critical gaps in her understanding of Tiwi and to tie together the "apparent discrepancies in social structure" that had left her with loose ends (1971: xix). In *Tiwi Wives*, Jane's own center is social structure and kinship; its centrality in her work is not coincidental, I think, to her mathematically inflected concern for pattern, for something complicitous with ethnographic explanation. That she located a circus ring in field methods within a foundation course in social organization and kinship tells us something about how Tiwi defined a particular kind of anthropology for Jane.

Similarly, in West New Britain, Kaulong shifted her preoccupations to their own concerns with the concept of person. Jane uses shell exchange as the singular symbol to be interpreted; the analysis of that exchange leads her to the rediscovery of a Melanesian truth, which is the centrality of relational configurations as a way of understanding the relationship between the individual and society. If shell exchange is the thread, pulling it leads her to this distinctively Melanesian analysis. Here (in *To Sing With Pigs Is Human*) we find yet again another evocation of patterning, of pulling the right thread:

> The use of a single symbol for the wide range of contexts becomes understandable if one interprets the ultimate message I am giving my trade partners with every shell exchange as follows: that I am saying something (always somewhat ambiguously) about my personal efficacy in producing things and in relationships by which my social ranking is established. But the shell itself cannot be used as a standard of that rank alone, for just as any person's rank is relative and dynamic, so is the value of each shell used to symbolize the rank. What has never been set by using a standard symbol (such as words) can always be renegotiated. For the Kaulong, verbal communication is always evasive and ambiguous, for once an explicit statement is made it is rarely forgotten. No personal evaluation is absolute unless one is nothing, without any worth, a so-

cial nonperson, a rubbish man, without efficacy or the ability to make or produce anything. Such individuals do exist in theory and fact, and they form a bottom line from which to measure one's own self-development. . . . To be human is to be judged only in relation to other humans and by activities understood to be human. To be competent, perhaps exceptional, in shell exchange is tantamount to being human, *potunus*. (Goodale 1995: 107–8)

Although not located within a narrative of world events, we do have here what John and Jean Comaroff (drawing upon Edmund Leach's *Political Systems of Highland Burma*) have referred to as the "fluid, fragmentary character of social reality," a complex multiplied thread. Recall that Leach's was a canonical text in the Primitive Society course, and Mauss, then as now, a bedrock text. We have their working definition of culture that my students used in a seminar in anthropology and literature—"culture [is] the semantic space, the field of signs and practices, in which human beings construct and represent themselves and others, and hence their societies and histories. It is not merely an abstract order of signs, or relations among signs. Nor is it just the sum of habitual practices. Neither pure *langue*, nor pure *parole*, it never constitutes a closed, entirely coherent system. Quite the contrary: Culture always contains within it polyvalent, potentially contestable messages, images and actions" (Comaroff and Comaroff 1992: 27).

In beginning to confront the "Baining Problem," Bryn Mawr undergraduate alumna Jane Fajans tried several "Goodale-like" tactics to address the problem—a problem of amorphousness, characterized by Gregory Bateson, whom she quotes, as "the lack of any formulable culture or social organization," a problem, as it turns out, that is an "artifact of various theoretical and cultural lenses used by other anthropologists, administrative officers, and missionaries." Fajans opted to:

follow the Baining's example and concentrate on learning, and integrating myself into, the mundane routine of everyday life. I spent many months sitting in the hamlet observing and participating in Baining family life. I tried to record the *patterns* and *activities* of hamlet life and garden work, of child socialization and casual visiting. This concentration on the mundane and the minute bore fruit. In the *activities* and *practice* I observed and queried I discovered patterns and consistencies which pervaded Baining life. These tendencies were the expressions of important Baining values, ideas, and motivations. They were not explicit but they infused everything that happened. Through understanding these *patterns* of behavior and values I found that I could generate a systematic description of Baining persons, behavior, culture and society. (Fajans 1997: 6; emphasis added)

Jane Fajans's solution to the Baining problem—resting in the discovery of endogenous but inexplicit patterns and reconceptualizing activity as "social interactions in which people transform their world to satisfy their needs, and in so doing transform themselves"—parallels not only Goodale's Kaulong patterns quoted above but also South Asianist Margaret Trawick's *Notes on Love in a Tamil Family,* by far the most attractive and successful ethnography that I have taught in Introductory Anthropology. In my students' favorite passage, Trawick invites them to test a metaphor with her; Trawick replaces Goodale's feminine metaphor of the thread with that of waves. She writes:

> Let us not think of the person, the native, as a sphere, with a surface to be stripped off or gotten through to the real stuff, the contents. Let us think of consciousness, or better yet, culture . . . as activity—culture/consciousness as an activity not done by one person, but done among people, leaving its traces in memory . . . which will be part of the matrix for the next cultural act, the next interaction. Let us say that culture is in the interaction. After all, where else would it be?
>
> Then when we view things this way, we find that there is no surface or depth. Instead there is only the turbulence of confrontation, with ourselves as part of it. . . .
>
> In all this churning, surface and depth are commingled. Now our aim is not to get to the bottom of things, but to stay afloat. Now what is most important is not what we or others are, but what happens between us—what others present to us, and how we receive it, and what we present, and how that is received by them, and what comes out of it all, continuously, what is being formed, the eddies, the patterns of waves. (Trawick 1992: 89–90)

Jane's students share an ethnographic stance and a commitment to ethnographic inquiry, characterized at its best as an "ethics of attention" by Deborah Rose (this volume), although our gaze in this cultural moment of epistemological angst is far less confident than that of our mentor. What has changed for us is that ethnography itself as a cultural practice has come under scrutiny and is invested in locating its own subjectivities; we are also invested in articulating a mode of ethnographic persuasion that goes beyond the rhetorical, one of ethnographic force and application, which is embedded in the work of some of Jane's former doctoral students: in Fred Myers's formulation of an applied hermeneutics; in Deborah Rose's commitment to the political economy of indigenous knowledges and her attention to colliding intersubjectivities (1993: 46); and in Annette Weiner's call for a comparative approach. Weiner's approach "would reintegrate the best of anthropology's past traditions—among them the ethnographic enterprise and our global concern with diversity" (1993: 17). Annette's comparativism is its global perspective.

In responding to the fallout of an ethnography that ceases to be a noun and becomes an adjective, Fred Myers iterates both the theoretical and practical significance of ethnography and of signifying practices that take place in concrete contexts (1988: 609). Sherry Ortner also captures it well as she confronts the problem of "ethnographic refusal" by articulating the "ethnographic stance" as being as much "an intellectual (and moral) positionality, a constructive and interpretive mode, as it is a bodily process in space and time" (1995: 174). Essential to such a stance is a commitment to a kind of Geertzian/Ortnerian hybrid of "thickness," which bears "traces [of the kinds] of exhaustiveness" Jane practices in detailed description (see Kahn, this volume) and continues to seek "an understanding [that comes] from richness, texture, and detail, rather than parsimony, refinement, and . . . elegance." (Ortner 1995: 174). What Ortner adds is the imperative to locate and contextualize data within "the global processes of the world system" (1995: 174). Reality is fractured into pieces; pieces that Sherry argues—also in a textile metaphor—are woven from within and without. It is the "deep attack on anthropology's most fundamental methodology" that most troubled Annette in the reception of Clifford and Marcus's *Writing Culture* (as quoted in Tumulty 1994: 192). Indeed, Jane's students consistently have retained their commitment to the discipline's ethnographic imperative.

Methodologically, in my own work, this imperative led me to unravel the thread that could explain the relationship of high-country farmers to their land. My fieldwork has focused comparatively on place attachment in two mountain regions in Australasia, where I sought to develop an ethnographically based set of methods that help to define the anthropology of place. As a student in Primitive Society, I began to learn the data-driven, inductive, comparative, indigenous, knowledge-based ethnographic craft that defines Jane Goodale's pedagogical and anthropological legacy. The relationship between people and place has been central to Jane's ethnography of the Pacific and to the work of her students. Jane taught us to examine place not as setting but as a physical site of cultural activity and imagination. Essential to this work has been the concept of the domestic domain, the role of land tenure, and the interplay between nature and culture (Goodale 1980).

In New Zealand my work examined the connections of pastoral high-country families to the land. It documents the ways in which these inhabitants' affinity to land is sustained and claimed through social practices and linguistic, symbolic, and narrative forms. From Jane, I knew to document these patterns through time (across generations, seasons, and multiple field residencies) and through space (across valleys, elevation, and sites), from the wool shed to the auction house.

- *Social practices:* I documented rules of land tenure and patterns of property transfer between the generations to show how patricentric partible inheritance practices create gender-based structural tensions, which must be reconciled to preserve family harmony and estate integrity. Against the precise, descriptive detail of mustering, shearing, and lambing activities, I described traditional pastoral productive processes and indigenous ways of knowing land. The practices are labor intensive and structurally important for the organization of social life, for the preservation of continuity of the past in the present, and as markers of cultural transformation.
- *Linguistic forms:* Toponymy and lexicon, as well as legal, geologic, and indigenous linguistic categories of land, define and convey the conceptual systems that shape and reflect the relationship of high-country people to the land. I drew upon materials ranging from geological maps, to resource surveys, to vernacular categories and idioms of orientation and containment, and to conversations with local people to address the ways New Zealand landscape forms the ground of high-country people's consciousness.
- *Symbolic forms:* By mapping the social cartography of the homestead and station layout, I examined the built environment as an identity marker denoting the generational continuity of family habitation as well as the particular historical and personal experiences of individuals.
- *Semiotic qualities of narratives:* My work also focuses on the testimony of high-country pastoralists before the Waitangi Tribunal. These data demonstrated the ways in which these people voice their sense of belonging when land is at stake. Finally, I examined an emergent "land ethic" by exploring the legislative arenas within which competing discourses of sustainability are defined and by examining the relationship of sustainability to "country" both historically and contemporaneously.

Comparative research in Australia and New Zealand suggests that mountain inhabitants systematically formulate their own perceptions of their surrounding environments, and the methods delineated above provide an ethnographically grounded way in which scientific research can take account of these perceptions. Comprising habitation, work, sociality, identity, memory, and affectivity, these mountain lands are invested with cultural meaning. The social science that I practice has directly addressed not only the ways in which both the natural and cultural aspects of mountain regions might be understood analytically but also, as important, understood with the kind of deuterolearning that Deborah Rose describes (this volume) as essential to Jane Goodale's ethnographic legacy.

Jane's ethnographic imperative shaped my ethnographic study. In *Calling the Station Home*, I argue that people are an extension of country and country an extension of people; so much so that the mutually inscriptive processes linking people to land and land to people—through inheritance practices, wool production, linguistic practices, and the built environment—seem ineluctable, unremarkable, and generic to them (Dominy 2001: 45). In the settler-descendant context, inheritance is about acquiring opportunity as much as it is about property transmission. These ideas privilege challenge as an equalizer and measure of worth and value achievement and hard work over ascription and privilege. Through naturalizing attachment, family is the vehicle for nurturing country and protecting individual attachment is sacrificed for protecting family continuity on the station. Traditional practices, such as mustering stock and producing wool—where men know how the land falls and see the traces of the land in the fleece—are embodied experiences signifying cultural identity rooted in the specificity of place. Formulaic phrases, such as "taking it on the chin" or "you cannot fight nature," reflect a progressive and resilient ethos of "getting on with it" in the face of economic, climatic, ecological, and geographic adversity, which linguistically create a capable, coping mentality that moves people forward. In this way, landscape becomes encoded in character. Thus, naturalizing conventions and discourses prevail as humans culturalize nature and naturalize culture in ways that script them physically, sensually, emotionally, cognitively, and socially as part of habitat. Embodied knowledge and rhetorically naturalized attachment are essential to the ways in which my high-country interlocutors understand the relationship between their identity and their place. Natal attachment to land, like that of lambs to land, and mutual inscription of land on people and people on land was the puzzle piece that rendered the latent visible. In this way, Jane's thread is more than a key to unravel the skirt hem; rather, it becomes multiple, woven, denser—the textile covering the body of culture.

In a powerful defense of the concept of culture (as a noun), John and Jean Comaroff write: "We require ethnography to know ourselves, just as we need history to know non-Western others. For ethnography serves at once to make the familiar strange and the strange familiar, all the better to understand them both. It is, as it were, the canon-fodder of a critical anthropology" (Comaroff and Comaroff 1992: 6). If I am reading the Comaroffs correctly, and their complex statement is, I think, redemptive for anthropology, ethnography as canon-fodder is an essential resource for an anthropology that matters, the deployment of which involves the risk and confusion of a high-stakes enterprise. I think Jane would find the substitution of a military metaphor, canon-fodder, for her domestic metaphor of pulling the right thread an acceptable maneuver to protect the ethnographic heart of the discipline even though its (and her) "tent in the village" (Clifford 1997: 60) has been decentered.

3.   It's Not about Women Only

Anyone unfamiliar with Jane's ethnography and teaching may assume—on the basis of her sex and the title of her iconic *Tiwi Wives* (1971)—that she privileges women and female anthropologists above men. Such is not the case, however. Jane has been a forerunner in the investigation of the many gender roles both women *and* men play over the course of their lives. She has also promoted a keen awareness among her male and female students of the pivotal roles gender and sexuality play in both their fieldwork experiences and the lives of those they study. Examining my own and others' work in the context of Jane's legacy, I explore the influences of reflexivity and gendered participation in the coming of age of the anthropologies of gender and development. Particular attention is given to insights gained from the 'games people play' and to the ongoing commitment and participation—beyond dissertation and tenure—of anthropologists who, like Jane, keep returning to the field as aging male and female players, local "ancestors," and cultural translators.

The Anthropology of Gender— It's Not about Women Only!

In 1991, a midwestern university hired me because I am a woman. There were other qualifications, of course, but a woman was needed to lend diversity to a five-man sociology/anthropology discipline housed within a male-heavy social science division. My male colleagues were also keen for me to introduce an Anthropology of Gender course, something they apparently believed can best be taught by a woman. During their review of my job application materials, they duly noted that I had taken such a course at Bryn Mawr College *and* been mentored by Jane Goodale of *Tiwi Wives* fame. This was all well and good, except that several male colleagues also wanted me to be a female terminator of a proposed women's studies minor. My colleagues saw the Anthropology of Gender course as an uncomplicated demonstration of how—with the exception of Western feminists—the world's women were satisfied with their culturally appointed roles. Some of the campus feminists who had conceived the proposed minor at once saw me as a threat and pawn of my male colleagues. Both sides rushed to malign the other. That first year was a nightmare. Drawing upon Jane's teachings and example, however, I created a course that not only satisfied my sociology/anthropology colleagues but also became one of the most popular courses in the women's studies and honors programs. Within a few years, I achieved tenure *and* befriended my women's studies colleagues. And during the twenty semesters I taught the course, my students and I engaged in a mutual learning experience that rivaled any I had ever experienced. I felt deeply satisfied when, in one semester, I had nine men in a class I deliberately limited to only twenty students a semester. Although I sometimes had to protect them from the occasional überfeminist during heated class discussions, the men had much to contribute and learn about the varieties of men's and women's gendered experiences at home and in other cultures.

Even so, I was dismayed by a persistent bias that "gender" equals "woman," a bias within and outside anthropology. This is our own fault. Textbooks favor women's topics when they are classified as gender studies. Even Brettell and Sargent's otherwise excellent reader (2001) has no articles on men in the section on colonialism, development, and the global economy. And elsewhere in the reader, the few articles that do address male gender include an excerpt from David Gilmore's annoying *Manhood in the Making* (1990). Gilmore classifies some societies—those that don't fit his psychological model of masculinity—as "neuter" societies in which men are supposedly free from the need to prove themselves and are allowed a basically androgynous script. One of Gilmore's examples of neuter societies is Tahiti, of all places! Frustrated, I got together with Jeanette Dickerson-Putman to organize a session on Men and Development in the Pacific at the 1994 American Anthropological Association meeting. With Andrew Strathern as invited discussant and ten presenters (six of whom were men) representing different areas of the Pacific, the session attracted a large audience of male and female scholars. Our primary goals were to challenge the proposition that development necessarily favors men over women and to clarify how gender and other cultural differences play into Pacific Islanders' strategies and motivations as they participate in the capitalist world system. After the meeting we sought publishers for the many excellent papers, but at that time few publishers were interested in highlighting *men* and development. Participants were forced to seek publishers on their own or to embed their findings in other papers. Sociology has done better in realizing the plenitude of men's issues that had not been addressed in earlier studies, so—back in my Anthropology of Gender class—I assigned Kimmel and Messner's *Men's Lives* (2001) to complement books on women. I began to realize how radical my education had been and what Jane meant when she cautioned against taking sides and getting lost in all the "isms" of the late twentieth century.

Reflexivity and Gendered Participation

Of course, setting the anthropological record straight has required the publication of many myth-busting books on women (and women anthropologists) such as Margery Wolf's *Women and the Family in Rural Taiwan* (1972) and Peggy Golde's *Women in the Field* (1970). In my course, the first four weeks focused on fieldwork, gendered participation, and the historical rise of reflexive anthropology. Readings and discussions centered on ethnographic cases where women had been given short shrift by male and sometimes female anthropologists and then later—on closer, often female examination—were revealed to be active participants alongside men in all or most aspects of their cultures and societies. I discussed how anthropologists were slow to recognize the important role of women in Australian Aboriginal societies in spite of early studies such as Phyllis Kaberry's on Aboriginal women and religion (1939; see also Burbank 1989). I pointed to Jane's *Tiwi Wives* (1971) and her student Annette Weiner's *Women of Value, Men of Renown* (1976) as groundbreaking ethnographies that present balanced accounts of men and women's gendered activities and cultural involvement. I contrasted these gender-sensitive studies with earlier ethnographies focusing almost entirely on the activities of Tiwi (Hart and Pilling 1960) and Trobriand Island men (Malinowski 1922). I discussed male bias in archaeology and physical anthropology, instructed students to follow Catherine Lutz's example (1990) and check bibliographic references for the erasure of women's writing, and, when it came out, had students read most of the articles in Behar and Gordon's *Women Writing Culture* (1995) to learn how stubborn male bias has been.

I wasn't content to leave it at only women setting the ethnographic record straight, however. So I introduced issues of male and female sexuality, gender, and reflexivity with Gilbert Herdt's *Guardians of the Flutes* (1981), Don Kulick and Margaret Willson's *Taboo: Sex, Identity and Erotic Subjectivity in Anthropological Fieldwork* (1995), and Tony Whitehead and Mary Ellen Conaway's *Self, Sex, and Gender in Cross-Cultural Fieldwork* (1986). In the Whitehead and Conaway reader, male and female anthropologists consider how age, sex, race, and other variables (their own and their informants') affect their field experiences and perspectives on the societies they work in. Interestingly, none of the articles suggest that one's gender necessarily prevents one from learning more than one side of the matter. And in his article, Tony Whitehead (1986) demonstrates that sometimes privilege—or the anthropologist's perceived class—prevents him (or her) from relying on such characteristics as shared race or sex as a means for obtaining an insiders' point of view. The West Indians he worked with did not perceive his 'blackness' as something they had in common with him. Rather, they perceived his American nationality as synonymous with wealth and power and kept him at a distance by persisting in calling him a "big brown pretty talking man." Similarly, Jean Briggs found her perceived privileges as a white American to be a roadblock, at least initially, for her acceptance into Eskimo society (1970).

Jane and Her Men

How fortunate that Jane studied the Tiwi. And, in spite of her book's title, *Tiwi Wives: A Study of the Women of Melville Island, North Australia* (1971), she made use of Hart and Pilling's research (1960) along with her own observations of Tiwi men and women to give us a nuanced view of Tiwi social structure and relations. Although her gender gave her greater access to women and she prevailed upon Hart and Pilling to drop their awful practice of calling older women "hags" (see Hart, Pilling, and Goodale 1988), Jane did not turn her own book into a feminist diatribe or use it to bash male colleagues. Indeed, when Charles P. Mountford of the South Australian Museum in Australia invited a young Jane to join him and others in an ethnographic study of the Tiwi of Melville Island in 1954, Jane quietly bridled at the idea that she was expected to focus only on "the women" and took every opportunity to interact with both Tiwi men and women during her time in the field. Unlike anthropologist Jean Jackson—who believed there would be little of interest in studying Amazon women and as a result had difficulties establishing close relationships with the women (Jackson 1986)—Jane quickly connected and enjoyed going into the bush with Tiwi men and women and being instructed in the "intricacies of their ways and philosophy of life" (Goodale 1971: xviii). For Jane, getting the Tiwi's story straight was paramount. After her first field trip, she discovered many discrepancies between her data and interpretations and those of Mountford, Pilling, and Hart. Much of the difference was related to Jane's greater understanding of the special roles older Tiwi women played in Tiwi ceremonies and economic life. More fieldwork was needed, however, before Jane was able to publish her analysis of Tiwi society, using the life cycle of women as a framework for discussing Melville Island culture.

It is worth emphasizing that the strength of *Tiwi Wives* (1971) lies in Jane's understanding of the bigger picture of Tiwi cultural dynamics and the participation of both genders. Jane was aided in this understanding of Tiwi social relations by being accepted into Tiwi society in various kinship positions. In his paper in this volume, Eric Venbrux makes reference to some of Jane's more significant kin ties. One such relationship was to Paddy Puruntatameri—her Tiwi "father"—who gave Jane her Tiwi name, *Tutangantilauwayu* ("female spear"). Paddy's wife Rachel had her own close relationship with Jane, beginning in 1954 when Jane would sometimes look after the younger Rachel, and continuing over the years as Rachel became Paddy's much younger wife and by extension Jane's "mother." Venbrux relates how Paddy and Rachel had many fond memories of Jane taking them hunting in the mangroves during subsequent field trips in the 1980s and 1990s. Venbrux points out a further kinship connection Jane has to Tiwi history and social life: that of the old man who—back in the early 1900s—sang about mainland magic being the cause of a serious epidemic being investigated by an Australian medical officer (and the subject of Venbrux's paper). The old man was Paddy's grandfather, and thus Jane's "great-grandfather." Such historical connections are common in anthropology and say something about the social importance of many of the people who go out of their way to interact with us when we first go to the field. My Gende "father," the big man Ruge Angiva, was the son of one of the first Gende men to work for the German missionaries who "first contacted" the Gende in 1932. Ruge's father thought there was much to learn from the missionaries. Ruge, himself, made a practice of overseeing the activities of all outsiders who came to the Gende's highland home, heading up a group of his clansmen and their wives and children to greet me after my plane landed at Bundi airstrip that very first time.

Jane took her understanding of complex Tiwi social relations and gender complementarity with her when she traveled to Papua New Guinea to study the Kaulong of West New Britain. She also took the knowledge that women are likely to have significant relations not only with husbands but also with other male relatives such as their fathers, sons, and brothers. Such knowledge encouraged Jane to look into many different kinds of relationships in her search for cultural understanding. Again, Jane established close relationships with both male and female Kaulong, although Kaulong women were at first less open with Jane and her relationships with them were not based on kinship. Two of Jane's earliest and most helpful informants were her two assistants (or "house boys")—Ningbi and Debli. In letters to Ann Chowning, Jane noted that Debli was the best language teacher, that she trusted both men, and that she found Ningbi to be an "excellent informant" (Goodale 1996b: 17, 57). It was through Ningbi—who married Ihimei while he was working for Jane—that Jane learned much about Kaulong marriage. Indeed, chapter 7 of Jane's The Two-Party Line (1996b) is entitled, "This Marriage Is a Gold Mine." Precisely because Ningbi worked for Jane and had no fictive kin relationship with her, he was free to talk about men's (and his own) fears of marriage and sexual intercourse and the Kaulong's notable separation between individuals who were married and those who were not (1996b: 151). When Ningbi's outspoken sister, Udwali, visited, Jane learned much about men's easier and important relations with their sisters (1996b: 164). What Jane learned from her two assistants (and other Kaulong) allowed her to write significant essays on Kaulong gender, sexuality, and marriage in the groundbreaking Nature, Culture and Gender (1980) edited by Jane's former student Carol MacCormack and Marilyn Strathern and on the nature of Kaulong sibling relations in Siblingship in Oceania (1983) edited by Jane's fellow ASAO colleague Mac Marshall.

Jane's openness, her painstaking accumulation and sifting of data from many sources, her respect for her subjects, and her graciousness toward colleagues are reflected in her students' accomplishments. One stellar example is Annette Weiner, who went to the Trobriand Islands in Papua New Guinea to study tourism and art and happened onto a major anthropological coup (see Weiner 1976). Here was a society studied by Bronislaw Malinowski, long thought of as one of the "fathers of anthropology" whose writings on participant observation (1922) are still included in books on methodology. Within days after her arrival, Annette realized that Malinowski had overlooked the importance of women's exchanges in the Trobriand scheme of things. Although some critics have since faulted Malinowski for being blinded by his youth and Western male prejudices, Annette did not use this oversight against Malinowski's work and memory. Rather, she wisely used his research and her own to better understand Trobriand society and gender relations as a whole.

Being reflexive then does not mean that because one is a woman you will necessarily understand other women better than a man might. Rather, one may acquire important insights into women's activities that, when put in the context of other research, may result in a kaleidoscopic shift in understanding. In Jane's "final postscript" to *The Two-Party Line*, Jane tackles the issue of "feminist voices in anthropology," declaring how refreshing it now is that volumes like Bell, Caplan, and Karim's edited book *Gendered Fields: Women, Men and Ethnography* (1993; see also Whitehead and Conaway 1986) "contains chapters written by men as well as women" and that "the topic of gendered fieldwork now includes both a discussion of the voices of female and male anthropologists as well as that of their male and female cultural guides" (1996b: 184). The only female advantage that Jane concedes is that "women"—in this case, she and Ann Chowning—may indeed "more easily than men reveal the emotional impact on themselves of the stresses of cross-cultural understanding" as she and Ann did in their "conversations in the field" (1996b: 186).

Big Men and Empowered Women in the New Guinea Highlands

By the time I first went to Papua New Guinea in 1982 and 1983, I was grounded in Jane's methods of doing fieldwork and well-versed in Melanesian ethnography. The first of only two of Jane's students to do fieldwork in the New Guinea highlands, I looked forward to meeting my first big man but was apprehensive about getting to know the mysterious highlands women, often portrayed as shy, hardworking, and kept in the background by their antagonistic and overbearing husbands and fathers intent upon using them to advance their own political interests (cf. Berndt and Lawrence 1971; Brown 1972, 1978; Brown and Buchbinder 1976; Glasse and Meggitt 1969; Langness 1967; Meggitt 1964; Salisbury 1962; Strathern 1971). There had been—it is true—whispers that it might be otherwise with at least some highlands women. In *Women in Between* (1972) and "No Nature, No Culture" (1980), Marilyn Strathern noted women's motivations and structural importance as they worked hard in expectation that their production might go to their relatives and that they might achieve a more "social" (as opposed to "wild") standing in their society. Elizabeth Faithorn went farther, showing Kafe women not only working hard but also commanding respect and agency in the affairs of their own clans, especially with their brothers (1976, 1986). Brother–sister relationships were much talked about by Jane, Mike Lieber (this volume), and other ASAO members around the time I was preparing for my first fieldwork, although never in the context of Papua New Guinea highlands societies (Faithorn's work was largely ignored by highlands ethnographers who then saw it as an anomaly). And Jane and several of her students (Judith Huntsman, DeVerne Smith, and Robert Rubinstein) had articles in Mac Marshall's ASAO Monograph, *Siblingship in Oceania* (1983), published shortly before my first field trip to Papua New Guinea (1982–83).

Coming from such an intellectual environment, I was excited to discover how forthcoming the Gende are about women's vital roles in all aspects of Gende society and culture, including their exchange system. In "Empowered Women" (Zimmer-Tamakoshi 1997a) and "Moga-Omoi's Daughters" (Zimmer-Tamakoshi 1997c), I described how—over the course of their lives—Gende women may achieve power and influence by actively participating in the Gende exchange system. A key exchange for women is *tupoi*, which literally means "returning the pigs." The size of a girl's bride-price is determined in part by her demonstrated value as a hard worker and potential mother of many children. Married women who pay back (or redeem) their bride-price to husbands' kin when they are middle-aged and have also helped their husbands pay childwealth for their offspring do so at large pig feasts known as *poi nomu*. From the time they make *tupoi*, these women are considered free agents in the exchange system. They are free to leave husbands who abuse them or do stupid things. And they are free to invest the pigs they raise in others' futures (such as helping a young man with bride-price), thereby building reputations of generosity and importance, sometimes as great as men's. Most wives of Gende big men do *tupoi* as part of the exchanges during which their husbands first achieve the status. Being a big man—*wana nambaio*—is synonymous with having "good women" for wives. Women who have achieved the status of "good women," or *ana mogeri*, are rarely shy and they rarely take a browbeating from husbands without a fight, usually threatening to return to their brothers and their own clan and to divorce their husbands—a disaster for men.

Gende women's rise to *ana mogeri* status is a function of both individual ambition and hard work and a life course structured in such a way that both men and women may achieve power and influence in their later years. Jane was one of the first anthropologists to fully explicate life course transitions (and opportunities) when she wrote *Tiwi Wives* (1971), showing how Tiwi women might amass influence as they grew older and became the wives of younger husbands and were in charge of younger, incoming wives. In the mid-1980s, a flurry of works documented the importance of life course studies in understanding changes in women's status over time (Brown and Kerns 1985; Counts 1985; Counts and Counts 1985). An important conclusion of many of these works was that earlier studies tended to focus (if at all) on younger women (as brides and young mothers) and not older women. Such studies painted women as having lower status than men, overlooking older women whose children were grown (or very nearly) and who had the time and inclination to engage in prestige-building activities and politics. They also tended to overlook the lower status of young men who, like young women, had to prove themselves worthy of others' respect. Studies from Melanesia and beyond were showing that the thorny issues of female inequality exercising Western feminists might not be relevant in all societies (Strathern 1987). They were also showing that gender is not a simple referent for "female" and that age and kin relations and a host of other factors have to be considered when one looks at gender issues.

Gender and the Anthropology of Development

The questions that drove my doctoral dissertation research among the Gende—at least at the beginning—focused on how a high rate of rural-urban migration, few and unreliable local developments, and the unequal distribution of urban remittances were impacting the lives and social and political fortunes of both men and women, villagers and migrants. At the time, the anthropological literature on development in the Pacific and elsewhere suggested that new, younger, and more Westernized leaders and big men would emerge to replace old-style leaders (cf. Finney 1973), that the majority of young male migrants in Third World cities were pursuing rural-oriented strategies of investment that would put them in the competition for such leadership roles (cf. Salisbury and Salisbury 1972), and that for the most part women's situations would deteriorate both in town and village as women suffered unequal participation in the development process with less access than men to education, jobs, and technical support (Boserup 1970; Charlton 1984; Cole et al. 1985).

A few studies suggested that neither women's nor men's respective situations were so homogeneous. In fairly wealthy coffee-growing regions of the Papua New Guinea highlands (in contrast to both the Siane's and Gende's more remote highlands homelands), villagers looked down on young migrants for "wasting time" in town versus growing cash crops at home (Strathern 1975). Although highlands women continued to be respected for their child- and pig-raising, in many areas men controlled the income from cash crops, even when women helped in tending the crop. This aggravated women because the cash was often spent on drinking and men's political ambitions and not on women's and children's welfare and education. In Papua New Guinea and elsewhere, however, small groups of women were inventing ingenious ways to benefit from or mold development to their own ends, while yet others stoutly—and sometimes successfully—fought against development and discrimination that threatened their traditional social equality and political influence. Etienne and Leacock's 1980 collection, *Women and Colonization,* and Van Allen's 1976 chapter in Hafkin and Bay's *Women in Africa* come to mind as important depictions of women's resistance to the loss of their traditional economic power and Igbo women's war against British taxation. Closer to home was Lorraine Sexton's work in the Eastern Highlands with the women's saving and exchange system known as *wok meri,* or "women's work" (cf. Warry 1986). Selling their vegetables in the Goroka market, nearby village women pooled their earnings, taking turns using the accumulated profits to finance even more profitable projects such as a food bar and trucking business. Women's motivations included wanting to show their men how to save and invest in development rather than spend all their coffee earnings in increasingly expensive beer-drinking and exchange competitions. Many of these women were middle-aged or older and able—because of their position in the female life course—to spend more time on marketing and *wok meri* business. Sexton's *Oceania* article was published in 1982 while I was in the field in another part of the highlands. But I was familiar with Lorraine's findings through listening to her talk at a small gathering of female anthropologists and students in the greater Philadelphia area who met monthly to discuss women and development. Jane had introduced Jeanette Dickerson and me to this particular circle and it was there that we began to ponder the possibilities of complex gender and development issues (cf. Dickerson-Putman 1986, 1992; Dickerson-Putman and Zimmer-Tamakoshi 1994).

One variable that especially interested me—and that was bound to interact in interesting and profound ways with other variables—was economic inequality. In the 1970s and early 1980s, Louise Morauta and Dawn Ryan were among a small cadre of anthropologists studying migrants from the lesser-developed areas of Papua New Guinea. Morauta and Ryan were finding that many of the migrants from swampy coastal areas were becoming permanent townsmen (and women). With little or no development at home, they were more usefully occupied in town. Parents and other family members remaining in the village were becoming increasingly dependent upon urban remittances. In some cases, older relatives were moving to town also, especially those whose migrant sons and daughters were not well-employed and were therefore unable to support their parents' village obligations (Morauta and Ryan 1982). For comparative reasons, Louise—who at the time was working at the Institute of Applied Social and Economic Research in Port Moresby (now the National Research Institute)—strongly encouraged me to work in the Gende area, an undeveloped highlands area of high outmigration with a still strong big man culture and patrilineal bias. The question of what was going on with women—old and young—in an area where there were no nearby towns in which to earn cash selling garden vegetables and men dominated the few opportunities for earning cash was only one of many intriguing questions waiting to be answered.

Gambling Men and Women

The stage was set for me to expect some surprises when I went to the fabled New Guinea highlands. In the event, the Gende outdid themselves. On the night of my arrival in Yandera village, the big man, Ruge Angiva, and his three wives who had chosen to look out for me left me alone in an unused schoolteachers' hut while they went off to play cards. From the beginning it was obvious that most Gende were passionate card players. Huddles of card players and onlookers were a common sight at almost any time of day. And I was told repeatedly that "good men and women" played cards; that people who played always had money even when they were losing because others would give them credit. My initial resistance to believing that there was any positive social or political significance to gambling broke down when—after keeping records of income and cash flow—I realized it was a parallel exchange system in which both men and women could earn money to be used in the regular exchange system; that persons with more cash than others (e.g., persons receiving higher urban remittances from prosperous migrant children) were easily coaxed into playing as a way of showing their generosity; that women would often play against their husbands (or vice versa) in order to earn some cash through the long and hard work of card playing; and that there really was a net flow of cash from richer to poorer (Zimmer 1983, 1984, 1985, 1986). It was crucial, however, that no one lose on purpose because that would put the winner—raised in an egalitarian society (that was now seriously out of whack)—in a position of receiving handouts and shame.

When I gave a post–field research seminar at the University of Papua New Guinea (UPNG) in May 1983, my gambling findings aroused excitement and I was invited to write papers on the topic for both UPNG's *Research in Melanesia* journal (1983) and *Oceania* (1986). Cases like the big man Ruge playing against his wife, Elizabeth, in order to milk some of her trade-store earnings (and money sent to her by their oldest daughter, then an Air Niugini hostess) in order to turn around and lose it to others demonstrated card playing's usefulness for redistributing cash and easing social pressures in an increasingly unequal society. When I returned to Bryn Mawr, Jane and I had lots to talk about. She, too, had interesting gambling data, so we organized two ASAO sessions (1985 and 1986) on the topic of playing with cards in Oceania. Papers from those sessions were published in a 1987 special issue of *Oceania*. In Jane's paper (Goodale 1987), the fact that older Tiwi women were the most numerous, most dedicated, and most skilled card players is striking. Jane related these gender differences to men's greater access to cash and to older women's ongoing role as primary providers for their families.

Having published my wider findings on gambling (Zimmer 1983, 1984, 1985, 1986), I wrote a new paper for the *Oceania* special issue entitled "Playing at Being Men" (Zimmer 1987b). Although both males and females of all ages participated in the Gende gaming system based on Lucky and Seven, only young men and boys played Last Card with any regularity. In my paper, I interpreted this bias as being related to the failure of traditional male initiation to provide an adequate context and means for young men to distinguish themselves and to attract the attention of potential bride-price supporters. Competing against their more fortunate peers, unemployed village youths played Last Card to demonstrate their self-control and mastery of others and to increase their income and ability to participate in exchange relations with older clan members. Interestingly, Lorraine Sexton's paper on card playing in the Daulo region (Sexton 1987) showed that although a majority of Daulo men and women play cards, women who were active in the *Wok Meri* movement were openly critical of card playing, perceiving it to be anti-social and economically unproductive. Unlike Gende and Tiwi gambling, gambling among the Daulo does not effect a more equitable distribution of cash income. Rather, a higher percentage of winning card players are persons who have relatively greater access to and control over money than losing players and nonplayers.

The Marriage Game Transformed

Migration and economic inequality have had considerable impact on the marriage chances and conjugal relations of four generations of Gende. The inability of many young men to contribute large amounts of cash to bride-prices has meant increasing numbers of bachelors as more and more Gende women are marrying prosperous migrants and non-Gende men from wealthier areas. Based on data I gathered in 1982–83, only half the male population of Yandera village—including migrants, or "absentees"—between the ages of twenty-five and thirty-five were married (Zimmer-Tamakoshi 1993a). Many of the bachelors then living in Yandera had previously attempted (and failed) to find work in town in order to improve their chances of marrying. Several approached me with persistent requests for special "American" love magic that might appeal to young women whom they perceived as "arrogant" or "conceited" (bik het). Over many years of working in Papua New Guinea, I have heard many more expressions of male insecurity and resentment toward marriageable women, especially those—such as university students—with many prospects and little inclination to settle down.

Higher bride-prices, however, mean that women have to work harder and longer if they are to pay back and justify their bride-prices. In the case of women living in town without gardens or jobs, many are finding it impossible to make tupoi, resulting in an obvious shift in the balance of power between husbands and wives within marriage and in women's status within their husbands' family and the larger community. Older men and women are also negatively affected, experiencing difficulties arranging large bride-prices for their sons' marriages and at the same time forcing their daughters to marry men who take the daughters far away, perhaps abuse them, and often end up treating the parents with disrespect.

There are quite a few differences in young women's situations and responses to their predicaments and I have discussed these in several articles, including two in Rick Marksbury's ASAO volume on *The Business of Marriage Transformations in Oceanic Matrimony* (Rosi and Zimmer-Tamakoshi 1993; Zimmer-Tamakoshi 1993a). In the paper coauthored with Pam Rosi entitled "Love and Marriage among the Educated Elite in Port Moresby," we concluded that while there were difficulties in elite marriages for both husbands and wives, elite women—particularly those who were well-educated and employed—were forced to be more innovative in their approach to love and marriage than their male peers. While most elite women maintain ties with villagers and promote their husbands' interests in the contexts of both village and town, many do so in a style that they feel elevates them above a dependent status to equal partnerships in marriage: dispensing, for example, with bride-price or other traditional payments in favor of more personalized giving. In the other paper, "Bachelors, Spinsters, and 'Pamuk Meris,'" based entirely on Gende cases, I discuss the dramatic bachelorization of Gende society and the stresses facing young men, many of whom will be in their mid-thirties or older before they can afford a wife—or a wife will take them on—and many others who will never marry.

Although the Gende are not likely to alter their exchange system any time soon, parents' sadness and regret over the distance that comes between them and their beleaguered children was often very obvious. They were also at the heart of breakthroughs in my establishing a close rapport with older villagers. In the early months of my first fieldwork, many older women shunned me for being a "bad mother and wife" who had left my family behind in America. When my teenage children and husband visited for a month in the middle of my fieldwork, I was admonished to wait on and defer to them. After they left, I was of course bereft but the older women were more censorious than ever in their glares and character analysis. During the rainy season, a month went by before mail made it to the village. When it finally arrived on a Sunday morning, an officious local school committeeman stowed the mail in the school office and told me I couldn't get it until Monday morning when the school was officially open. While he and other villagers were off playing cards, I "broke into" the school office and took the mail that was mine back to my house to devour. Late in the afternoon, an angry committeeman arrived at my doorstep and began berating me. A crowd gathered—in fact, almost the entire village along with visitors from other villages—to enjoy the show. When I started to cry, the older women present turned on the committeeman. They lambasted him—and all other men—for being insensitive to women's feelings of longing for their children. After the crowd dissipated, the old women and I went into my house to drink tea and I listened to them discuss how much they missed their own migrant children and how lucky I was to be an American woman who, apparently, could come and go as I pleased, but who was, nonetheless, a caring "human being."

Gende Women and Development

Ever larger bride-prices and women's desire to achieve balance in their relations with men have produced interesting responses to development on the part of Gende women in village and town. In a special issue of *Pacific Studies* edited by Jeanette Dickerson-Putman (1996) on women, age, and power, I wrote about a new development that promised steady work for hundreds, possibly thousands, of Gende men and women. Kobum Spice Company's main interest was cardamom, a highly desired spice in India and Southeast Asia. Very quickly, a gendered division of labor evolved in which men cleared and planted the rainforest and constructed buildings and women picked and sorted the mature cardamom. Age played a factor as well, with older women doing most of the picking (primarily because they could bring infants and young children with them) and young women doing all of the sorting into various grades of cardamom. Because they were paid more and could work longer hours, the sorting girls were earning two or more times as much money as were their mothers and aunts. This reversal of female power did not sit well with the older women. Within a few short years, the women pickers pulled the plug on Kobum Spice Company by withdrawing their labor. Exhausted with double workdays, dismayed that their earnings failed to keep up with runaway inflation in the Gende exchange system, and angry with the young female sorters for "wasting their money" on frivolous purchases and contributing to the inflation (their parents were asking higher bride-prices for them because they were obviously more valuable than girls who were not so employed), the older women convinced the younger women to join them in their walkout, telling them that they would never be able to pay back such inflated bride-prices once they were married and looking after gardens, pigs, and children (Zimmer-Tamakoshi 1996b). Interestingly, gambling was less social at Kobum, with outsiders coming in and aggressively challenging the Kobum workers to play cards in order to drain them of their earnings. Young women were especially preyed upon, one reason many of them readily agreed that Kobum was not for them.

In Jane's paper (1996a) in that same volume, she shows that although the polygyny of the past is gone, senior Tiwi women still gain influence and control over younger women (once their cowives) and men by heading households composed of several nuclear families and widowed men and women and by managing the household's wages and pensions for the good of all. These Taramaguti are considered the best card players, earning cash to supplement household income. The Taramaguti's economic and political influence also offset some of the negative effects of development and nuclear families such as alcoholism and spousal abuse.

Some Gende women in town have also used the management of household funds as a way to manage urban husbands' behavior for the advancement of the couples' interests both in town and with their network of village kin (Zimmer-Tamakoshi 1998). Choosing to marry less wealthy migrants, the women at the Okiufa settlement outside Goroka earned their husbands' loyalty and respect through their careful use of the men's wages for everyday needs and exchange commitments and by standing between the men and urban temptations such as drinking and loose women. Willing to live in squatter settlements rather than spend money on more expensive housing, the Okiufa women and their husbands used their money to invest in their children's education and in land rights back in their home villages. Investing in children's futures has already paid off for many of the Okiufa families I stayed with during numerous field trips in the late 1980s when I was teaching at UPNG. And domestic violence is rare at Okiufa, rarer than among elite marriages and even village households.

Men and Their Discontents

That some men benefit from development more than other men (and women) has never been an issue. Ben Finney's coffee barons (1973, 1993) and Joe Leahy—all making it big in the New Guinea highlands—come to mind immediately, driving Mercedeses and sending their children to private schools in Australia. Looked at from the bottom up, however, many men—in some cases many more than women—are actual losers in the development game. This has been most apparent in the Gende case, particularly when one looks at marriage and men's relations with women. On the one hand is the bachelorization of Gende society; on the other are conflicts with and over women as fathers and brothers threaten or succeed in "selling" daughters off to the highest bidders and unsuccessful and disinherited urban males come home to the village only on special occasions to drink beer and wreak havoc on a society that can't abide persons who can't keep up with the exchange game (Zimmer 1985, 1990a).

In a paper in *Oceania*—"The Last Big Man: Development and Men's Discontents in the Papua New Guinea Highlands" (Zimmer-Tamakoshi 1997d; see also Zimmer 1990b)—I describe how even big men may suffer from uneven development. In spite of a keen business sense, what looked like the right moves, and a sincere concern for his followers, Gende leader Ruge Angiva could not prevent his society from being ravaged by inequality or help a growing number of bachelors afford expensive bride-prices as more and more village girls married wealthy strangers from other parts of PNG. In 1991, a clan brother killed Ruge in an argument over land, making Ruge a victim of capitalist development's indifference to local traditions of family, reputation, and leadership.

When I began my research in Papua New Guinea in the early 1980s, I was unprepared for the degree of conflict and violence associated with the growing inequality throughout the country and especially evident in places like the swampy Sepik region and the Gende's homeland. While I had heard of roving rascal gangs terrorizing Papua New Guinea's towns, rural areas were, for the most part, considered havens of generalized reciprocity ready to absorb disappointed migrants back into the fold with few or no questions asked. Thanks to Jane's emphasis on looking at the whole of any situation and at all the different players, however, I was prepared to witness conflicts and adjustments as Papua New Guineans grappled with capitalist development. In a master's thesis (Zimmer 1979) supervised by Jane—*Man in the Middle*—I had reviewed the existing literature on leaders in three New Guinea societies (the Tolai, Trobrianders, and Hagen people) and concluded that while big men might effectively introduce economic changes and new development, they were "middle men" with reciprocal obligations and not simple entrepreneurs who lead the way. Being at the center of numerous exchange relationships with other men and women, older and younger persons, persons in other groups, and so forth, they would be obligated to make sure everyone benefited and that society maintained an even keel. Ruge's death was stark evidence of how difficult, even impossible, that task might be.

In recent years, the Gende have renewed hopes of finally making it big with the Kurumbukare nickel and chromite mining operation on the northern slopes of their territory near the Ramu river. That only some Gende are receiving large compensation payments, however, has triggered a scramble of ancestral gerrymandering as kinship ties and ancient claims to the land are bargained over and redefined in large, expensive exchange ceremonies (Zimmer-Tamakoshi 1997b, 1997e, 2001a, 2006). Men are already in trouble with women over what the potential of this development means to them. Even before they received land compensation, many landowners acquired second or third wives on credit. Many of these men are living in urban areas like Madang with their new, younger wives, leaving older wives and bachelor sons behind at Kurumbukare to work gardens on land near the mining camp as a way of maintaining claims to the land. The older wives and sons are not happy. The Gende ethic of everyone (or no one) a winner is not being upheld by the men, as far as the women are concerned. Kurumbukare is a hot, virgin rain forest with death adders and malarial mosquitoes real risks. Clearing virgin timber is no easy task. And most wives had something else in mind for any compensation their husbands might receive, such as obtaining brides for their sons, educating children, and generally better circumstances for themselves and their families. The recent start-up of a second mining venture near Yandera village by the Marengo Mining Company may also exacerbate intergenerational and gender conflicts, although the more clear-cut land ownership situation of a long-occupied village may lessen ancestral gerrymandering.

The Mature Anthropologist

Another thing Jane taught was the value of returning to the field repeat-edly, growing old with our informants and maturing in our understand-ings and contributions. In Jane's case, she has become more than the Tiwi's anthropologist. She has become their daughter, sister, potential wife, mother, grandmother, friend, confidante, adviser, teacher (literally, as she was a principal lecturer at the Darwin Institute of Technology in 1986–87), opponent in card games, and, someday, an ancestor. I, too, have returned to the field many times and in many capacities. In the summer of 2000, knowing I was soon to take early retirement and lose easy access to university travel money, I made an effort to get around to all my old haunts in PNG as well as a few new ones. In a late-night, fireside con-versation with an old leader and twenty or so younger Gende residing in a settlement near Kurumbukare, I was caught up in the enthusiasm of the moment and agreed that one day my granddaughter Samantha would bring my bones back to PNG to be buried beside the oldest landowner at Kurumbukare. The importance of the evening's conversation lay not in where I am going to be buried, but that it was a multigenerational, multiperspectival discussion of things happening at Kurumbukare and in the larger world. It was a bull session and none of us wanted to end it even though several of us had to get up early to hike further into the mountains. We were connecting on many levels and as Jane would have us do (see Debbie Rose's paper in this volume)—by paying serious atten-tion to one another.

All my returns to the field have been as gratifying. My first return, in 1986, was to teach anthropology at UPNG. For three and a half years I had many great opportunities: to live in the nation's capital (Port Mo-resby) and to befriend and work with Papua New Guineans at the Uni, to work as a government consultant to the Jimi area (Zimmer-Tamakoshi 1988), and to be a member of the Papua New Guinea women's political group, Women in Power, Politics, Parliament (WIP). I also made many visits to Gende settlements throughout the country as well as back to the villages in their homeland in southern Madang Province. Those years taught me much about Papua New Guinea women and men, about devel-opment issues, domestic and sexual violence, nationalism, the politics of sexuality, and more.

I had a chance to develop some of my ideas (along with twelve col-leagues) at the first of Monty Lindstrom and Geoff White's eight-week-long, National Endowment for the Humanities–supported *Politics of*

Culture in the Pacific seminars at the East-West Center in the summer of 1991. Several publications came out of that including my 1993 *Pacific Studies* article, "Nationalism and Sexuality in Papua New Guinea" (1993b); a double issue of *Ethnology* on the *Politics of Culture in the Pacific Islands* (Feinberg and Zimmer-Tamakoshi 1995); and my article in that special double issue—"Passion, Poetry, and Cultural Politics in the South Pacific" (Zimmer-Tamakoshi 1995). Teaching at UPNG, where the female student body was only about 10 percent of the total, where I met scholars from many fields and students from many parts of Papua New Guinea, and where I worked with and taught some Gende youth afforded me insights that—along with the epiphanic experience of Lindstrom and White's seminar—made those articles and subsequent works richer. Teaching a Study of Society class to 300 students a semester at the University of Papua New Guinea—a class in which thirty or so sophisticated and worldly young women were usually huddled together in one corner of the lecture hall, seeking safety in numbers from the young men—taught me things about elite gender relations I wouldn't have seen in a village context or in a squatter settlement like Okiufa where women and men interact in a more relaxed manner. While Pam Rosi and I were right to say that in some ways educated Papua New Guinea women had more freedoms and possibilities than their male peers (Rosi and Zimmer-Tamakoshi 1993; see also Brown 1988), female students' fear of sexual violence was a significant constraint on their university experience (Zimmer-Tamakoshi 1992).

Some of my most rewarding experiences at UPNG were taking Papua New Guinea students to the field and teaching them research design and ethnographic field methods. When I was back in America and teaching American students, I found it useful to create a Web site on fieldwork (1996a) so that my students could study the process from beginning to end. *The Anthropologist in the Field* site has resulted in many further opportunities, such as opportunities to connect with Papua New Guineans who have seen and in some cases used the site and invitations to create other Web sites such as *The Anthropology of Gender* for Bell and Howell (Zimmer-Tamakoshi 2000) and to write a comprehensive encyclopedia article on Papua New Guinea (2001b) that puts the nation in a global context and does not exoticize it. In 1998–99, I used a sabbatical leave to set up an in-university Web course on Cultures of the Pacific. Using the Internet-based course allowed the students to interact and collaborate with Pacific scholars and students at other universities, many of them fellow members of the ASAO community and easily accessed through ASAO's Web site.

Since dissertation research in the early eighties (1982–83) and teaching at UPNG (1986–90), I have returned to Papua New Guinea as often as possible to continue my work with the Gende and other Papua New Guineans (1994, 1995, 2000, 2007). Each time, I have deepened my involvement in their lives and they in mine. One of the more profound threads of my quarter-century engagement with Papua New Guineans has been an enduring focus on the topic of gender violence. While it may be best not to be identified with a particular "cause," what I have seen and heard in Papua New Guinea (and elsewhere) has captured my attention and inspired me to write articles and reviews on gender violence, in particular rape and other sexual aggression (e.g., 1992, 1993a, 1993b, 1997f, 2004). As Jane often reminded us, being an anthropologist is not for the faint of heart. She also taught us that it is in our *relationships* and in our willingness to commit to whatever our work requires of us that truth is found. It is not possible to put societies under a cold, objective microscope and to stand apart from the fray. Rather, staying with our subjects, it is possible to see a society (and ourselves) from many angles. This is what reflexivity is all about. It involves knowing that we are part of the fabric of our research.

Just how intertwined things can be struck me a few years ago when I was preparing to write an encyclopedia article on rape and sexual aggression in Papua New Guinea and around the world (2004). Reading many, many disturbing studies about widespread sexual violence against women and girls *and* boys and men, I painfully recalled the sexual violence committed against me as a child and teenager—memories I had kept to myself and pushed to the edge of consciousness. For the first time, I seriously considered how that violence has affected me and may account for a fierceness that energizes my research and that must be kept in line if I am to produce anything of value. This is the first time I have written about this, Jane. And I have yet to unravel all the complexities of my embeddedness in the subject. But I intend to keep tugging at the threads of my research and personal reflections. And one day I hope to *pull the right thread* and make practical sense of *all* my experiences, at home and in the field. Meanwhile, it has been redemptive to recognize not that I necessarily have anything in common with other victims of violence, but that I may be part of the solution. Coming out of "retirement," agreeing to be a discussant in an ASAO session on gender violence, returning to the field in 2007 to further study "troubled masculinities," and looking forward to pondering the causes and policy implications of intergenerational and gender tensions associated with the Ramu and Yandera mines as an upcoming visiting research associate with the State, Society and

Governance in Melanesia program at the Australian National University in Canberra, I have picked up the threads of my earlier research on men and their discontents (see Zimmer 1984, 1987b, 1990a; Zimmer-Tamakoshi 1993a, 1993b, 1995, 1997b, 1997d, 1997e, and 2001a). The reflective anthropological discipline you taught us is surely guiding my search for *the right thread*. And, yes, though gender violence is a serious "women's issue" in Papua New Guinea and elsewhere (see Zimmer-Tamakoshi 1997f, 2004), it's never been about "women only."

4. *"Every Action Is a Human Interaction"*

Introduction

More than thirty years ago, in 1973, I was a student in Jane Goodale's graduate seminar in field methodology. And it was thirty years before then that Jane first studied anthropology as an undergraduate at Radcliffe. To illustrate the vast changes that had occurred since her own exposure to the discipline, she once told me stories about her anthropology classes in the mid-1940s, which incorporated some entertaining drama. Ernest Hooten taught brachiating by swinging across the pipes on the classroom ceiling, and Patrick Putnam, to teach about Pygmy hunting techniques, would lead a line of Radcliffe women down the corridor as he pretended to beat bushes to the sound of his Pygmy cry while Carleton Coon, who stood at the other end of the hall, bellowed like an elephant.

Anthropology and the teaching of it have changed tremendously, not only in the sixty years since Jane was at Radcliffe, but in the thirty years since I began studying with Jane at Bryn Mawr. Even thirty years ago, anthropology was a very different discipline than it is today, believing, for one, in the notion that communities were relatively bounded, penetrable, and knowable if you just had the right tools to unlock the cultural door. As a student of anthropology in the mid-1970s, I was sent off to "the field" armed with a toolbox full of techniques. I was trained in how to observe and record data, which, once I had gathered enough of, would lead me to theory, all of which I did in a relatively fixed setting where the techniques actually mapped quite well onto what I wanted to learn.

When Jane first went to the field in the 1950s, such training was nonexistent. As she wrote about her own graduate training in her book, *The Two-Party Line: Conversations in the Field,* "Field methods—how the data were collected—largely remained a mystery. . . . None of my professors at the University of Pennsylvania, where I was enrolled as a graduate student, seemed able to tell me anything more than just 'to go there, live with the people and learn what you have to learn'" (Goodale 1996b: 2).

Thus, it was quite remarkable that only a decade later, when Jane was teaching at Bryn Mawr, she developed a course in field methods as part of a required curriculum for anthropology majors. "It was a difficult topic to teach. With very little literature, I resorted to anecdotal accounts of my life in the field, illustrating different methodological truths and realities, as nearly every fieldworker has done for their students since before Malinowski's time" (Goodale 1996b: 4). She realized that "the process of cultural data gathering is at best, an unpredictable and serendipitous affair . . . learning is . . . experiential and not experimental, in that control of the learning environment is largely in the hands of others" (Goodale 1996b: 5).

By the time I was a graduate student at Bryn Mawr, Jane's field methods seminar was well established. In this particular seminar, our principal guidelines came from two sources: Pierre Maranda's book, *Introduction to Anthropology: A Self Guide* (1972; a large paperback with a bright-pink cover that I still own), and Jane's insightful wisdom. The sequence of the book's chapters charted our course throughout the semester. As we progressed through the text and its various exercises, we slowly got closer to people and understanding what was important to them. In the first set of exercises, we made our way from mapping large geographical areas, to diagramming people's living rooms, to asking the inhabitants personal questions—always linking close observation to the formulation of hypotheses and, eventually, to more questions. While taking these methodological baby steps under her tutelage, we were exposed to Jane's formidable lessons about connections—what Deborah Rose (this volume) describes as "the method . . . is the ethic . . . becomes the encounter . . . becomes the knowledge . . . becomes more questions."

The first exercise entailed making a map of an area that was about twenty-five square miles (mine included the entire Bryn Mawr/Haverford part of Philadelphia's main line). The next exercise narrowed in on roughly one square mile of it in detail, including stores, schools, churches, houses, roads, and railroad tracks. After I completed my map, I formulated a (probably obvious) hypothesis about how, judging from details like the average size and condition of the houses, it appeared that the closer people lived to the railroad tracks, the lower their socioeconomic status seemed to be. Next we had to map one street in exacting detail and I chose Franklin Street, a street of modest brick row houses that ran parallel to, and was only twenty feet away from, the tracks. I tested my powers of observation, noticing how each house, while identical to the others in basic construction, showed individual variation in details like the style and arrangement of chairs and rockers on the front porches. We practiced our skills further by drawing what we observed; I carefully sketched several of the houses, recording the differences in their picket fences, cyclone fences, bushes, front porch chairs, bicycles, hanging plants, and television antennae.

Then we had to move from keen detached observation to knock-on-the-door participation and I began to panic—but persevered. We had to conduct a census: Who lived in the houses? How were they related to one another? Where did they work? Where did they shop? In the process, I met a retired postal worker, a housewife, a retired painter, a liquor store employee, a grandmother, and many other individuals. The next exercise required that we make diagrams of the rooms inside the houses, indicating the placement of every item: tables, chairs, couches, radiators, televisions, radios, bookshelves, lamps, ashtrays, framed photographs, wall decor, and curios like plastic flowers, stuffed animals, porcelain figurines, and religious statues. I devised another hypothesis—about the sedentary, family-oriented tendencies of the inhabitants of Franklin Street.

At the end of this first set of exercises, we were asked to comment in class on what practical problems we had encountered, what techniques we had learned, and especially what insight we had gained about the relationship between observation and the formulation and testing of hypotheses. Certainly, I felt a great sense of accomplishment at having mastered several helpful techniques. But what I remember most vividly about that whole experience was the precariousness of establishing human contact, how dependent I was on it, and how, without it, my knowledge remained vague and inaccurate. When I rang the doorbell and asked to do a diagram of the living room at one of the houses, where only a week earlier the owner had welcomed me in to conduct my census, this second time he looked at me and abruptly said, "Sorry, we're busy today," and closed the door. If doing quality fieldwork depended on getting close enough to strangers to have them welcome you into their private lives, I seriously wondered whether this was the profession for me.

But, fortunately, along with Maranda's structured exercises, we had a second source of guidance, namely Jane. In class she encouraged us to discuss our strategies, accomplishments, and fears and helped animate our seminar discussions, which usually continued long after the class period had officially ended. Jane always laid our fears to rest. She believed in the science of the discipline and kept this faith in the foreground. As she told us (and I quote from my class notes, which I've kept all these years), "Anthropology is a science and your laboratory is the field. You need to test your powers of pure observation. You need to record everything on the spot rather than rely on memory. Keep your eyes and ears open and your notebook out." Her advice was always laced with practical tips as well, such as, "Wear clothes with large pockets for your notebook and pen."

Jane always emphasized the interconnection between data and analysis, reminding us that "the relationship between data and analysis is crucial. Your data will allow you to move to analysis, and from careful analysis you should come up with new questions, which will bring you to new data." She highlighted the connection between what we were trying to find out and how we should best go about it. For example, if I wanted to learn about symbolic messages embodied in food exchanges, I needed to understand what kinds of questions to ask in order to get the information I wanted. These questions would determine the data I could gather, which, in turn, would influence the analysis I could do.

In Jane's class there was always a focus on reflection as well and, for 1973, Jane was way ahead of her time in this regard. As she told us, "What makes fieldwork so strenuous is that you have to constantly reflect back upon yourself and what you are doing. When things don't go as you imagined or hoped, you have to contemplate why. You need to ask yourself: Why did I dislike visiting so-and-so? Why does such-and-such frustrate me? Why did so-and-so say that to me?" In other words, when I did my fieldwork exercises on Franklin Street, rather than wallow in feelings of frustration, I had to ask myself why the man shut the door in my face, thus turning that disheartening episode into a positive learning experience.

Through all of her advice, what shone through most clearly—and even overshadowed the techniques of "science"—was the importance of the human component in fieldwork. As Jane reminded us, "An anthropologist cannot decide the boundaries of an action. Every action is a human interaction, connecting you more and more with the people in the community. Early on, establish a role for yourself. Decide who you are, what you are doing, how you will fit in, and even how you should dress (other than in skirts with large pockets)." She conveyed that, as ethnographers, and as observers and participants, we would *always*—first and foremost—be part of a cultural community. As Michele Dominy says (this volume), Jane taught us that participant observation was "an experiential dialogic process." Jane told us (and I still remember her words), "Becoming part of a community is the hardest, but the most rewarding, aspect of fieldwork. The process of doing fieldwork is that of going from being an outsider to becoming an insider. Without becoming part of the community, nothing else happens." From Jane, I became aware that, when in the field and unable to control things, the best I could do was to put myself in situations that might allow me to deepen the friendships and (with my handy toolbox of techniques by my side) to learn from these continually intensifying human interactions.

Papua New Guinea: Sharing Food and Mapping Stones

In 1976, three years after taking Jane's field methods seminar, I was at Kennedy Airport saying tearful good-byes to my family and friends, boarding the first in a series of planes that would eventually take me to Papua New Guinea. Influenced by the work of Reo Fortune (1932) and Bronislaw Malinowski (1922, 1935) and everything I had read about the Melanesian preponderance for treating certain domesticated plants (especially taro and yams) as though they were anthropomorphic beings, I wanted to study the plant world, horticultural ritual, and food symbolism in order to learn more about Melanesian concepts of personhood (see Kahn 1986, 1988).

And, greatly influenced by Jane's work, I was fascinated by how people achieve, maintain, and express their humanity. In her book, *To Sing With Pigs Is Human: The Concept of Person in Papua New Guinea* (1995), Jane explored Kaulong ideas about personhood, status, theories of knowledge, and social communities. Even though her book was not yet published when I left for Papua New Guinea, her ideas invigorated our classes and appeared in papers that she presented at professional meetings (Goodale 1976, 1977, 1978). Jane was deeply aware of the socially interactive nature of human nature, both in her own life and in that of the people with whom she worked (Goodale 1985). As Kaulong friends instructed her, "If a person wants to live in peace, he or she lives in the bush alone" (Goodale 1995: xi). But living all alone in the bush is inhuman and antisocial behavior. "To be 'human' one must live with others" (Goodale 1995: xi). Jane also connected Kaulong ideas about humanity to their production of resources and their systems of exchange. For her Kaulong friends, being human entailed controlling one's needs and desires and mastering self-control. Jane, with her mind tuned to symbolic systems, was keenly aware of elaborate systems of codes—how people communicated one thing (such as how to be human) through other means (such as making art, exchanging shells, growing and exchanging food, or singing songs).

When I took those first daunting research steps by going to Papua New Guinea, Jane's intellectual ideas influenced the directions my own work would take. Moreover, the techniques I had learned in Jane's class all felt like appropriate tools to pursue my chosen focus on horticultural ritual, food exchange, and concepts of personhood.

After arriving in Papua New Guinea, I settled into Wamira, a village in the southeastern part of the country. Nestled between an expansive blue sea and a grassy plain at the base of precipitous mountains, Wamira lay in an atypical savanna landscape in an otherwise tropical world. I lived with a family of three, which included my "mother" Alice, her brother Aidan, and their elderly mother Sybil. Alice's husband was living in the town of Lae and their daughter, whose acquaintance I had made in the capital city of Port Moresby, was then a student at the University of Papua New Guinea.

On my very first day in the village, I joined with several others (albeit very clumsily) who, in a communal effort, were building a house for a family in the hamlet in which I lived. I quickly learned how to weave coconut fronds into wall panels and to sew them onto the sturdy posts to construct the house's walls. As some of us stood inside the house and others stood outside, poking a long wooden needle laced with bush fiber back and forth through the panels that we were attaching to the frame, I had my first language lesson when people taught me the words for "toward the mountains" and "toward the sea," which are two of the main directional markers in Wamira. Each day, when the work was done, we all sat together in the hamlet and ate food that was donated and cooked by the family whose house we were building.

During those first few days—when not helping with the house—I often sat with Sybil, who was teaching me how to gather a creeper from along the path, remove its inner fiber, roll this fiber on my leg to make twine, and then weave it into a string bag. In addition, I often went to the river, a twenty-minute walk from the hamlet, to wash dishes and pots with the village women, getting to know them, gaining a better sense of their individual personalities, and all the while learning more of the language.

Jane's phrase about every action being a human interaction was brought home to me within the first few weeks of living in Wamira. One day, Alice and I had returned from the local market carrying heavy string bags of food down our backs. As we approached our house, Alice made what seemed like a slight detour. But, eager to put down my heavy bag, I went directly up to the house, walking in front of our neighbor, Osborne, who was sitting outside his house chewing *areca* nut. Once Alice and I were inside, she immediately asked me, "What will you give him now?" When I expressed confusion, she explained that I shouldn't have walked so close to Osborne, thus flaunting the food I had purchased. Because I had passed in front of him, I had to share the contents of my bag with him. "Our life is like that," she tersely explained. Indeed, that one split second of seemingly innocent behavior on my part became a profound lesson. From that action and interaction, I began to learn about the many rules and taboos that revolved around food, the customs of sharing and hiding it, and the jealousy that a display of food could elicit in others. I also gained a better understanding of my relationship with Alice, who was a patient and firm teacher as well as a concerned and loving mother. Moreover, when I later went to Osborne to share my food, I initiated a neighborly reciprocal relationship that deepened over time. In fact, Osborne became one of the key people who generously helped me when I recorded mythology.

In those early days in Wamira, recalling Maranda's exercises and my experiences on Franklin Street, I also made meticulous maps of everything. I mapped the entire village and included every house, path, and garden plot. I also made a more detailed map of Inibuena, the hamlet in which I lived and, while doing so, was told by various onlookers, who gathered by my side and peered over my shoulder, that I needed to include every tree. That one "technique" opened a veritable flood of "data." That day, I began to learn about the importance of food trees; the difference between ownership rights and usage rights; and the names, life spans, and values attached to the different trees and their fruits.

While doing the mapping, I noticed prominent stone arrangements in various hamlets and people began to tell me the stories associated with these. Many of the stones were believed to anchor the taro in the gardens and to ensure abundance by "tugging at the taro roots to hold them down." Some of the stones were thought to be capable of moving around, especially at night. I learned that in Wamira people anchored their personal narratives and communal histories to specific landforms, such as escarpments, plains, gullies, and rocks, and that cultural heroes and heroines were seen as capable of turning into stone and inhabiting the landscape as daily reminders of history and morality. Each stone arrangement marked and recalled the past as recounted in mythology.

In one instance, my desire to map some stones was made conditional upon my later having two dozen rugby shirts printed—in America—with my map of the stones on the front of the shirts. Members of the clan-based rugby team hoped that, by wearing the powerful shirts while playing against their rivals, they could ward off jealousy in their competitors. My map on the shirts would prove that they owned the land on which the stones were located and would demonstrate—through their ability to win—that they gained power from the stones. While I later had the rugby shirts made in the United States, I mused about the ironic twist to the many layers of inscription and how a seemingly innocent field technique like mapping could take on new meaning. The clan's "power," originally inscribed upon the land, could be transcribed onto an anthropologist's map and then further reproduced on sports shirts. These numerous permutations seemed to enhance, not lessen, the sense of power embedded in the stones. As the rugby players, with the anthropologist's map on their chests, scrimmaged aggressively against their opponents, they would feel empowered through their association with the original stones and the land to which these tied them, all of which was intensified by the map's brief journey to America. These initial forays into mapping provided me with a better understanding about people's relationships to land and the status and power that comes from such relationships (Kahn 1990, 1996). They also led to my interest in senses of place, something I would pursue in Wamira and, in later years, explore more fully in another region of the Pacific.

Not only did I feel Jane's guiding presence when I remembered her lessons—about human interactions and mapping, for example—but she occasionally entered into my fieldwork setting in relatively tangible form for Wamirans as well. Whenever one of her letters arrived, people eagerly gathered around me as I opened the envelope, asking me: "What does your teacher in America say? Is she pleased with your progress? Are we telling you the right things? What else does she want you to learn?" Little did Jane know when she wrote to me that her letters expanded Wamirans' webs of interconnected people and, as a result, opened even more research opportunities for me. Wamirans wanted me to succeed with my work, in part, so that my teacher, the American equivalent of a Melanesian "big woman" in their eyes, would recognize their generosity in helping me.

Halfway through my stay in Wamira, a friend came to visit for several weeks and the residents of my hamlet thoughtfully decided I would appreciate more space and privacy. They organized work groups, gathered the necessary materials, and built a house for me, adding special touches like a desk and chair, which they imagined would be useful for my work. This time, unlike a year earlier when I first arrived, I was not allowed to help with the construction. Instead, each day I gathered, purchased, and cooked food for the workers to feed them when they were done. Rather than listening to other people discuss and decide on feasting details, I was now in charge of making these decisions. When the house was completed, I was told that because I had paid for it by feeding the workers, I now owned it, thus making me even more of a Wamiran (in their eyes) than before.

In Wamira, it was relatively easy to become part of the community simply by being there because the community was all around me. By merely stepping outside my house I was immediately surrounded by neighbors—children eager to bring me shells they found on the beach or flowers they picked from the bushes, and adults who came with an array of questions ("Had a man really traveled to the moon?" "Why were American relations between black people and white people full of tensions?" "Weren't my mother and father in New York lonely when I was so far away?"). I was also privy to discussions that occurred inside the walls of our house. When feasts were being planned, I could listen to the discussions about who should give what to, and get what from, whom. When feasts took place, I was smack in the middle of all the activity, even lending pencil and paper to the hamlet leaders to make lists of the distribution details. And, when all the festivity was over, I sat among the hamlet residents as they took stock of, and dissected, every detail that had transpired.

In short, the methods I had learned on Philadelphia's main line worked well for the kinds of things that fascinated me about Melanesian village life in the 1970s. The deepening friendships that blossomed from simple actions—walking in front of someone while carrying food, mapping hamlets and trees, designing rugby shirts, opening a letter from Jane—allowed me to gradually enter into a cultural community. Techniques I had learned under Jane's tutelage did indeed seem like handy tools that allowed me to initially break the ice, to make new friendships, and to continually explore new research territory.

I ended up spending two years in Wamira on that first trip, and then returned again for another year in 1981–82; I have since visited Papua New Guinea again in 1995. But in the early 1990s, I felt the desire to broaden my horizons and become familiar with a second research area as well. I wanted to stay in the Pacific, where I felt comfortable with the geography and customs, and where the Austronesian languages seemed relatively easy for me to learn. But I also wanted a location that reflected the changing nature of anthropology and the world. I wanted to work in a more multisited setting where social and political life would be more diffuse. I wanted to do research in a place that was more obviously enmeshed in the global world, where instead of carrying water for twenty minutes from a river I could get it by turning on a tap inside the house, and where fieldwork might include electricity, television, and telephones. I didn't necessarily want these things because of the comforts they brought, but because I longed for a new kind of challenge. I specifically wanted to be in a place where I wouldn't be able to step directly from my house into "the field," but where I'd have to search out my data in more strategically planned ways. By now, in the 1990s, the currents that swept the world reached to the remotest, formerly inaccessible, areas. Very few places could still be thought of as being like a "scientific laboratory." Thus, I wanted to test my skills at careful observation and description of empirical data, and the formulation of theories based on those data, in a new setting where daily life was more visibly intertwined with these worldly currents.

Tahiti: Tasting Ice Cream and Hosting Dancers

In 1993, now twenty years after having taken Jane's field methods seminar, I (together with my husband and our daughter) went to French Polynesia. My stone mapping in Wamira had led to my growing interest in senses of place—an interest also shared by Jane (Goodale 1995: 112–17) and evident in the work of many of her students (Dominy 2001; Myers 1986; Rose 1992, 1996, 2002). When I went to French Polynesia, it was with the goal of understanding how various, seemingly conflicting, senses of place—which included both inhabited and imagined realities—articulated with one another (Kahn 2000, 2003, 2004, 2006). I was influenced by Henri Lefebvre's (1974) ideas about the production of space and how different senses of place clash and collide and, in doing so, generate a more politically charged space of experience. I wanted to know how Tahitians define and relate to their own place (even while living in a place that has a life of its own in the imagination of others). And I wanted to know what it is like for tourists to visit a place that already exists in their mind before they get there. In short, I wanted to understand the complex politics of the coexistence of contradictory locations. Furthermore, I wanted to learn about the relationship between Tahitians and the commercial forces that shape their landscape and influence their lives. How is "Tahiti" created, for example, by a complex tourism industry whose business it is to make places and create desires? And how is the product embraced, disregarded, or sabotaged by Tahitians who spend their lives in French Polynesia, a colonial outpost in today's postcolonial world?

As I planned the details in preparation for my first research trip to French Polynesia, I assumed from the start that I'd leave most of those "outmoded" techniques at home. And, as it turned out, in French Polynesia I gathered most of my data by other means. I sipped drinks with government ministers at airport bars, attended international tourism conferences where I listened to PowerPoint presentations, participated in antinuclear protest marches, interviewed tourists in their lounge chairs on cruise ships, analyzed print media and Web sites, and invited Tahitians to Seattle where my family and I took them, according to their wishes, to shopping malls and tattoo parlors.

How could Jane's field methods seminar possibly have prepared me for any of this, I wondered? How could I make maps of imagined places? And how could I become part of a community when its members are not only scattered all over the globe, but also are packing their suitcases even as they talk to me? How could those trusty field methods help my research on "place" and "tourism" when my research is temporarily derailed because my Tahitian friends decide to take a vacation to Disneyland?

On my various trips to French Polynesia (in 1993, 1994, 1995, 1996, and 2001), during most of which time I lived on the island of Huahine, I attempted some mapping, conducted a general census, jotted down kin relations, and recorded some mythology. I never, however, completed any of these exercises with the same thoroughness as I did in Wamira. At the third house that I visited for my census, for example, the owner, Cyriaque, invited me in to taste the ice cream she was in the process of making. Being a resourceful young woman, she had decided to open an ice cream business with the goal of selling her homemade product, with flavors like mango, guava, and coconut, to tourists who passed by the house in their air-conditioned vans and, ultimately, to large grocery stores on the island of Tahiti. A few days after my curtailed census, Cyriaque arrived at my house asking if I could help her. Because I had a computer and printer, she wanted me to design and print various materials that she could use for publicity for her ice cream business. I gladly agreed and we stayed up late into the night designing posters, price lists, and even snazzy container lids with computer-generated clip art.

In Wamira, Jane had arrived in the form of letters. But on Huahine she arrived in person! I was honored, in 1995, to have her visit us for several days. In typical Jane fashion, she wasn't content to just "visit" and watch me work, but asked probing questions about everything she saw and experienced. Naturally, one of the people to whom I introduced Jane was Cyriaque, who had become a close friend (and who gave us generous helpings of ice cream).

If time-honored techniques, like mapping or census taking, weren't directly useful on Huahine, it didn't matter. I began to understand that such techniques were best viewed as ways of connecting with people, of making initial contacts that would later unfold in a myriad of unanticipated and exciting directions, taking learning into "contexts we can neither predict nor prescribe" (Rose, this volume). What continued to be helpful, however, were "actions that were human interactions" that eased my ability to become part of a community, even if the community wasn't neatly bounded, mappable, or countable.

Because my fieldwork was now multisited, I could engage in actions almost anywhere and experience the results as they rippled ashore thousands of miles from the source. As my husband occasionally joked, one of the most helpful things I did for my research occurred when I wasn't even "in the field." The particular chain of events he had in mind was triggered one spring day in 1997 while I was watching a Hawaiian hula performance at Seattle's annual Folklife Festival. As I sat in the audience, my mind wandered to my Tahitian friends and how their dancing would certainly be as interesting as that of the Hawaiians, especially for Seattleites, who were accustomed to seeing hula but were not necessarily familiar with Tahitian *tamure* or *aparima*. When I got home that evening, I contacted the organizers of the festival, who in turn suggested I contact yet a different organization, namely the Seattle International Children's Festival, because they (unlike the Folklife Festival) had a budget that allowed them to bring people from overseas.

One year later, in the spring of 1998, I was at SeaTac Airport, anxiously awaiting the arrival of eighteen Tahitian dancers and musicians from Huahine who had been invited to participate in the Seattle International Children's Festival. The group, *Tamari'i Mata'ire'a Nui* (Children of the Island of Playful Wind; i.e., of Huahine), had been preparing for months, choosing dances that would be most appropriate for Seattle's children and designing and making elaborate costumes, which they transported together with all their instruments in what seemed like mountains of luggage.

Although most of their ten-day stay was consumed with dancing, they managed to find plenty of time for what they, as tourists in Seattle, really wanted to do—shop. Just as I had made rugby shirts for people in Papua New Guinea two decades earlier, I soon found myself in a T-shirt store again, this time ordering several dozen shirts, some for Huahine's top volleyball team and others as promotional giveaways for Cyriaque's ice cream business, all of which were carried back to French Polynesia with the dancers.

Three years later, in 2001, when my family and I again went to Huahine, we were surprised to be festively greeted at the airport by the *Tamari'i Mata'ire'a Nui* dancers, who performed magnificently for our arrival. A few days later, several of the dancers arrived at our house with pots of food, wanting to prepare lunch for us. We soon learned what was uppermost on their minds: a burning desire to return to Seattle to dance. Along with the pots of food, they also brought photo albums of their various trips to the United States; as we talked, I gained more insight into their ideas about place and why they, too, like to travel and be tourists.

On this particular research trip, many of the dancers became close friends with whom we often socialized and who also helped me with my work. Bianca, the star dancer, occasionally took us fishing, pointing out details in the landscape and recounting the accompanying legends. Jean Yves, the costume designer, visited regularly and it was with him that I went on board the luxury cruise ship where he sold his artwork and danced, and where I learned more about the interactions between cruise ship tourists and Tahitians. Marietta, the leader of the dance group, had since been put in charge of Huahine's cultural museum in the village of Maeva, the main tourist attraction on the island, which was one of the places where I often conducted research on tourism and place. Through my friendship with Marietta I was able to learn more about the politics involved in the development of this particular tourist site. It was also Marietta who then invited my husband and me to go along on a trip to the island of Taha'a with a group of ninety *matahiapo* (elders) from Huahine, where my husband and I made our dance debut when we were pulled into the Huahine contingent during competitive dances, and where Huahine—even with us as part of the group—won first prize.

These same dancers often invited me to the hotel at which they performed the weekly floor show. On these occasions, I was able to pursue my research on tourism and especially on how space is managed to meet tourists' expectations. Dance is an activity in which spontaneous Tahitian behavior meshes well with tourists' expectations. Dance—once brutally suppressed by missionaries because of its erotic character—since the 1950s has become the main cultural activity that is extracted from its context and presented to tourists for entertainment. In the process it has been transformed into a staged business enterprise. Dance elements are now combined into a marketable pastiche, always with the aim of keeping the performance dazzling, the cameras clicking, and the income from tourism flowing.

On one such occasion, having arrived at the hotel about thirty minutes before the group was to perform, I visited with individuals while they got ready. They were sitting on the floor in the hotel's main lounge area and its adjoining corridor, surrounded by their dance paraphernalia, which included plastic bags of fresh leaves and flowers that they were carefully adding to their costumes before the show began. The musicians were already seated on their stools in the back of the dining room providing music for the guests as they ate.

When the dancers were ready, the musicians began to beat their drums more forcefully. The performers appeared, flowing swiftly and gracefully onto the stage to the rhythm of the thundering drums. They began dancing—with feather headdresses bobbing, shredded-leaf skirts swaying, and, most important of all, torsos steady and hips gyrating. The tourists were mesmerized. The men, especially, focused intently, many abandoning their dinner as they watched with rapt attention. With video cameras poised, many watched much of the performance through their camera lenses.

I learned a lot on occasions such as this. Within the carefully controlled hotel space, dance plays an extremely valuable role—perhaps the most crucial—by providing tourists with the ultimate cultural encounter they may hope to have. On the one hand, dance brings the brochure images to life for the tourists. Dance takes place in spaces that exhibit an increasingly pronounced visual character, ready-made for tourists to watch, photograph, and film. From what tourists told me, it seems that they interpret sight, or seeing, as life itself. Yet, dance is also emblematic of the distortions that occur in how Tahitians are involved and represented within a staged touristic space. The dancer's life becomes a decipherment of messages by the tourist's eye, which relegates the dancers to a safe distance and renders them passive, turning their life into spectacle.

That evening, soon after the dance performance ended, the dancers and I were sitting in the hotel transfer boat, surrounded by costumes and instruments, speeding across the lagoon on our way back home. Shrouded by the blackness of the night and listening to the sounds of the water against the sides of the boat and the strumming of their guitars as the dancers relaxed after the performance, I reflected on my varied experiences. How in my life did I end up in that boat with these wonderful friends with whom I had just spent the evening at Huahine's most luxurious hotel? Unreal as the moment seemed, there was nonetheless something natural about the meandering path my research had taken. On the one hand, I was a long way from Franklin Street and my diagrams of knickknacks in people's living rooms. And I was far away from Wamira where I had first settled in by helping neighbors I didn't yet know build their house. Yet as I sat in the boat skimming across the Pacific waters, all these various experiences seemed to flow together seamlessly, and did so, I'm convinced, because of what I learned from Jane.

Musings

During all of my various field trips—both in Papua New Guinea in the 1970s and 1980s and in French Polynesia since the 1990s—I realized that the most fundamental things I learned from Jane were more than techniques. What made a profound and lasting impression on me was what she communicated about the aspect of anthropology that was not always rational science and did not necessarily occur in the laboratory. At the heart of her engaging narratives in that field methods course was always her deep understanding of the nature of cross-cultural interactions and human friendships. Although I can still make a good map and produce a kin chart, it's these personal insights that have stayed with me, grown with me, and continue to guide my research as I carry out fieldwork today. From Jane I learned that the process of doing field research is a personal journey of gradually going from being an outsider to becoming a more knowledgeable and accepted member of a community—from helping others build a house to feeding workers who had built a house for me, and from watching a hula performance at a folk festival in Seattle to sitting in a boat with Tahitian friends and dancers as they relax after their own performance. No matter where one conducts fieldwork, it is always a creative combination of focused attention to detail (where techniques can actually help) *and* interpersonal engagement in friendships and in a community. It is these actions and human interactions, the personal involvement and the deepening friendships, that nourish all learning—indeed that even make the learning possible. And no matter how many theoretical twists and turns anthropology takes over the decades, whether it is 1973 or 2003, the reciprocal nature of field methods remains like bedrock at the core of the discipline.

5. *Remember Malinowski's Canoe and* Luk Luk Gen

Introduction: Jane's Legacy and the "Bryn Mawr Mafia"

As the last of the Ph.D. students Jane Goodale mentored in Pacific ethnography (we have been named the "Bryn Mawr Mafia"), I pay tribute to her in my paper as an anthropologist of "high degree" and acknowledge four aspects of her work that have influenced my own research and its theoretical underpinnings: first, her insistence that fieldwork be inductive if ethnography is to be grounded in the lived experience of indigenous people in local, regional, national, and, increasingly, global networks; second, her belief that fieldwork can take place anywhere; third, her perspective, influenced by her work with the Tiwi (of Northern Australia) and the Kaulong (of New Britain), that art making and aesthetic objects must be understood not in the restrictive Western modernist concept of "art for art's sake" but as sociocultural practices and products that are embedded in dynamic contextual matrixes; and fourth, her recognition that successful fieldwork depends on engaged involvement so that anthropologists need to be culturally sensitive to how their actions and values influence or even change the lives of those they study and befriend (Goodale 1971, 1995, 1996b; Goodale and Koss 1971).

Influenced by these four factors, my research since 1986, when I did fieldwork for my dissertation at Papua New Guinea's National Arts School in Port Moresby, has focused on the ways that new contemporary art forms in Papua New Guinea (PNG) have been created in response to modernization and national independence—achieved from Australia in 1975. Given the great cultural diversity and strong tribal allegiances held by most PNG people when statehood was officially declared, my primary interest has been in documenting how contemporary arts are contributing to nation making with imagery that engages debates about making national culture and the controversial question of how, amid diversity, national identity is to be conceptualized and imaged (Rosi 1991, 1994, 1998a, 1998b).

As other scholars concerned with nation making in PNG have noted (Foster 1995, 2002; Otto and Thomas 1997; Zimmer-Tamakoshi 1998), the process is contested and volatile—even to the point of bitter civil war—among peoples who speak over seven hundred different languages and whose emotional loyalties are embedded in immediate ties of kinship or emerging class (Brash 1987; Gewertz and Errington 1999). Fundamental to popular debates and conflicts over policies of nation making is the ongoing problem of how ancestral traditions and desires for modernization are to sustain one another in equitable ways that uphold Melanesian values (*pasin bilong tumbuna*).

In a country that, until recently, has been anthropologically associated primarily with village life and the art world's recognition of the aesthetic value of traditional Melanesian village arts (Linton and Wingert 1946; Gathercole, Kaeppler, and Newton 1979; Lincoln 1987; Meyer 1995), my work has instead been directed to the little-known or -valued urban-dwelling artists caught up in the dislocations of modernization and the cultural politics and economics of national, regional Pacific, and global art worlds (Rosi 1998b, 2002; Rosi and Zimmer-Tamakoshi 1993; Venbrux, Rosi, and Welsch 2006).

Having developed personal relationships with a number of these artists, I recognize with some concern that these connections have affected their lives as well as their cultural expectations in ways I had not always anticipated or been able to satisfy (Rosi 2003). In this respect, my experience of fieldwork speaks to the ethnographic and political reality of lived life and the importance of reflexivity that Jane Goodale has encouraged all her students to think and write about either in single or collaborative authorship.

As Mike Lieber emphasizes in his paper in this volume, one of Jane's most important legacies as teacher is the attitude she has consistently fostered in her students to be supportive of each other's work and to relish the mutual exchange of intellectual ideas, arguments, and diverse viewpoints. In other words, while encouraging intellectuality, Jane has sought to discourage competition between students in favor of working together in an ethos that has supported collaboration and mutual respect and, as far as possible, downplayed hierarchy while stimulating high performance. As an Englishwoman accustomed to the imperative of marking social distinctions, I remember how first-year graduate students were supposed to address her as "Jane" and not "Professor Goodale." As she would remark, "at Bryn Mawr, we are all colleagues who are learning from one another." So Jane's familiar call for "brown bag lunches," described by Joy Bilharz (this volume), was another of her persistent efforts to get members of the department together to talk and to experience collegiality. It took prodding.

Several contributors have referred to the "Bryn Mawr Mafia" as the bonding of Jane's Oceania students. Although this description fits, I think this group loyalty is better characterized as an extension of Jane's wider efforts to encourage collaboration not only within the Anthropology Department at Bryn Mawr, but also to provide students the skills needed to carry out culturally sensitive fieldwork (see Debbie Rose's insightful discussion, this volume, on this) and for later professional networking. As Eric Venbrux notes in his chapter in this volume, other anthropologists who have worked with the Tiwi during the past forty years, including himself (Venbrux 1995, 2002a, 2002b), have "gained enormously from Jane's invaluable support and encouragement" (1995: 226). By setting a personal example, Jane has encouraged her students to appreciate that working with other colleagues—through the ASAO or elsewhere—can reap many rewards. Indeed, I am a good example of the benefits of collegial goodwill and academic collaboration that have been generated from being a member of the "Bryn Mawr Mafia."

By a fortunate coincidence, in 1986 Laura Zimmer was appointed to teach at the University of Papua New Guinea at the same time that I arrived in Port Moresby to begin my fieldwork at the National Arts School situated adjacent to the university. Knowing this, Laura generously invited me to share her official housing. This not only helped me to eke out my limited budget, but also allowed us the opportunity for several months to discuss and exchange ideas about what each of us observed in the lives of PNG students and staff at our two respective institutions.

We also shared many of the realities of life lived in the capital: for example, coping with frequent water cuts, observing incidents of violence against women, seeing the eruptions of ethnic conflicts, observing the problems of weekend drinking, trying to understand the volatilities of national politics, and having the opportunity to meet with Papua New Guineans and expatriates from all over the country who participated in the rapidly modernizing life of Papua New Guinea. At social events, including exhibitions at the National Arts School, we also encountered diplomats and other PNG dignitaries. To move within a short period of time from a squatter settlement on a town "dump" to rubbing shoulders with a minister of culture was mind-boggling—but such were the contrasts of life in Port Moresby at the time we experienced it.

Back from the field, we coauthored an article about the conflicts of contemporary love and marriage among the PNG elite, which grew out of our lived familiarity with urban Papua New Guineans and the discussions we had during that period. Later, when Laura returned to teach at the UPNG for three more years, I contributed an article on contemporary PNG artists to a volume that she was then editing on *Modern Papua New Guinea* (Rosi 1998b). And, based on each of our research, we continue to share an interest in the problems confronting Papua New Guinea women as they challenge the traditional authority of men by seeking modern jobs and education.

With the four aspects of Jane's legacy now singled out, let me elaborate how they acquired their first importance when I was a graduate student and later continued to affect my fieldwork and analysis of contemporary PNG art. Included here has been the need to ask new questions and to think reflexively about an anthropological approach to art that looks at the entangled connections between contemporary art worlds, critical discourses about art, indigenous artists and their audiences, and the contexts and creation of aesthetic value (Kasfir 1998; Marcus and Myers 1995; Mullin 2002; Phillips and Steiner 1999).

Although Jane set me on the path to thinking about these complex relations as I prepared for my preliminary Ph.D. examinations, applied for research grants, and later struggled to conceptualize my dissertation data within new theorizing about nation making, I also want to acknowledge my debt to the work of two other scholars with whom I am connected through Jane and the ties of the "Bryn Mawr Mafia": Fred Myers, whose dissertation *To Have and To Hold: A Study of Persistence and Change in Pintubi Social Life* Jane supervised, and Eric Venbrux, who, as his paper in this collection eloquently demonstrates, has continued Jane's search to interpret and understand Tiwi culture and its interface with Australian and global modernity.

Both Fred and Eric have critically investigated the integration of Aboriginal art into the global art market (Myers 1995a, 1995b, 2002, 2006; Venbrux 2002b, 2006) by focusing on how Papunya and Tiwi artists have come to achieve national and international acclaim. In drawing on their ideas about the dynamics of critical art discourses, establishing regimes of value, and the need for anthropologists to now analyze art systems from a global perspective, I have gained useful insights into explaining why the imagery of contemporary PNG artists has been largely ignored or dismissed as inauthentic by audiences at home and abroad (Rosi 2002, 2006). After being introduced by Jane Goodale at the ASAO meetings in 2000, Eric and I began collaboration based on our mutual interest in studying world art. In 2002, we cosponsored an invited session for the Society of Visual Anthropology entitled *World Art Worlds and the Future of the Anthropology of Art.* Two years ago we coedited the papers from that panel in two journal volumes (Rosi and Venbrux, *Visual Anthropology* 17, nos. 3–4 [2004]; Rosi and Venbrux, *Journal of International Anthropology* 18 [2003]). In 2005, with Robert Welsch, we coedited *Exploring World Art* (Venbrux, Rosi, and Welsch 2006). If, as Michelle Dominy writes, Jane regards the key to good ethnographic explanation as akin to "pulling the right thread" in unraveling a skirt hem, the key to collaborative endeavor is, to borrow a metaphor from Laura Zimmer-Tamakoshi, like "making a daisy chain" that expands if new links are constructed.

The Focus on Inductive Fieldwork

As a first-year graduate student, I became aware of Jane's commitment to inductive fieldwork when I enrolled in her Melanesian Ethnography course. For starters, all students had to read *Argonauts of the Western Pacific* (1922) to learn why Malinowski accorded such significance to "the imponderabilia of everyday life." However—and this point is crucial—a commitment to inductive fieldwork was never equated with being untheoretical, or what Jane calls "unmirrored" (Goodale 1994b). Rather, inductive research meant being open to the concerns of informants, with the lesson being "informants know more than you do" (Goodale 1994b: 13).

For example, living in Port Moresby with its national institutions, national symbols, and visibly modern lifestyles, it was hard for me to initially recognize what Papua New Guineans kept telling me—namely, that national sentiments were very shallow and easily dissipated whenever kin-based (*wantok*) loyalties were called upon. I only came to fully appreciate this after I repeatedly encountered actions and attitudes that corroborated what I was told and I realized that I needed to think within this framework if I wanted to grasp the problems of making national culture in Papua New Guinea.

But beyond listening carefully to informants and refraining from asking them leading questions, Jane also stressed to students the importance of collecting detailed data. She argued that data had historical reality and, even if incomplete, would be available and valuable for reinterpretation. Against the postmodern mode that labeled all facts as cultural constructions, Jane, the scientist, was insistent that there were always data that "didn't need a reality check . . . or become pre or post something." (Goodale 1994: 7). For her, these facts included making a census; recording events, such as the opening of an art exhibition; and noting births, deaths, or the documented collection of material "things"; that is, data that had concreteness and were not, in her view, imaginary or illusory, although culturally embedded.

During the early stages of my fieldwork at the National Arts School (NAS), Jane's advice to follow the flow of daily events was most valuable. In an urban setting, I could easily have spent time conducting formal interviews with artists or following prearranged schedules of class visits. Instead, by hanging out, I engaged the lives of artists in unanticipated ways and thus came to learn more about the problems they encountered living in town—for example, getting evicted and then having to cancel a scheduled exhibition; having no money to take a sick child to the doctor; facing the threat of reprisals from traditional enemies; being beaten up by a drunken husband or, worse, experiencing the brutality of rape.

I learned that the distress of these and other incidents sometimes found expression in images created by contemporary artists and reflected their views of Port Moresby as both a city of "progress" and dislocation. For example, Martin Morububuna designed murals for the PNG Telecom Company that illustrated that the development of a modern telephone system would eventually connect even the most remote PNG villages. Similarly, his murals at Port Moresby's hospital imaged the benefits to health brought by modern medicine. Yet, on a personal level, he also created images that metaphorically equated the problems of his urban existence with the sufferings of Christ or the dangers of a *kula* canoe sailing at night (Rosi 1994). Such ambiguity about the direction and consequences of social change spoke to contemporary debates about where Papua New Guinea was going and the difficulty of framing national identity when ideas of what constituted PNG culture were so often in dispute (Narokobi 1980; Kasaipwalova 1987; Lindstrom 1998).

The Propriety of Field Sites

Beyond Jane's emphasis on the importance of inductive fieldwork, I am also indebted to her flexibility about field sites. In 2006, this may appear to be an anomalous topic to raise but, in 1998, an article in the *Chron-*

Figure 5.1. Martin Morububuna. Mural, Modern Medicine, Port Moresby Hospital. Courtesy of Martin Morububuna. (Photo by Pamela Rosi, 1986)

Figure 5.2. Martin Morububuna. Blue Kula. Screen print. Courtesy of Martin Morububuna. (Collection of Pamela Rosi)

icle of Higher Education (Passaro 1998) discussed why attitudes still prevailed among anthropologists that questioned the value of research done in urban as opposed to village (read primitive) places. This issue has personal resonance because, at ASAO meetings in 1986, I remember the quickly masked shadows of disbelief that passed over some faces when I mentioned doing fieldwork in Port Moresby. Moresby, as most people thought of it at the time, was a depressing (Westernized) place to pass through as quickly as possible on the way to "the field"—meaning the village where one would find "authentic" culture. Moresby did have culture, of course, but it was hybrid and, in 1986, not yet "proper" (read valuable) to study. Fortunately for me, constructing my project and getting a grant concerned Jane the most—not the choice of field site. As it turned out, far from being a peripheral location from which to investigate the realities of Papua New Guinean life, Port Moresby was the hub in which to encounter the dynamic effects of modernization and the forces linking village and town, including the presence of diaspora communities continuing to practice local ceremonies and traditions. Three months after arriving in Moresby, I attended a Highland girl's initiation ceremony where she was secluded after her first menstruation, and I learned that several village artists at the NAS converted the cash from the sale of their paintings to buying pigs to engage in traditional village exchanges and/or to contribute to village bride-price payments.

In fact, my choice of field site was linked to another Bryn Mawr Mafia connection. At the 1984 International Symposium of the Pacific Arts Association meeting held in New York, Laura Zimmer introduced me to Professor John Waiko of the University of Papua New Guinea, whom she had met during the course of her earlier fieldwork. He told me about the recent development of contemporary art in PNG and sent me an exhibition catalogue of Kauage paintings from the National Arts School (NAS 1977). When I saw these striking images, I recognized immediately that here was something culturally and politically significant to study, write about, and—which became a later committed interest—to curate and exhibit.

Contexts of Creativity—Remember Malinowski's Canoe

With her abiding interest in cultural holism, Jane's long-term research among the Tiwi and (to a lesser extent) the Kaulong has included careful descriptions and interpretations of rituals, including their aesthetics and associated objects. As the title of her monograph on the Kaulong under-

Figure 5.3. National Arts School Kauage Exhibition Catalogue, 1977. Courtesy of Dr. Regis Stella, Melanesian Institute of Arts and Communication, University of Papua New Guinea.

scores, singing for these Melanesians is a key symbol (Ortner 1973) for defining humanness as well as their primary aesthetic locus (Goodale 1995; Macquet 1985).

Among the Tiwi, the *kulama* yam ceremony and the *pukamani* mortuary rites—with their associated paraphernalia, painted objects, body decorations, songs, and dances—configured, connected, and incorporated primary values of Tiwi cosmology and symbolism of daily life, glossed today as "The Dreaming" (Holmes 1995: 10–14; Sutton 1988: 14).

A consistent focus of this analysis, elaborated in her coauthored article, "The Cultural Context of Creativity Among Tiwi" (Goodale and Koss 1971), is to deemphasize Western ideas of "art as object" and direct attention to the dynamics and significance of artistic processes and creativity. "An art object" Goodale and Koss write, "is not simply a means to a particular end but represents the incorporation of a number of values, sought or achieved during the process of creation as well as after it" (190).

In one of our first discussions at Bryn Mawr, Jane made this same point to me, but with another famous illustration: "Remember Malinowski's canoe. In a museum, you can admire the beauty of a Trobriand canoe prow, but there is so much more to the meaning of that prow than aesthetics—though they are important. There are the associations of context. You can't bring these into the museum, but Malinowski wrote a whole book about their intersections in the Kula . . . and others are still writing about that" (Rosi, personal notes, 1978).

Today, anthropologists and art historians studying non-Western arts investigate the dynamic contexts of production in which art objects and performances are embedded through observations made from various locations in the "field"—including vectors of time and space. As was discussed by the participants in the session that Eric Venbrux and I organized at the 2002 AAA meeting, this expanding and intersecting environment is necessary today because the contexts of Third and Fourth World art making can include local, regional, and global domains that engage several art worlds. From this current perspective, as argued by Fred Myers and George Marcus, anthropologists interested in studying world art need to discard paradigms largely interested in mediating non-Western objects and aesthetics to Western audiences, and turn to refiguring the relationship that exists between anthropology and Western art worlds themselves (Marcus and Myers 1995; Myers 1995a, 1995b, 2002).

Contexts of Contemporary Art Production at the NAS

When I began research at the NAS in 1986, art production was linked to and affected by state educational and economic policies: first, state efforts to create a new national culture to develop what Benedict Anderson has called "imagined community" (Anderson 1991); second, the intent to promote and commoditize PNG art and culture at home and abroad to build knowledge and respect for PNG identity, with art seen as the highest form of nationness (Narokobi 1980, 1990; Rosi 1998a). This policy of promoting art as the embodiment of PNG culture was initiated prior to independence in 1975, with Michael Somare, PNG's first prime minister, as its leading spokesman (Somare 1974, 1979).

In probing the relationship existing between PNG art and nation making, I have therefore been concerned not only with the meanings of art objects in imagining and framing relations of PNG identity, but also with the cultural and economic contexts that foster or curtail the creation of domestic and global markets for this art. As Nelson Graburn (1976) discussed in his important volume on arts of the Third and Fourth

Worlds, social identity is a two-way process that needs to be directed inward to symbolize group solidarity, but also outward to mark difference and distinction to outsiders.

In PNG, the production and value of art has been affected in both these contexts by two important factors: first, the continual erosion of government funding that, since 1972, has underwritten the production and promotion of contemporary art to domestic and foreign audiences; second, critical judgments or indifferent audience responses that operate at home and abroad to question the authenticity of new contemporary art forms as being Papua New Guinean or even genuine "art" (Rosi 1991, 2002, 2003, 2006).

Contesting Authenticity and Requesting "Luk Luk Gen" (Look Again)

Domestically, because they are urban products inspired by Western notions of what art should be, contemporary paintings and sculpture have little meaning for most "grassroots" Papua New Guineans. In *Tok Pisin*, they are spoken of as *samting nating* (no significance) as opposed to *samting tru* (having power and sacred value) (Berman 1990). This attitude is changing, however, as more PNG children learn about Western art media in school, enter national art competitions, and are exposed to new art forms through television, radio, videos, concerts, and theater performances (Powell 1987; Rosi 1994; Taylor 1988). Their parents also encounter new art forms in Christian imagery created by PNG artists and through purchases of locally designed T-shirts and *lap laps* (sarongs) screen prints (Cochrane 1997; Narokobi 1990).

In the mid-1980s, in an effort to introduce new aesthetic media into traditional ritual contexts, PNG's foremost textile designer, Wendy Choulai (who died in 2001) began making traditional decorations in modern fabrics for the village celebrations of her Motu-Koita clan relatives (Lewis-Harris 2006; Nijmeegs Volkenkundig Museum 2002). She substituted (or mixed) fine strips of silk or recycled plastic for/with the natural fibers of grass skirts (Choulai 1996) and, at the same time, she started teaching these techniques to other women in local village workshops in other regions of PNG (Choulai 1996: 46). In diverse ways and in a variety of media, new PNG arts are therefore being integrated into modernizing PNG society, but the process is slow and often encounters resistance.

Beyond encountering the problem of public apathy, contemporary PNG arts, including new architecture, also face the problem of disputed authenticity because many Western critics consider new artistic expres-

Figure 5.4. Larry Santana, Hepi Krismas. *Christmas card series AktinRuts. Courtesy of Larry Santana.*

sions to be syncretic and overly Westernized. A prime example is the new PNG Parliament House, which, as I have described elsewhere, has been labeled "inauthentic regionalism," a "compromised and enervated architectural pastiche," and an "example of cultural abortion" (Rosi 1991: 311).

Almost as dismissive was a remark I overheard in April 1998 about an exhibition of contemporary PNG art that I had curated at a college in Boston. While I was attending a lecture on traditional Melanesian art at the Boston Museum of Fine Arts, a man in the audience stood up to say that he had just visited an exhibition of contemporary PNG arts displayed nearby that was "just a step above tourist art." This derisive comment reflects critical Western views that Papua New Guinea art is tainted and lacks the true spiritual power of village art because it utilizes modern

Figure 5.5. The Papua New Guinea Parliament House designed by Cecil Hogan. Courtesy of A. C. Crawford. (Photo by A. C. Crawford)

media and is a commodity. Yet most elite PNG commentators, including former Prime Minister Somare and playwright and constitutional lawyer Bernard Narokobi, valorize all new forms of art as "genuine, dynamic, and exciting" and the "soul expression of what is deep within" (Narokobi 1990: 20).

These diverse discourses about contemporary PNG art reflect the cultural dynamics of establishing artistic value in the contemporary arena of world art. Without support from museums, galleries, critics, and assorted patrons, contemporary artists and their work have little chance of establishing aesthetic and financial worth in today's global fine art market.

Nevertheless, from a personal perspective, contemporary PNG artists find the lack of appreciation for their work painful and frustrating. They feel unsupported by the government, which, while generous with official rhetoric, substantively gives them little help financially or by providing regular exhibition facilities. Artists are, moreover, confused that Westerners, having been instrumental in modernizing their country, now fail to understand new indigenous art forms that address the changes taking place in PNG culture and society (Narokobi 1990).

In 1986, the resulting emotions of frustration prompted Gickmai Kundun, a young sculptor who forges images from metal scrap scavenged from the city dump, to mount an exhibition that he entitled *Luk Luk Gen* (Look Again). He selected this title to alert Papua New Guinean and expatriate viewers that his work deserved to be evaluated on its own terms and for its own cultural sensibilities (NAS 1986).

Engaged Involvement

My reference to *Luk Luk Gen* in the title of this paper is intended to reaffirm Gickmai's judgment that contemporary PNG art does, indeed, deserve "another look." However, this re-looking must also include awareness of the growing importance of urbanization and modernization in

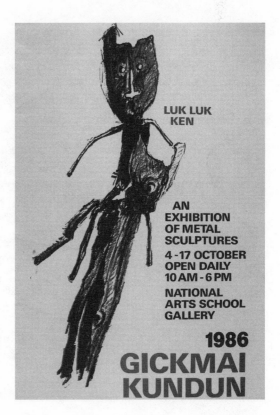

LUK LUK KEN

AN EXHIBITION OF METAL SCULPTURES 4 - 17 OCTOBER OPEN DAILY 10 AM - 6 PM NATIONAL ARTS SCHOOL GALLERY

1986 GICKMAI KUNDUN

Figure 5.6. National Arts School, Luk Luk Gen: An Exhibition of Metal Sculptures by Gickmai Kundun, *1986. Courtesy of Gickmai Kundun.*

PNG life, which includes the fluid relations that exist today between village and town (Knauft 2002; LiPuma 2001; Smith 2002). Contemporary artists, like most Papua New Guineans today, regularly travel between these two spaces—and even beyond. Consequently, this experience of living between intersecting worlds finds expression in their art and the cultural sensibilities underpinning it. Following the trajectories of this traffic is therefore one of the challenges facing anthropologists doing contemporary fieldwork in PNG. While I am following Jane's scholarly tracks to Papua New Guinea, I am doing so at a different time and place and, in this respect, am taking a new perspective on fieldwork that now extends to include global connections (see also Mimi Kahn's and Michelle Dominy's chapters in this volume for further discussion). Nevertheless, Jane's heritage of stressing the importance and value of direct observation (including the need for double-checking) as the hallmark of culturally sensitive anthropology still remains vital.

Figure 5.7. Painting a panel carved with a design from the Trobriand Islands. National Arts School, 1986. Courtesy of Martin Morububuna. (Photo by Pamela Rosi)

Regarding cultural sensibilities, Jane has frequently reiterated that fine-tuned ethnography depends on the importance of empathy and the development of friendship or fictive familial ties with those we study. But these special relations also bring with them obligations, or what Papua New Guineans today call being a *"wantok."* Consequently, anthropologists must be conscious of how our decisions and actions impinge on the lives of those who, through fieldwork, have become friends and/or family.

To conclude my tribute to Jane, I want to raise the question of engaged involvement because it has presented me with a paradox—namely, has my work helped more than hindered the Papua New Guinean artists I have tried to support in their quest for artistic recognition?

Paradoxes of Being a "Wantok"

Several problems have emerged for me in becoming a *"wantok."* First is my inability to live up to the unrealistic expectations of several artists that I am their road to artistic success in the United States. Unwittingly, I have therefore been the cause of unrealistic hopes and frustrations for them. Second, although I have curated several exhibitions of contemporary PNG art in the United States and, recently, the Netherlands (Nijmeegs Volkenkundig Museum 2002), the outcome for the artists has not been of immediate value because, as businesspeople, their immediate priority is to sell their work. But because the exhibitions have been displayed in educational venues serving to promote knowledge of PNG art and culture, artists consider them of little practical value.

Nevertheless, artists are anxious to travel abroad to build their reputations. Procuring sponsorship is, however, difficult and veiled competition develops among artists over funding. Several of my informants have therefore been disappointed—even resentful—that I have not enabled them to visit the United States as compensation for what they regard as their contribution to my research.

Still, even when such a visit takes place, emotional repercussions occur and life expectations are changed. In 1998, I obtained funding to arrange for Larry Santana, a PNG painter and designer, to spend five weeks in Boston as an artist-in-residence.

Accompanied by his family, Larry had a very successful visit and received good publicity from local media. However, the Santanas found the contrast with life in Port Moresby so great that no one wanted to return to Papua New Guinea. And, after the family did return home, the children refused to return to school for several weeks.

Figure 5.8. The Santana family with PNG ambassador Nagora Brogen at the opening reception of the exhibition Nation-Making and Cultural Tensions: Contemporary Art from Papua New Guinea. *Pine Manor College, Boston, April 1998. Photo courtesy of Pine Manor College.*

In 2002, after another devaluation of the PNG kina, which brought with it further inflation in local prices, Larry was unable to pay his rent or school fees for the children. Fearing to move to one of the crime-ridden Port Moresby squatter settlements, he asked me to buy some of his paintings so he could use the money to fly his family to Madang to live with his relatives there in a more secure situation, albeit one that would restrict opportunities to promote and sell his artwork.

Such dissatisfaction leaves me with a sense of unease about my part in changing the life expectations of this family. Was it a good thing to have brought the Santanas to the United States when the better material conditions of life here could only enhance their frustrations with the difficulties in their own country? Reflecting this, one of the paintings Larry recently sent me depicted PNG metaphorically being pulled down by various forces of development—including the World Bank (Rosi 2004).

One of the first questions the Santana children asked me when I met them at the airport at the beginning of their stay in 1998 was "where are the fences and the dogs?"—a reference to the violence and crime that is a part of their everyday lives in Port Moresby. Jane has noted that cross-cultural experience should provide both sides with the opportunity to learn about one another (Goodale 1996b: 189). Inevitably, changes will happen in this interaction but, as anthropologists, we need to be continually alert to the personal consequences of this intercultural exchange and the responsibilities we bear for the results.

When outcomes are mixed, it may be difficult to remain professionally detached from those with whom we have developed what Fortes termed "the axiom of amity" (Fortes 1968: 219)—no matter how fictive. However, in confronting the glitches and bumps of fieldwork, Jane has never had any hesitation in telling her students what to do. Accept them, try harder to understand and resolve them, and keep on going. For Jane, fieldwork has been a labor of love and this is the model of commitment she has held up for both her students and colleagues as her special legacy.

6. *Ethics of Attention*

Dear Jane,

I have long forgotten the exact difference between Crow and Omaha types of kin terminology, but I remember vividly much of the content and most of the philosophy of your field methods course. Of all my anthropology course work, "field methods" was the best: the most useful, engaging, and continuously relevant of them all. Now that I train grad students, I draw on your course and continue to discover its importance. I recall, re-learn, and re-teach with pleasure and commitment the idea that in good anthropology methods and ethics are enmeshed. In my own practice I have come to put ethics first—ahead of theory, ahead of prescriptions of any sort. This leads me into sometimes strange waters, and frequently I take comfort in the fact that I can still hear your voice saying "anthropology is . . . what anthropologists do."

Sincerely, Debbie

Jane Goodale drew on the work of Gregory Bateson to teach us that in our learning from others in the field, a central method was deuterolearning, or learning to learn. Our task as anthropologists, it seemed, did not allow us to transfer our epistemologies into another context. Rather, it required that we learn how other people learn, that we open our minds and our bodies to other people's epistemologies. For this reason, and as a result of her own extensive field experience, Jane taught that good field learning is a whole-person experience. Our most important research tool, we were taught, was our own self; self-observation and self-awareness were not to be suppressed in the work of observing and gaining understanding of others.

The implications of deuterolearning take us into an anthropology that is wonderfully open. Canadian anthropologist Jean-Guy Goulet, for example, writes of his work with the Dene Tha that "Dene informants are firm in their conviction that individuals, including ethnographers, who have not directly experienced the reality of revelation or instruction through dreams and visions do not and cannot understand a crucial dimension of the Dene knowledge system" (Goulet 1998: xxix). His narrative ethnography seeks to communicate this and other aspects of his deuterolearning over many years with these people.

As the work of Goulet, among others, makes clear, the issue is not only epistemological in the methodological sense, but also leads into a rich metaphysical domain concerning the human condition and the condition of life more generally. This openness leads to an anthropology that is dialogical, reflexive, attentive to process, and that extends beyond the human. Thus, for example, in *To Sing With Pigs Is Human* (Goodale 1995), the core question concerns the concept of the person, and the ethnography introduces us to forest and pigs, clearings and taro, song, and the weaving of the ephemeral into patterns of connection, along with the unexpected idea that people here hold that they share biogenetic substance with their place and its resources (Goodale 1995: 112). To be human is to be in dynamic relations that work between continuity and loss, and between sameness and difference.

The ethics/methods we learned from Jane already predisposed us to work outside the constraining structures, analyzed so eloquently by Johannes Fabian (1983), that produce representations of distanced others. The coeval chronotope of ethical ethnography is founded in attention to the actual here and now of the encounter. In my view, an ethical encounter demands of anthropologists that we engage attentively with our teachers and with that which attentively engages our research partners/teachers/informants. Such attention is demanding. As the years went by, I began to realize that I needed to improve my skills in history and geography. Then it was botany and ecology, and later environmental philosophy and ethics. "Holism or hubris?" Bradd Shore (1999) asks in an essay on anthropology's engagement with a holistic approach to humanity. Perhaps some of both, it seems to me, but in any case a legitimate demand on a whole-person research scholar. Deuterolearning is experiential, not experimental; as Kahn notes in this volume, experiential learning was one of Jane's great teachings.

Jane's approach not only presses one to exceed the boundaries of disciplines and categories, but also to exceed the boundaries of a normative or rational self. Fabian expresses the view that a lot of our research "is carried out best while we are 'out of our minds'; that is . . . when we let ourselves go" (1991: 399–400). He notes that *ecstatic* experiences are rarely reported, and he calls for more analysis of the *epistemic content* produced in this manner. As is the case with many others, my willingness to follow, to try to learn what my teachers were trying to teach, and to act on that knowledge in responsive and responsible ways has led me outside many norms. This paper tracks one such excursion. Contrary to Fabian's call for epistemic content, however, I examine the ethics of experience.

Like Fred Myers, I followed Jane's footsteps into Aboriginal Australia. The story I offer here primarily involves my relations with people in the communities of Yarralin and Lingara, in the Northern Territory of Australia, where I started my studies in 1980. In particular, it concerns my friend and teacher Jessie Wirrpa—she took me into her care not long after I arrived in Yarralin in 1980, and kept me under her wing until her death in 1995. One aspect of what I think is important to say about Jessie I have already written about in an essay called "Taking Notice" (Rose 1999). A brief summary will facilitate the story.

When Jessie took me walkabout she called out to her ancestors. She told them who we were and what we were doing, and she told them to help us. "Give us fish," she would call out, "the kids are hungry." Jessie's country included the dead as well as the living, and when she called out she usually addressed the dead. Her brother Allan Young explained it this way: "At night, camping out, we talk and those [dead] people listen. . . . When we're walking, we're together. We got dead body there behind to help. . . . Even if you're far away in a different country, you still call out to mother and father, and they can help you for dangerous place. And for tucker they can help you" (see Rose 2002: 73).

As Jessie and I walked, we took notice of other living things. When the cockatoos squawked and flew away, Jessie laughed because they were making a fuss about nothing. When the march flies bit us, we knew the crocs were laying their eggs, and Jessie began to think about going walkabout to those places. When the jangarla tree (*Sesbania formosa*) started to flower, we knew, or Jessie knew, that the barramundi would be biting. The world was always communicating, and Jessie was a skilled listener and observer.

In "Taking Notice," I wrote about paying attention to the world: about how the world is in communication, and how a person like Jessie understands that and becomes part of it. One of the points I made was that I came to know that Jessie's country gave her life because I walked with her and observed the process, and I knew it experientially because it gave me life too. She was a presence in her country, a known and responsible person who belonged there. I came to understand that Jessie lived an ethic of intersubjective attention in a sentient world where life happens because living things take notice. Tagging along behind her, I did my best to take notice too.

Whole-person deuterolearning required me to learn types of observation and communication that had formerly been unknown to me. I had to develop an awareness of several root principles: that the living world is filled with both human and nonhuman forms of sentience; that the world is filled with patterns and communications; and that living responsibly requires one to take notice and to take care. This was threshold learning for me; once across those cognitive leaps, it was neither reasonable nor possible to go back. Having learned to experience the vivid and expressive presence of other living things, there was for me no good reason, and probably no way, to return to a duller world.

My experience may constitute more than what is implied by the term *deuterolearning. Recursive epistemology,* a term Bateson used late in his life, according to his intellectual biographer Peter Harries-Jones (1995: 9), expresses more fully the dynamics of the ethical/epistemological process. *Recursion* itself is defined as conditions under which "events continually enter into, become entangled with, and then re-enter the universe they describe" (Harries-Jones 1995: 3). The term *recursive epistemology* depends on recent rethinking of organism and environment, focusing on relationship. This ecological perspective on connectivity asserts that each affects and enables the other in ongoing ways that continue to affect and enable. In the context of anthropological research, recursive epistemology connotes the situated connectivities within which knowledge comes into being. The anthropologist's thought is shaped by her teachers as her life shifts more deeply into relationships with people, places, and concepts that become increasingly constitutive of her own thought and being. Although fostering porous proximities, recursive epistemology does not lead toward homogeneity. Rather, it works productively with difference, change, and exchange. In addition, it demands a rethinking of ethics. I return to this latter point shortly.

Recursive epistemology helps me account for the ongoing entanglement of my own learning. Jessie's teachings were not just in my notebooks, but were becoming formative of my own experience of the world. They were shaping my questions, my perceptions, my hypotheses, and much that I would later write.

Another aspect of what I would like to say about Jessie is published in a paper by historian Peter Read (1997). Read's paper draws on interviews with people who have spent many years learning from Aboriginal people. I spoke about some opportunities I have had to experience country differently. Most of these experiences took place while I was with Jessie. They were experiences of vastly heightened perception of the life and connectivity of the world around me. Everything I could see looked vibrant, tingling, connected, and shimmeringly alive. When I was with Jessie and first experienced this awareness, my sense of it was that this was new to me. Over time, however, I came to realize that at some level the experience was not as unfamiliar as I first had thought. I began to think that perhaps the world had been like this a lot of the time.

I never asked Jessie about what she saw. Sometimes I asked about what she heard. Mostly I stayed with her and watched what she did—how she turned her head, who she talked to—which birds, for example, and why, and what she was learning from them and from other events going on around us. Who she called out to, when, and why.

Jessie was a great hunter—the Ngarinman term is *Mularij*. Everybody wanted to go with her all the time because they knew they would get a feed. Her forte was fish. She never missed. Jessie and I have been to just about every junction, every permanent water hole, and most creeks and billabongs within her sections of the Victoria and Wickham rivers. Sometimes we went on foot, more often by motorcar; sometimes we went with a large group; occasionally she and I would take a couple of kids and strike out on our own. Some of those days were so glorious that they remain among the most beautiful times of my life. Others, of course, were dreadful. If I never again sit on a steamy river bank in 113-degree heat with my head about to explode from the reverberations of the screaming cicadas, and with blood running down my legs from the march flies, that will be okay with me. Jessie almost always seemed happy, but sometimes there were too many kids, too much nuisance, everybody wanting to borrow her gear, messing it up, and then sitting around waiting for her to catch fish so that they could have dinner. We hunted together in good times and tough times.

The same year that Jessie died, I had reason to take a group of indigenous people from North America to Litchfield National Park (just south of Darwin) for a day. I had been working with a group of the traditional owners of that area for a few years, and my plan was to take the visitors to the park and then to stop by the little bush town of Batchelor on the way home and introduce them to Nancy Daiyi, a senior woman from the country. I called her first to ask if this was okay. She said yes, and I asked if I could take them into an area called Makanba, where the water is free of tourists and where the mermaid custodians of the country are said to live peacefully (see Rose 2002). She said yes to that too. Late in the day we got to Batchelor, and I told her what we'd done, and said that I'd made sure to splash water on the visitors at Makanba. She asked if I had called out, and I said no. In her grumpy and imperious way, she said I should have called out to the old people. I was not aware that I was authorized to do that, and I had to tell her that I didn't know how. She told her daughter Linda to show me, and Linda did.

I should state that Nancy's pedagogy works like this. Her default position is that the people around her are intelligent and competent, have observed what to do, and know how to do it. She doesn't praise people for getting things right, she just growls at them for getting it wrong. I knew why she was saying what she was saying, and I could appreciate why she was annoyed. However, the following year I made the same trip with my young niece, and although I knew I was supposed to call out, I could not bring myself to do it. I just couldn't. What I remember is that my throat wouldn't work.

I now jump to 2001 when my sister Mary visited me for the first time. She came to Canberra and we drove to Darwin by way of the Birdsville track, the Victoria River District, and Kakadu National Park. We were out in the Vic River district, having come across the Murranji, and when we got to the Dashwood Crossing of the Victoria River, we stopped. I took Mary down to the riverside, I got a cup of water and splashed her, and I called out loud and clear. I addressed Jessie, and my voice was absolutely right.

A question I ask myself retrospectively is: why was I able to call out in one area and not in another? The quick answer is that in one area I had spent years of my life fishing with Jessie, we were there together all up and down this river. On top of that, Jessie, my friend, was dead, and thus when I called out I could address someone I had known and been close to. These are good personal and social reasons for the difference, but they actually are not experientially what the difference consists of. The experiential difference is this: in one place I could hear, and in the other I could not.

Along the Victoria River on that day I could hear something I had experienced often with Jessie, but hadn't quite realized and hadn't quite thought to try to articulate. I could hear a listening presence. The world at that time was not just a place, it was a presence. I could hear awareness, and so I could call out.

The temptation with using the written word in academic contexts is to find reasons and explanations that fit the existing discourse. And yet, what happened was embodied responsiveness. It did not matter exactly what I knew or thought I knew. It mattered that here I heard something around me and here I had a voice. Here it seemed that that which was beyond me called forth my voice. All I had to do was let it move.

I am not saying that Makanba and Dashwood Crossing are qualitatively different places; I am only saying that my experience of them was qualitatively different. For me, the difference is that my ability to hear gave me a voice. In contrast, at Makanba, where I had every good reason to call out, I heard nothing and thus could voice nothing.

This experience seems to lie outside the general domain of what is sayable in normative anthropology. Povinelli (1995), for example, contends that such matters fall well outside the normative modernity in which anthropology and other social sciences ground their legitimacy. So the experience of finding my voice has had a paradoxical effect: when I return to the academy, I feel voiceless. The finding of a voice in one context renders me nearly voiceless in another. My silence in the academy is built up from my knowledge and experience of boundaries and censure, but perhaps it is also influenced by the silences that pervade the place. These boundaries, these limits to what is sayable, are made evident primarily by being breached and that rarely happens, so usually it may not be apparent that in an academic context that is founded in seminars, lectures, letters, articles, books, and coffee breaks, there are actually some terrible silences. They are overcome from time to time by works of passion and daring that leave one longing for more such riches.

Colin Turnbull wrote just such an article, published in 1990, in which he contends that anthropological methods and boundaries, linked with a constrictive ideal of objectivity, have limited us and incapacitated us in our fundamental endeavor of understanding. He notes the criticism (leveled by "third world scholars and laymen alike") that we fail "to be fully human and [thus fail] to use our full human potential." This failure leads us to treat others "as though they were indeed not full human beings themselves but things that could be satisfactorily examined and explained through the artifice of reason alone." He goes on to describe our superficiality as a major weakness of anthropology (Turnbull 1990: 51).

Anthropology and its silences: I have been thinking about theories of absence, and I have become intolerant of the strictly discursive approach to these issues. To put it abrasively, normative anthropology's silences are not so much signs of repression as they are signs of amputation. These silences do not produce an excess of meaning and desire; rather, I fear, they diminish meaning while producing complacency. They dumb down toward instrumental modes of explanation and they excise vast amounts of experience, including the encounter with mystery and the experience of joy.

I have been developing a concept of double death, drawing on Bateson's insights concerning entropy and the disorganization that starts to ramify with the loss of metapatterns (Harries-Jones 1995: 169, 210). The work seeks to develop real-world analysis with these abstracted concepts. Long before Jessie's death, I had written about death, life, and what becomes of human beings after death, according to Yarralin people. I want to return to some of this earlier discussion, to look at the twisting together of life and time, so that death is bent back to affirm and contribute to the life of country.

As I discuss in *Dingo Makes Us Human* (Rose 1992/2000), Yarralin people talked about the components of the human person in ways that suggested at least two animating spirits (and I also expressed caution about the use of the term *spirit*). One of them keeps returning from life to life, so that death becomes an interval leading into transformation into new life. Often the genealogy of *spirit* includes animals as well as humans—this life force moves through life forms and continues to bind death and life into the ongoing and emerging life of the place. Another *spirit* returns to the country to become a nurturing presence. These are the *dead bodies* I spoke of earlier—the dead countrymen who continue to live in country and to whom people appeal when they go hunting. This ecology of emerging life sets up recursive looping between life and death; country holds both, needs both, and, most important, keeps returning death into life. The return is what holds motion in place, and in the dynamics of life and death, life is held in place because death is returned into place to emerge as more life.

Double death breaks up this dynamic, place-based recursivity. The first death is ordinary death; the second death is destruction of the capacity of life to transform death into more life. In the context of colonization, double death involves both the death that was so wantonly inflicted upon people, and the further obliterations from which it may not be possible for death to be transformed. Languages obliterated and maybe gone forever, and clans or tribes eradicated and maybe gone forever are examples of double death.

Ecological violence performs much the same forms of obliteration. Thus, species are rendered extinct, billabongs and springs are emptied of water, and soils are turned into scald areas. This violence produces vast expanses where life founders. It amplifies death not only by killing pieces of living systems, but also by diminishing the capacity of living systems to repair themselves, to return death back into life. What can a living system do if huge parts of it are exterminated? Where are the thresholds beyond which death takes over from life, and have we exceeded those thresholds violently and massively in the conjoined process of conquest and development? These processes are not always irreversible, but in many areas the answer is yes.

In Jessie's way of life and death, she has joined the other *dead bodies* in her country, and, like them, is becoming part of the nourishing ecology of the place. In life she was a great hunter; in death she joins the providers. Double death puts her in double jeopardy. The rivers are rapidly deteriorating from erosion and, even more severely at this time, from invasions of noxious weeds. It is probable that in the near future, riverine ecologies will collapse, and with that collapse the possibility for the living to go fishing and feed their families will be radically impaired, if not completely obliterated. For Jessie, then, there is a doubling up: first her own death as a living person, and, subsequently, her obliteration as a nurturer within a flourishing country.

I can imagine that there could be yet another form of obliteration—a triple death, perhaps, with anthropology as a contributor. Our boundaries around what is sayable, and our elisions that treat as real only that which can be subject to constricted modes of social analysis, either excise a great range of experience and knowledge or drag it back into the familiar, thus depriving it of its own real power. As scholars we are vulnerable to being colonized by reductionisms and to reinscribing their legitimacy by refusing to name and challenge their power.

The concept of multiple death requires us to think about what is happening in the world. Death is overpowering life, and some of our practices facilitate this violent thrust of entropy. The term *derealization* seems to me to endeavor to grasp the quality of this powerful death work. Normative modernity's progressive emptying of the human capacity to imagine nonhuman life in subjectively vibrant forms of self-realization, self-repair, and self-organization is matched by practices outside and beyond anthropology that progressively are emptying the living world of its subjectively vibrant life forms. Social and ecological derealization go hand in hand. Anthropology's silences have the potential to derealize much of what people have to say about the process, and to excise much of the evidence of violence from the record.

Fabian (1991) demonstrates that anthropology has consistently allowed itself to be deflected from the challenges of epistemology and enabled itself to find a zone of security. In contrast to security, Fabian contends that ethnographic knowledge is a process. His passionate and perhaps risky protest in favor of a processually engaged anthropology returns me to a basic question: who or what was I addressing when I called out to Jessie Wirrpa on the banks of the Victoria River a few years ago? The short, pithy answer is "I don't know"; in Aussie vernacular, "I wouldn't have a bloody clue, mate." That is factual, but I can also say that I was not indulging in clueless behavior.

A significant point that Fabian did not discuss, and that I believe follows directly from a recursive epistemology, is faith. I would say that when I called to Jessie, I acted in faith, and I mean the term in several senses. The first is that of faithfulness or holding fast, such as is implied in the idea that I acted in good faith. My action was faithful to Jessie's teaching, and in good faith it continued the mutuality we shared in life. I claimed an enduring bond of connection, implicitly asserting that just because one of us was dead, it did not follow that the relationship was finished. And indeed it is not. As this paper shows, Jessie's gifts continue to shape my life, and clearly I intend my work to analyze and make publicly explicit some of the perils she and her country now face.

Another meaning goes to the question of the nonsecular. A number of scholars today pursue a distinction between faith and belief. Turnbull, for example, describes *belief* as a domain of mere reason and rational forms of religious experience (1990: 70). Similarly, Debjani Ganguly (2002), one of the new wave of postcolonial Indian subaltern scholars, insists that while belief can be reduced to political-cultural calculation, the force of nonsecular language and experience challenges, and may fracture, the apparent hegemony of modernity. Along with these and other scholars, I suggest that faith is not defined solely by cognition; it can be located throughout the body, and it may often erupt mysteriously, being called into existence by that which is outside us or precedes us. Faith, in my view, is action toward intersubjectivity. It is called forth by that which is beyond the self, and thus equally is action arising from intersubjectivity.

Jessie taught me about a communicative world by taking my hand and walking me in it. Through her own listening, she taught me to listen. Having held her hand and followed in her footsteps, I know that my life takes a twist into life-affirming action when I ground my life's work in her intersubjectivity of place. I call out as a gesture of faith: that country matters; that life has its own vibrancy, intensity, and modes of attention; and that my voice has a place in this world.

In calling out I take a stand, and I now clarify this position. I noted that recursive epistemology leads one directly into ethics. This is so for several reasons; for me, the most interesting point is the convergence between biological theory (see, e.g., Maturana and Varela 1998) and late-twentieth-century philosophy's turn toward ethics. Emmanuel Levinas is one of the great twentieth-century philosophers of ethical alterity, and his life's work moves away from the insular totalizing self and toward relationships. "Self is not a substance but a relation" Levinas writes (1994: 20). Recursivity between subjects posits a similar mode of becoming, and thus requires "abandoning the ontologies of our time" as Levinas (1994: 24) so forcefully puts it. A recursive epistemology positions the anthropologist to become embedded in intersubjective encounters and engagements. It must, therefore, give primacy to ethics. Ethics involve relations between self and other, and thus actively abjure homogenization, appropriation, objectification, and amputation. Both self and other matter in their difference: in their capacity for relationships and for mutual influences.

Methods for intersubjective encounters depend, I believe, on a radical theory of dialogue. Although Fabian (1991: 394) objects to the term *dialogue* because he thinks it sounds soppy—"anodyne, apolitical, conciliatory," I think that the term has a good history and an excellent future. Granted that the term *dialogue* is often used loosely, I mean it quite precisely. Dialogue is a form of ethical practice among subjects (not a subject–object relationship, but a subject–subject relationship). Dialogue seeks connection with others, and need not be restricted to human others. Philosopher Emil Fackenheim (1994/1982: 129) draws on the work of Rosenzweig to articulate two main precepts for structuring the ground for ethical dialogue. The first is that dialogue begins where one is, and thus is always situated; the second is that dialogue is open, and thus the outcome is not known in advance.

The situatedness of dialogue is context-specific. It includes the here and now of the encounter—its place and its time. It includes the history of the place and the personal and social histories of the parties to the encounter. The situatedness of dialogue means that our histories precede us, and that the grounds of encounter are never abstract or empty. In the Victoria River valley, for example, the ground between me and my Aboriginal teachers was occupied in the first instance by Captain Cook. A history of conquest, white rule, dispossession, and cruel decades of colonization stood between indigenous people and any outsider, particularly a white person, in the first instance. That was the situatedness of our encounter. Other possibilities were open to us, and Aboriginal people's efforts to assert the existence of, and to specify, moral others (in Burridge's 1960 term) offered generous paths toward alternative grounds of encounter. But such developments depended on the process of the relationships through time, as we revealed our selves to each other through our actions. Other contexts, in Australia and elsewhere, have their own unique situatedness. Situated dialogue is never abstract, and thus is always specific.

The concept of openness may sound obvious, but is actually equally challenging. Openness is risky because you do not know where you are going to get to. You cannot have a mission statement, a set of goals, targets, charters, and performance indicators. You would have to be clever in your proposal writing if you hoped for funding. To be open is to hold one's self available to others: you take risks and make yourself vulnerable. But this is also a fertile stance: your own ground, indeed your own self, can become destabilized. In open dialogue one holds one's self available to be surprised, to be challenged, and to be changed. This ground of openness is the place where knowledge arises. It seems important, therefore, also to assert that openness depends on an underlying faith in pattern, connection, and communication. That is, while the outcome is not determined in advance, one works with an expectation that random or chaotic outcomes will be the exceptions rather than the rule.

From an anthropological perspective, this theory of dialogue is a position of situated availability. One is situated in one's own history, training, desires, and self, and is available to be called into change through the teachings of others. One holds one's self open to recursive epistemology both by knowing and learning one's own situatedness and by being available to become enmeshed in the teachings one has struggled to encounter.

Situated availability poses a further challenge. One of my favorite philosophers, Lev Shestov, says that for us moderns, faith is audacity: it is a refusal to regard anything as impossible (1970: 33). One can read Shestov's audacity as a theological claim, which may be part of his project, but one can also read it today as an ecological claim. From this point of view, as long as the living world is fully alive, it will be self-organizing and self-repairing, and thus it is a dynamic system in which the whole is greater than the sum of its parts. It is not knowable as a whole by any of its constituent parts.

Shestov's view that the desire to be able to encompass and explain everything constitutes a forfeiture of "the capacity to come into contact with the mysterious" (1982: 105) holds special significance for anthropologists, as our work brings us into contact not only with that which is mysterious to us, but also with that which is mysterious to our teachers. *Impossibility* in an ecological context defines the knowledge that life exceeds our capacity to understand it. In the context of anthropology, audacity can be read as faith in three conjoined propositions:

- That differences within the human family are real (see Hornborg 2001)
- That understanding is possible across differences
- That understanding never exhausts itself; there are always possibilities for more questions and more understandings

Jane's legacy as I experience it is this chain of connections associated by moral claims: the method . . . is the ethic . . . becomes the encounter . . . becomes the knowledge . . . becomes more questions. This anthropology is . . . what anthropologists do dialogically. I am not proposing a new dogma. Rather, as a constituent part, it seems to me that Jane's legacy has ecological qualities to it. It is a dynamic process, and it is greater than the sum of its parts. Those of us who have had the great good fortune to have come under her guidance and influence take her teaching into different fields, engaging with other teachers, and turning our learning into communicative forms that carry it into contexts we can neither predict nor prescribe.

Acknowledgments

I offer my thanks to the organizers of this session, and all the participants, for their work in helping us to identify the patterns that connect us and to revitalize these relationships. Special thanks to Michael Lieber and Eric Venbrux for extremely helpful feedback. A version of this paper is published elsewhere in *Extraordinary Anthropology: Transformations in the Field*, edited by Jean-Guy A. Goulet and Bruce G. Miller, and is reprinted here by permission of the University of Nebraska Press and by the Board of Regents of the University of Nebraska, c. 2007.

MICHAEL D. LIEBER

7. *The Squabbling Stops When Everybody Wins*

Jane Goodale and I might as well have had the same father. Both were New England doctors with a scholarly bent, and both loved intellectual contest and trained us to do it and love it as well. So Jane and I have spent over thirty years debating, contesting, and otherwise squabbling over theory, data, and interpretation and what Oceania is *really* about. From my point of view, each contest is intense, affectionate, and richly satisfying. From Jane's point of view, I think, it's more like little brother showing up for an argument. She straightens him out (once again by pointing out cases that falsify his generalization du jour) and then sends him on his merry way. Such is love.

When Jane invited me to teach at Bryn Mawr in 1985, I told her that I'd come so we could stop squabbling and do serious battle. I lied; I really was spying, trying to see how she managed to build the most successful Ph.D. training program in the country with a department of five people affectionately known as the Bryn Mawr Mafia (hereafter BMM). There was no formula and no secret, just a process that has characterized her entire career as a researcher, a colleague, and an educator—*collaboration*. For all their touting of interdisciplinary research, American universities rarely reward collaboration, particularly in the social sciences. Product differentiation is what confers prestige. In this academic-entrepreneurial context, Jane's career stands out not only as collaborative, but also as unabashedly and enthusiastically so.

Jane's first field research with the Tiwi was a collaboration with

Charles P. Mountford and later with Hart and Pilling (Goodale 1971; Hart, Pilling, and Goodale 1988). Jane's work with the Kaulong began as a collaboration with Ann Chowning, whose own collaborative work with Ward Goodenough had been so productive. Equally important and in some ways more important, Jane's work with her students has been a long series of intellectual collaborations.

The master–apprentice relation may characterize the early phases of her work with students, but by the time dissertations are being written, the relationship has typically become a partnership wherein both partners benefit from and learn from their mutual contributions. According to Jane and her students that I have talked with, the collaborative part of the relationship ranges from Jane acting as a sounding board (responding to specific arguments) to cooperative puzzle solving. What students get out of this is a set of alternative inferential pathways, counterexamples, and (sometimes to their consternation) more reading to do. What Jane has gotten from the collaboration have been three things:

1. An increasingly broader understanding of not only Oceania but also of the other ethnographic areas in which her students have worked
2. An increasingly deepened understanding of what constitutes comparative ethnography, what kinds of knowledge it yields, and what this knowledge tells us about human cultural variability in general and for specific regions
3. A deepened understanding of and facility with the symbolic approach to cultural analysis (see especially Goodale 1995)

And of course, there is the Association for Social Anthropology in Oceania (ASAO), the quintessential institutionalization of collaborative ethnographic inquiry. Jane has twice guided ASAO through very difficult periods of transition. She has taken a leadership role in the definition and redefinition of how ethnographic comparison might best be conceived and implemented in face-to-face engagement. This is how I first met Jane in 1972. A small group of us met to form ASAO from what was left of its predecessor, the Association for Social Anthropology in Eastern Oceania.

For all of the intellectual excitement of our early battles following that first meeting, I quickly learned that our relationship would never be one-to-one. To be involved with Jane is to be integrated into a personal and intellectual network that includes her closest colleagues, like Ann Chowning and Ward Goodenough, and her students. By students, I mean not only her Oceania researchers, but also people like Joy Bilharz (Seneca) and Adrian Stackhouse (Jamaica) and not only her doctoral students, but also her undergraduate students like Jane Fajans and Michelle Dominy and Gita Srinavasan. To be part of this network is, among other things, to reread Carlton Coon with new eyes and—I don't know how to put this any other way—to stand in utter awe of Freddy de Laguna.

What it means to be part of the Bryn Mawr Mafia, even an adopted member such as me, is being part of ongoing conversations that one can start, join in, or be invited into. The conversations are multilayered. That is, they are always "about" something, such as gender issues or exchange systems, but they move up and down a ladder of generality from theory to data (or vice versa) to midlevel empirical generalizations to the patterning of instances that generated the empirical generalization to counterinstances (always) and back. It takes a bit of practice to follow the conversation, since no one seems to feel compelled to flag the points at which he or she moves up or down the escalator of logical types. A question about where we are on the escalator usually gets answered by someone posing an ethnographic instance or counterinstance. Another feature of these conversations is what computer geeks call hibernation. A conversation can be interrupted or dropped—sometimes for years—and then be picked up again from where it left off without any preamble other than "Remember when you said . . . ?" The "when" could be four or five years ago. No one seems to find this disconcerting or even remarkable.

The settings of this flow of communication vary from telephone conversations to visits to meetings. We are forever going to hear each other's presentations at ASAO or AAA meetings, or at visiting lecture series (in Philadelphia, Chicago, etc.). We join each other's panels, symposia, and planning sessions, and we usually read one another's stuff. The reading punctuates the spoken part of the conversations, and if I didn't know that Ali Pomponio or Fred Myers or Laura Zimmer-Tamakoshi had just published something hot, I can count on Jane telling me to read it. Sometimes there is general agreement on the current issue under discussion, but more often there is some exception taken. That's what keeps any conversation going.

What makes these conversations collaborative is their outcomes. Research planning and conduct, theses, dissertations, books, articles, panels, symposia—all of these are typical outcomes of the conversations described above. All are results of conversations with and around Jane Goodale combining complementary competencies to produce outcomes that are otherwise difficult or inconceivable for each partner working alone. Let me illustrate BMM collaboration with my own experience.

Collaborative Outcomes: The Development of Oceanic Epistemology

As a cofounder of ASAO, I can say it—the 1977 ASAO sessions in Charleston, South Carolina, sucked. You could infer the participants' boredom by all the parties they were having in their hotel rooms at night. When the sessions are good, people are too tired to party at night. The only saving grace was the preliminary (informal) session on knowledge in Oceania. It was clear from the ideas and the data participants shared that we had good stuff. Marty Silverman's admonition that we were treading on turf occupied by the greatest minds of the past three millennia only served to heighten our appetite for the venture. I agreed to organize and chair the symposium for the next ASAO meeting. By the time the meeting was about to begin, only two of the promised eighteen papers had been written and circulated—mine and Jane's. Goody, another tiff.

Our papers were different but complementary. Mine focused on knowing as a patterning of meanings using lexical data: epistemological terms "to know," "to learn," "to practice," "to accustom oneself to," and the logical and substantive connections among them. I used this approach to make the case that the structure of the concept of *knowing* was identical to the structure of the concept of the *person* on Kapingamarangi, a Polynesian atoll in Micronesia. The person is defined as a relatum, one end of a relationship, while "to know" is awareness of differences (distinctions), difference being a relationship between some X and Y. The phrase "to learn" is literally to disengage something from the matrix within which it is embedded. What one learns about and comes to know about are relationships.

Jane's paper, by contrast, focused less on lexical issues and more on understanding knowledge by observing what Kaulong people of New Britain do with it. Kaulong use what they know in the same way a card player uses his own and his opponents' cards in a poker game. Knowledge is deployed in those situations whereby its use gains its user maximum advantage given the costs of publicly revealing what one knows. While I described a world of concepts and their logical links, Jane described a world of strategies and the contexts in which one is more effective than another. However, for both Kapingamarangi and Kaulong people, all knowledge is personal (because it is the result of repeated experience). It is not a body of stuff from which all can draw equally. Indeed, knowledge as we understand that term does not exist among Kaulong or Kapingamarangi (hereafter Kapinga) people. What I needed to know from Jane was more about the terms Kaulong use to talk about knowing, while what she needed from me was more about how Kapinga use what they know.

By the summer of 1978, I was back in Micronesia for what was to be two years of field research between 1978 and 1982. With Jane's paper in hand for comparative reference, I began trying to answer her questions using three research strategies. First, I tested a hypothesis logically derived from my lexical analysis: I reasoned that if knowing was awareness of relationships, then Kapinga fishermen should be optimizers who understood the relationship between human activity and the relationships between fish and their habitats; that is, they should be conservationists. I was wrong about that; they are maximizers who take every fish available until the canoe can hold no more. I redid my interviews on the lexical terms and their connections looking for falsification of the original analysis, but these data only confirmed what I originally had. Puzzled, I started a different line of questioning about how information is imparted.

The first thing I found was that the English phrase "to describe" is untranslatable into Kapingamarangi. What we think of as a unitary communication process is, for Kapinga, a set of different communicational operations that include the following:

> painting a verbal picture of X
> comparing X to some Y
> locating X
> clarifying details about X
> exemplifying X
> demonstrating or showing X
> recounting experience with X
> verifying statements about X

All of these operations are responses to requests or demands on someone made by the person seeking information. The seeker of information, in other words, has to specify what he/she wants to know and answer questions about why he/she wants to know and about what he/she already knows (although the nature of the question implies that). The seeker's relationship to the information sought is part of the relationship of seeker to informant.

Whether a question is likely to be answered depends on a number of things, one of which Jane predicted I would find: does the person seeking information have the right to know it? Depending on what information is being sought, relative age, gender, family membership, men's house membership, and relationship with the person being questioned can qualify or disqualify the seeker to receive the information. Another question constraining the likelihood of an answer is that of the costs and benefits to the informant of revealing the information. For example, if the information sought is of the sort that a number of people could provide, then the costs of providing it are lower than if the informant were the only expert. But the costs also depend on the relationships between the seeker, the person asked, and the other people who could provide the information. If there is someone with the information who is closer to the seeker such that he or she *should* be the one asked, then the costs and benefits vary with the relation between the one asked and the one who should be asked. If these two are close, then the former will refer the seeker to the latter to forfend risking the latter's ire at being ignored. If the two are not close or are competitors, the costs are low, and there is a double benefit of obligating the seeker for future considerations and embarrassing a rival. If the information sought is specialized such that few people know it, the specialist incurs a high cost by answering the question. Because people use specialized information only when commissioned to do so, revealing the information is creating a competitor. Apprenticeship, by contrast, involves gradually revealing specialized information over a period of years. The master benefits from the labor of the apprentice and from the prestige of being sought out as a mentor.

The result of these interviews was that my data quickly began to look a lot like Jane's. My third collection method was participant observation, focusing on a single kind of activity, traditional fishing, and observing what people did and said about it, often while fishing with them. I worked from observation to interview and vice versa with a heightened awareness of epistemological implications of what people did and said about what was done in conversations, meetings, gossip, and the like. This procedure helped to fill in the nuances of how people come to know and use (conceal and reveal) what they know. Planting taro or mat making or house or canoe construction or a feast would have been productive inquiries, but fishing had the advantage of having immediately observable outcomes—the provision of food; the establishment, enactments, and maintenance of social rank; and the capacity to cope with dangerous spirits who inhabit deep water. The links between these three things made it clear that pre-Christian religion, which was about food, was a just as much a technology for food production under variable environmental conditions as fishing methods were. Their differences in form are less important than the class of contexts to which each technology is applied.

Fishing techniques are applied to largely predictable environmental conditions subject to known ranges of variation. Ritual practices are knowledge applied to largely unpredictable activities of spirits with a small range of known constancies. The two kinds of knowledge are complementary but asymmetrically ordered. Knowledge of fishing techniques is applied if and only if environmental conditions are such that the application of ritual knowledge (to unpredictable environmental changes as a result of spirit activity) is unnecessary. Ritual knowledge contextualizes fishing knowledge. It was this asymmetry that explained age and ritual class stratification privileging unequal access to fish habitats, canoes, and sacred and secular leadership positions. Political competition among Kapinga fishermen was as intense as among Kaulong big men and women, but social stratification muted the outward forms of competition in activities requiring reliable responses to variable conditions by fishing groups.

As I was learning all of this, Jane was busy with her own spin-off from her knowledge paper. The "poker game of life" was more than a metaphor for her presentation of Kaulong epistemological data. The Tiwi of Australia were literally inveterate gamblers (and I've heard it said that Jane is, too), and as she pondered this aspect of her Tiwi data, she did it like everything else—collaboratively. After Laura Zimmer-Tamakoshi returned from her first fieldwork with interesting data on gambling in another context (Zimmer-Tamakoshi 1983, 1985, 1986), Laura and Jane organized a series of ASAO sessions on gambling in Melanesia and Australia. Laura then edited a special issue of *Oceania*. In her paper in that collection, Jane examined the gambling activities of Tiwi women and men in the context of their respective traditional work roles—foraging and hunting—and in relation to men and women's efforts to achieve personal status (Goodale 1987; see also Zimmer-Tamakoshi 1987a, 1987b).

Jane and I worked together again in 1984 and 1985 in ASAO sessions on cultural identity and ethnicity in Oceania organized by Lyn Poyer and Jocelyn Linnekin. James B. Watson joined this session, introducing to participants the idea of Lamarckian identity (Watson 1990). That is, the people of the Kainantu region of the New Guinea highlands understand procreation in Lamarckian terms—the inheritance of characteristics acquired by the fetus's parents before and during the pregnancy. What parents eat and do, for example, can alter their biological substance, and this alteration can be passed on the fetus. I had found the same thing on Kapingamarangi. For example, when my wife was pregnant with our first child, Kapinga women told her not to look at misshapen fruit lest the baby be born with a similarly misshapen head. Children from an atoll house compound are said to inherit propensities, such as for carpentry or fishing or sexual promiscuity, that supposedly typify the descendants of the family inhabiting the compound. Watson found the same with descendants of former inhabitants of villages among Tairora people. Through intense conversations with Jane and Watson, I worked out a logical chain of reasoning whereby sociocentric personhood—the person as a relatum—is a logical outcome of Lamarckian-type concepts of procreation (Lieber 1990). But if the person is defined by relationships, then it follows that kinds of persons are results of kinds of relationships. Thus there is no logical discontinuity between gender identity, family identity, and ethnic (or cultural) identity. These are social categories arranged in nested levels of inclusion. Symposium participants had no problem with this part of the chain. It was the next part that only Watson and Jane found unobjectionable.

What distinguishes one as human is the capacity for knowing. What distinguishes one human from another is capacities for knowing different sorts of things and relations among things, what we might gloss as aptitudes, which in places like Kapingamarangi and Pohnpei (Falgout 1986) are part of one's somatic inheritance. In Oceania, aptitudes are observed as personal preferences for different kinds of relationships—for example, with fish, with wood, with the opposite sex, and so on—-and different ways of conducting those relationships, which adepts seem to learn and develop effortlessly. If this is true, then differing capacities for knowing generate different *kinds* of people. It is, thus, knowing that underlies social categories, of which ethnic and cultural identities are examples. Epistemology is the cultural infrastructure of ethnic and cultural identities. Reaction among participants to this was intense and brief. Participants wanted no part of this level of generalization, and it was dropped. But this is about Jane's world, so in typical BMM fashion, I will presently pick up the conversation where it left off in 1985.

If Jane got anything from me at all, I suspect it was the relationship between knowledge and personhood. In my 1994 book on traditional fishing (Lieber 1994), I concentrated on the relationship between personhood and knowledge to show that their conceptual patterning, applied to fishing, structures the social and political order on Kapingamarangi. Jane's book, *To Sing With Pigs Is Human* (1995), however, takes this relationship much further than I did with chapters devoted to food production, illness and healing, exchange, siblingship, political positioning, and song as critical arenas for the enactments of personhood and the distinctions between people that enactments engender, maintain, and augment. It is facile to say that one is what one knows. For Kaulong, it is more a matter of one being what one knows, what others think one knows (and/or what one might know), and successfully keeping people guessing about what one knows or might know by avoiding or confronting challenges to personal knowledge to one's own best advantage. It is the acquired skills in managing both one's knowledge and how others perceive it that define what sort of person one is. I have found in reading and rereading this work both remarkable correspondences and differences between Kaulong and Kapinga notions of the person and of knowledge. It is in this context of comparison that I take up the conversation that was truncated in 1985.

There were two fundamental issues on the table at that 1985 meeting: (1) the ethnobiological implications of Lamarckian inheritance, which were discussed but never clearly articulated, and (2) knowledge, which was clearly articulated but barely discussed. My thinking on the first issue has been profoundly influenced by Ali Pomponio's and Michelle Dominy's contributions to the symposium and the volume that followed. Ali contrasts the Mandok (middlemen traders of the Siassi Islands) with people like the Tairora, described by Jim Watson as the difference between "marigenic" substance versus "terragenic" substance. That is, just as Tairora people incorporate relationships between things in their mountain environment (e.g., drinking local waters incorporates local spirits in the water) through ingestion, Mandok incorporate things and relations between things from their ocean environment. These become parts of their physical bodies, and they can pass them on to their children. Marigenic substance represents Lamarckian inheritance with a "Mendelian" twist (Pomponio 1990). The twist, as I understand it, is the biological part—if it's biological, then it's biogenetic. I was unable to convince Ali that somatic characteristics do not necessarily imply a Western-style genetic understanding of the soma. When all of this came up again in ASAO sessions on race and racism in Oceania, I experienced much the same frustrations in trying to explain why there is no documented precolonial case of a concept of race in Oceania. My disagreement with Ali kept popping up in my head as I puzzled over an approach to the concept of race that would be clear and obvious. Michelle Dominy's (1990) work helped clarify the problem. Her Maori feminist informants contrast *pakeha* with local cultures as rootless (and portable) versus those rooted in specific places, echoing Watson's account. This contrast reframed my thinking about the Mendelian identity/Lamarckian identity contrast in concepts of constitution of the human soma. What I finally realized was that it was the issue of *biological substance* and its connection to place that had never been directly addressed by any of us in that 1985 session.

When David Schneider used biological substance in his account of American kinship (1968) to characterize the somatic side of what kin share, he used that phrase interchangeably with "biogenetic substance," contrasting it with "code for conduct" shared by kin. This nature/law (culture) distinction is a very old one, and it contextualizes Americans' thinking about kin relations. It was this distinction that was implied but never explicitly stated in the contrast between ethnic identity and cultural identity, which is one reason I never bought cultural identity as a useful concept. Rejecting it without further consideration cost me dearly, however, since it delayed confronting biological substance and its applications to Oceanic data.

Thomas (1999) and Carsten (2001) have pointed out that biological substance is an ambiguous term when one looks at its usages by anthropologists. But it is clear from data collected in Oceania from the early nineteenth century onward that Oceanic people have their own ideas about how the human soma is formed, how it grows, how it changes, how it responds to insults to its outer or inner workings, and what it is capable of doing. These ideas constitute an ethnobiology of the human soma. Indeed, Jane's account of Kaulong management of knowledge and personhood is a partly ethnobiological one, although that was not its purpose.

There are significant variations in Oceanic understandings of the human soma, as we might expect, but there are also some fundamental assumptions that appear to be shared throughout the Pacific islands. Procreation concepts are examples of the latter:

1. Multiple acts of sexual intercourse over a period of time (ranging from weeks to months) are necessary for pregnancy to occur.
2. The fetus is formed from the combination and coagulation of male and female fluids, and continual inputs of these fluids results in the growth and formation of the fetus.
3. The parents pass on not only somatic substance inherited from their parents but also increments to their own somas that they have acquired through interacting with their physical and social environments; for example, relationships with ancestral spirits buried in the ground through ingestion of food or water, relationships with people such as theft or promiscuity, and relationships between animals and their habitats or between part of an animal and the whole animal (as illustrated by prohibitions against eating crayfish lest the fetus cling to the womb as the crayfish clings to its crevice in the reef or against eating frogs lest the infant have webbed feet or hands).
4. The concept that the human soma is mutable and that changing location (as in migration) changes the human soma and, thus, group identity (see Stewart and Strathern 2001; Watson 1970, 1990).

It is the last feature that explains why one finds no indigenous concept of race in Oceania, even in the cases where ethnic differences are assumed to be rooted in somatic differences; for example, Kapinga people (Lieber 1990) and Pohnpeians (Falgout 1986). Whatever else race denotes, there is general agreement that racial characteristics are assumed to be immutable. It is ethnobiological differences that yield or cannot yield a concept of race.

From these four shared features of procreation we can infer a fifth one—the idea that a fetus is an outcome of processes of composition combining somatic resources from what its parents have inherited with those acquired by its parents' through their experiences with their physical and social environments (transformed into somatic substance in their fluids, which the fetus absorbs). In the case of environmental relations transformed into parental substance through ingestion or through what the parent sees or does, somatic features of the fetus are analogues of the environmental relations. The analogies are part-to-whole relations and are identical to the composition of magical substances, such as yam magic described by Malinowski in *Coral Gardens and Their Magic* (1935), and of riddles, common in Melanesia (Maranda 1971). The infant, then, consists of parts accumulated and combined in the composition process. There are ways to forfend inheriting some kinds of environmental features, such as using food and behavioral injunctions, but there few means to ensure the transmission of desired features in the composite other than food prescriptions (Stewart and Strathern 2001).

One sees this feature of the composite soma in both Kaulong and Kapinga ideas of the person (*potuna* and *dangada*, respectively). Jane glosses the Kaulong self as a denotatum of *enu*, which also means "shadow" or "spirit." The self can act independently of the body, leaving the body during dreams, being frightened out of the body, or leaving of its own accord. The closest Kapinga come to this Kaulong concept is the term *mouli*, which means "life, lifetime." Like the *enu*, one's *mouli* suffuses the entire soma, but unlike the *enu*, it leaves the body only once, at death. It is not independent of the body, as the Kaulong *enu* is. The term I have used to gloss the self for Kapinga is *lodo*, a person's "insides." For Kapinga, one's "insides" consist of emotion, desire, will, and thought, each of which appears in the infant at different times and none of which is controllable by the others; the self in this case is the domain of true chaos (Lieber 1994). For both Kaulong and Kapinga, control of the self is critical to living one's life. Jane describes control of self for Kaulong coming from the "mind," *mi*, which also means "inside" or one's "insides" and can be used to denote desire, emotion, and thought. Jane uses the term *self-control* to talk about the relationship between *enu* and *mi*. For Kapinga, self-control is an oxymoron. But for both Kaulong and Kapinga people, control of the self and control of one's insides, both independent parts of the person, are critical to one's viability as a whole person. It is the issue of control and how it is exercised that makes the Kaulong–Kapinga comparison so fascinating and potentially fruitful for larger concerns of Oceanic ethnography and for anthropological theory.

Both Kaulong and Kapinga must control their insides in order to interact with people and things in their worlds. Both a Kapinga's *lodo* and a Kaulong's *mi* are vulnerable to loss of control. It is understanding their differences in vulnerability that the meaning and role of knowing is crucial. The Kaulong *mi* is vulnerable to control through events and persons external to the self, including sorcery and magic used by another person and through possession by ghosts and through illnesses to which everyone is susceptible. Avoiding loss of control and coping with it when it does occur help to maintain one's control over one's own *mi*. For Kapinga, loss of control over one of the components of one's insides is the result of unconstrained desire, emotion, will, or thought dominating the other three such that one pursues satisfaction of only one of them without regard to the others or to how other people respond to one's obsessive acts. Since the locus of control is not internal, one depends on relationships with other people to control one's insides. So, for Kapinga, control of one's insides always comes from relationships with other people. When relationships are cut off, control ceases. For Kaulong, it is the opposite. Relationships with outside agents can interrupt one's control. For Kaulong, control comes quite literally from inside the person, whereas for Kapinga, it comes from outside the person. In both cases, it is what one knows that makes control of self and control of inside possible.

For Kapinga, one learns about relationships and the differences of each kind of relationship, especially differences in authority and what one expects from each. It is the maintenance of these relationships with others that constrains one's own expressions of what one wants and what one thinks. Knowing the consequences of how one conducts each relationship constrains what one says and does. If this is correct, then it follows that Kapinga people would avoid being alone for any more time than that necessary to complete some task. This is in fact the case. Unlike Kaulong, who seek the solitude of the forest and welcome its availability, Kapinga do not seek solitude and are suspicious of anyone who appears to do so. To be alone is to be *ongeonge*, "lonely," and to expose oneself to loss of control of components of the self, particularly of thought. Unrestrained thought, literally "thinking too much," is the cause of all insanity. Once a person ceases to become aware of what others are doing, saying, and expecting, then one's desires or will or emotions or thought can take over one's *lodo*. It is knowing, awareness of relationships, that maintains control of self; that is, that constrains (regulates) otherwise independent components of the self and, therefore, the person. Regulation is the result of integration of the person with others in ordinary interaction, where the demands of a particular interactional context delineate and delimit which and what kinds of expressions of one's *lodo* are appropriate. Knowing what is expected and knowing how to meet those expectations makes integration possible. Integration of the self, then, occurs at the level of interaction between persons, the integration of a person into a social nexus.

For Kaulong, knowing also integrates the person, but in a different way. To know, whether from hearing, experiencing, or seeing, is to fill up the self, which in turn serves to configure the body, creating its form, especially its curves. The more one knows, the more full and healthy the body. Knowing more makes one more attractive to others and better able to compete successfully for prestige and power. The full body of a knowledgeable person creates a place that one's *enu* is loathe to leave for very long. A body not filled with knowledge is a shabby place that one's *enu* can become disgusted with and leave permanently. For this reason, Kaulong men and women manage their knowledge carefully, since revealing what one knows potentially depletes one's store and potentially empties the person of content, inviting the disaster of an *enu* choosing to leave forever. In this way, knowing integrates person and self through the *mi*, where decisions about how to use what one knows are made. The *mi* serves not so much to regulate desire, thought, and so on, but rather to *synchronize* them. For Kaulong, timing is everything.

That knowing integrates what Marilyn Strathern calls partible persons in these two very different communities is striking, particularly in contrast to Americans where knowing serves to provide individuals with a complete set of intellectual resources necessary for acting and interacting as adults. We talk about completeness in a number of ways, formally and informally. Juveniles are not legally adults because they have not had the time to accumulate all of the knowledge necessary to operate as adults. They are not complete persons in a legal sense. We use metaphors like "one brick short of a load" and "not playing with a full deck" to talk about incompleteness of adults, not of children. Integration of the person is a separate issue and is talked about in a different way; for example, "has a screw loose," "get my shit together," and "coming unglued." Integration of self is also at a higher level of logical type, for it includes completeness (and knowledge). An adult is not competent to stand trial, for example, if he or she is not mentally integrated enough to know the difference between right and wrong, but knowledge is one of the things that is integrated; it does not do the integrating.

To Conclude, BMM Style

This account of a twenty-six-year collaboration with Jane and her students is a progress report on our development of the relationship between Oceanic concepts of personhood and knowing. We have reached the point of preliminary ethnographic comparison of that relationship. The comparison raises questions at several levels and of what we should do about them. Is the central role of knowing in integrating the person in these two communities fortuitous? Or is it an artifact of analytical procedure? Or is it somehow another one of those features of the Oceanic cultural landscape that is, like procreation theories, shared with a continuum of variation across Oceania? It seems clear in both communities that it is knowing that distinguishes humans from animals. Kapinga, for example, point out that "animals do not know who their relatives are" to explain why incestuous couples are "acting like animals." Does the difference in the level at which persons are integrated in these two communities imply different and mutually exclusive cultural premises or the same set(s) of premises distributed through different social organizations? Is *potuna* a fundamentally different construct from *dangada*? It seems to me that there are two ways of answering this question. One is more specific comparison; for example, is *potuna* defined as a relatum or an individual in the Western sense or is there some other alternative yet to be inferred? Another strategy is comparison across a set of communities in a symposium focusing on the relation between knowing and personhood. I suggest that the latter would be more productive (and more fun).

It would help if there was a theoretical framework for integrating the comparison, and my choice would be Bradd Shore's (1996) concept of culture as sets of models built on "foundational schema"; that is, what I have called cultural premises (following Carroll 1988 and Carroll 1977) elsewhere. This is a cognitive approach to culture, based on people's models of and for relations with their social and physical environments that are inferable and testable. Using this common framework facilitates comparison in a way that can visualize similarities and differences in concept maps. This comparative strategy also implements our shared goal of developing the concept of culture as the central construct that organizes our work.

So Jane, whaddaya say? Wanna dance? Invite our friends and get a band maybe?

JOY A. BILHARZ

8. *From Pig Lunch to Praxis*

I was very excited in the spring of 2002 when Laura Zimmer-Tamakoshi contacted me about the session honoring Jane Goodale that she and Jeanette Dickerson-Putman were planning for the annual meeting of the Association for Social Anthropology in Oceania (ASAO) and immediately typed out by e-mail my willingness to participate. It was only after I hit the send button and the message was irretrievably flying through the ether that a sense of panic set in. There they would all be, I thought, the Bryn Mawr Mafia, exchanging details of their most recent fieldwork (all in neo-Melanesian of course), and I would be there too, the outsider, forced either to pretend I understood their conversations or that it didn't bother me that I couldn't! As a graduate student, it had always seemed to me that Jane's Oceania students constituted a special group, and I was acutely aware that I was not a part of it—despite the fact that Jane never made this distinction. Too embarrassed to back out, I began to reflect upon what Jane's mentoring had meant in my career and life.

My first and most enduring image of Jane is from the reception for new graduate students at Bryn Mawr held in the fall of 1969. As I recall, it was a quite formal affair with servers in white gloves and I was feeling quite academically and socially out of place when I suddenly saw Jane in a striped shirtdress of various shades of blue, blue pearls, sneakers, and her matchless smile—and I knew things were going to be okay. From the beginning, she embodied feelings of strength, dignity, integrity, and, above all, a sense of adventure. Reading *The Two-Party Line* (1996b), I was again reminded of the physical adventure that her fieldwork has always entailed, but there was also the adventure of the mind and the spirit, the belief that anthropology was an endless quest for a better understanding of humanity, that no topics or people were outside its realm, provided they were approached with understanding and compassion.

The excitement of anthropology was conveyed in her courses, but, in a less formal context, developed out of Pig Lunch. This was a concept that Jane and her first doctoral student, Judy Huntsman, brought back from the Anthropology Department at Auckland. In its Bryn Mawr reincarnation, two graduate students were responsible for providing sandwich makings for an entire week. At noon, anyone who happened to be around could throw in a dollar, make a sandwich, and sit around and talk. Although the occasional seminar debate flowed over into Pig Lunch, it was usually a time of more informal discussions about what various students and faculty were doing in the field, ideas they wanted to run by peers, and a general bull session. Often the speaker for the monthly meeting of the Philadelphia Anthropological Society would stop by on a Friday and other visiting anthropologists made appearances. The institution of Pig Lunch provided a means of integrating students and faculty in a learning experience often far more significant than what occurred in more formal situations. The only parallel of which I am aware was the afternoon tea that Dr. Lawrence Angel held in the physical anthropology labs at the Smithsonian Institution. Whatever doubts I might have had about my choice of anthropology were eliminated by Pig Lunch.

It is ironic to me that the areas that have come to inform much of my fieldwork, gender and social organization, were topics in which I had no interest when I arrived at Bryn Mawr. Everyone had to take Social Organization and Jane was a spectacular teacher, but I still wasn't excited by the topic. As several of the authors in this volume note, there was no need for a "feminist" anthropology at Bryn Mawr; that women's lives were as important as men's was understood and it was recognized that women's perspectives had often been ignored. Three decades later and in an academic climate that has witnessed an overt concern with women's lives in many disciplines, it was not surprising to find that a common lament that we shared when we met in Vancouver was that the term *gender* is now being used as a synonym for women. What we learned is once again being challenged, albeit from the other side. As an Iroquoianist, what has intrigued me from the beginning about the lives of Iroquois women, especially the Senecas whom I know best, is the way in which they have achieved a balance between the rights and responsibilities of men and women so that although they may do different things, the value of their contributions is considered equivalent. Dominance is as easy as it is common; finding an equitable balance is difficult. Being well educated and politically astute, we knew that American society had not achieved anything approaching a balance, but Jane made sure that we examined sex roles rather a myopic focus on women if gender was our research focus. A brief glance at the contributors to this volume demonstrates that not all Jane's students or those she mentored are women and not all have gender as a primary research concern. That a majority of her students were women is probably a reflection of the history of Bryn Mawr as a women's college even though the graduate school accepted men from its inception.

This is not to suggest that Jane was not a feminist—she was and is—but that what we learned from her was always within the context of social science (with an emphasis on the *science* part). Those of us whose emphasis has been on women's roles did not go out burdened with political or social agendas to "prove" that women were important; we went out as anthropologists to answer questions that had not been asked, to talk with people who hadn't been listened to as well as those who had, to fill in some blank spaces in the ethnographic record, and to identify others. The postmodernist/literary critique emphasis on "voices" has always seemed inappropriate to me. Voices are disembodied; they can emanate from Nobel laureates, saints, and psychotics. To truly understand what they are saying requires a connection to the human being who uttered them and the social and cultural context in which they occurred. Gender is simply one element of that context, although it is one that many of us have found particularly interesting and significant. What we learned from Jane was to learn from *people*—not just to listen, but to observe, participate, empathize, and comprehend.

When I began my fieldwork among the Allegany Senecas, the issue of gender was clearly critical, given the role that Iroquois women had played in the past. Because they were first to accept the tidings of the Peacemaker, the fifty chieftainships of the Iroquois Confederacy were held by matrilineages. Only males in those lineages could be chiefs but only women could appoint and remove them. Sitting chiefs had the right to refuse the matrilineage's nomination but could not put forth a name themselves. Because the unanimous consent of a full complement of chiefs was required for any action, both men and women could independently shut down the system. Compromise and cooperation were therefore imperative. Women provided the "Three Sisters" (maize, beans, and squash) that were the staples of Iroquois diet and were responsible for the distribution of all food. Whether a war captive would be executed or adopted was also determined by women. Membership in the Six Nations was set by matrilineal descent and postmarital residence was accordingly matrilocal.

Males served as hunters, warriors, chiefs, and diplomats. A functioning system required men and women to do their respective jobs.

In 1848, the Senecas on the Allegany and Cattaraugus reservations withdrew from the confederacy and established the Seneca Nation of Indians. Eliminating chiefs,[1] they instituted an elective government reflecting nineteenth-century American practices. Although the Seneca Nation constitution referred to women as the "mothers of the nation" and enrollment was based exclusively on matrilineal descent, women were stripped of their political roles as the rights to vote and hold office were restricted to males.

This was still true in the 1950s when the federal government claimed roughly a third of the Allegany Reservation for the Kinzua Dam Reservoir. Lands historically held by the matrilineages were lost without any formal consultation with the women. This seemed to me to be an ideal topic for research. The literature on forced relocations throughout the world indicated that the status of women was negatively affected by removal. Would the traditional strength of Iroquois women and the fact that contemporary males consulted with women and respected their input (at the same time that they denied them formal political participation[2]) result in a different outcome for Seneca women?

The more time I spent in the field, the more I also realized that children were also crucial. Using a processual model developed by Thayer Scudder and Elizabeth Colson (1982), which examines forced resettlement as a multigenerational phenomenon, it seemed to me that one cannot understand the role relocated children will play as adults unless one understands what that forced removal meant to them as children. Unfortunately, there were no ethnographic data from anywhere in the world that dealt specifically with how children coped with the destruction of their physical, and frequently social, world. I remembered Jane talking about the first surviving twins among the Kaulong and wondering how different their social experiences might be from those of their peers and their parents. As I began to collect information on the lives of parents and children, it was apparent that the removal of the Allegany Senecas caused a massive dissonance between the experiences of parents and children of which neither generation was fully aware at the time. As both tried to minimize their fears and losses, communication about the ordeal between parents and children was often nearly nonexistent as each tried to spare the other a perception of their pain.

Jane's emphasis on comparison became more important to me as I revisited my data and as information on other forced relocations became available. Why, I wondered, had the Allegany Senecas survived their experience better than other groups? Why do their communities still exist, not without problems, but certainly without the total disintegration seen among the Ojibwas at Grassy Narrows or the Innus of Davis Inlet? The difference, I think, was social organization and, in particular, the role of matrilineal descent. What the women of Allegany had been telling me (and I had interpreted solely in terms of gender) had a much broader implication that involved the whole society. Matrilineal descent, beyond being the criteria for *being* Seneca, also provided an organizational framework far more compelling than any formal political structure. Although many women were angry or disappointed about their inability to vote, they were also secure in their ability to influence the course of events through informal means and in fact I have argued (Bilharz 1995, 1998a) that women's traditional concerns became the focus of the Kinzua Dam Settlement Act. Because the formal structure of the Seneca Nation's government, which consisted of a president, treasurer, clerk, and council, could not adequately address the issues posed by the Kinzua Dam, committees were appointed to focus on specific issues such as relocation of the nation's cemeteries, loss of the reservation school, allocation of settlement funds, and so on. Women were appointed to these committees and gained invaluable experience in dealing with American bureaucracies as well as the electoral politics of the Seneca Nation. Women dominated committees concerned with education and health, traditional female domains; in fact, the greatest allocation of the so-called rehabilitation funds was for education of the nation's youth. Once again reviewing my field data, I saw that the men of Allegany had been telling me the same thing. Following Jane's example, I went back to the people and asked, "Is this what you were telling me? Do I finally have it right?" And George Heron, the president of the Seneca Nation at the time of removal, said "95 percent of it!"[3] Subsequently, Thomas Abler, an anthropologist at the University of Waterloo who had been resident at Allegany during part of the removal period, and I collaborated on an analysis of the effects of women's suffrage (finally granted in 1964) and right to hold office (granted in 1966) on Seneca politics and government.

Now where does Oceania fit into all of this? I knew there were a few graduate students who had worked with Jane who were not Oceanists and wondered how or if their experiences coincided with mine. Jane faxed me a list (figure 8.1) of her doctoral students and I was quite surprised to see that of the eighteen, seven (40 percent) had done their dissertations in other areas, ranging geographically from Sierra Leone (Carol Hoffer) to Siberia (Kristin Barsness) and from Nepal (Premalata Ghimire) to Nashville (Julia Lydon)! Via phone or e-mail I was able to contact everyone but Prema and, sadly, the late Carol Hoffer. Fortunately, I knew both of them. Prema and I were graduate students together and, although Carol was finishing her research and writing up her results as I was starting my graduate program, she was a frequent attendee of Pig Lunch and meetings of the Philadelphia Anthropological Society. I also spoke with Sue Roark-Calnek, whose own dissertation about North American Indians was strongly mentored by Jane and whose success probably served as an incentive for Jane to take me on as a doctoral student.

The fact that my own feeling of isolation as a non-Oceanist was not shared by the others resulted in part, I think, because I was in the cohort that included Annette Weiner, Fred Myers, and DeVerne Smith and my interests at the time were in physical anthropology and archaeology. I was not unique in this; my earliest recollections of Annette are the gargantuan cockroaches that came back in her materials from Guatemala where she had done a field season in archaeology with Ben Reina at the University of Pennsylvania. To the dismay of the Dalton Hall custodial staff and many students, these bred eagerly with the local Bryn Mawr population, producing a classic example of hybrid vigor.

There was a strong agreement among the non-Mafiosi that Jane has had a significant effect on our work in four major areas. First, Jane insisted on a grounding in *empiricism*. From our initial seminar reports to the final dissertation, conclusions and interpretations had to be supported. With adequate data, one could move to comparative questions. Sue

---

Figure 8.1. Non-Oceania Dissertations Directed by Jane Goodale

1997—Kristin Barsness, *A Tlingit Community: A Century of Change*

1988—Premalata Ghimire, *Ethnicity, Class and Caste: Categories of Group Relations in Sunauli, a Village in Southern Nepal*

1988—Pauline Johnsen, *Women as Caregivers to the Elderly: The Filial Imperative in Anthropological Perspective*

1988—Julia Lydon, *Finding a Way: Cross-Cultural Adaptation at Home and School in Nashville, Tennessee*

1987—Joy Ann Bilharz, *Ghosts of Broken Hearts and Laws: The Allegany Senecas and Kinzua Dam*

1979—Marjorie Balzer, *Strategies of Ethnic Survival: Interaction of Russians and Khanty in 20th-Century Siberia*

1971—Carol Hoffer, *Acquisition and Exercise of Political Power by a Woman Paramount Chief of the Sherbro People*

Roark-Calnek and Kristin Barsness both noted the richness of the Melanesian material and Jane's insistence that we read entire monographs, and pointed out the lack of comparable material in native North American research. This had not occurred to me, but it is certainly true.

Second, Jane's *holistic approach* and the feeling that one could do anthropology anywhere made her the logical director for those with interests outside Oceania. Part of this reflects Jane's own enthusiastic quest for knowledge and insistence that we read as widely as possible. (One possibly unforeseen result of this is that several of us now share her passion for mystery novels.) When I asked Jane how she ended up directing Premalata Ghimire's dissertation on Nepal and Julia Lydon's master's thesis on Afghanistan, she told me that as a student she had taken more courses on central Asia (both ethnographic and archaeological) than she had on Oceania. The reality that one's research may not have a one-to-one correlation with academic course work is exemplified by Jane and represents one of the unheralded strengths of a broad four-fields preparation in anthropology. She recognized that anthropology was more than ethnographic research and encouraged me to present seminar papers on the prehistory of Oceania. I suspect that many of us may have had more courses in Oceania than we had in the regions in which we subsequently specialized. It should also be noted that Jane was an important mentor to many whose actual dissertations were directed by others, reflecting in part the small size of the Bryn Mawr department but also her own enthusiasm for the field and willingness to serve as a sounding board for evolving ideas. Her Oceania data and experiences served as useful sources of comparative material for students working outside the region and I believe she was the most logical adviser for those whose interests were *not* in Oceania precisely because of her emphasis on comparative research.

Third, all of us are extremely grateful for her *support for nontraditional fieldwork*, interrupted by the demands of family and/or employment. This is probably a significant difference between her Mafia and non-Mafia students, although Annette Weiner, Debbie Rose, and Laura Zimmer-Tamakoshi all had young children when they began their research but were still able to undertake extended seasons in the field. Reading the drafts of papers prepared for the Vancouver session honoring Jane, I was struck by the extended stays in the field undertaken by her students working in Oceania, which tended not to be undertaken by the non-Mafia for a variety of reasons. Jane saw all of her students through marriages, births, illnesses, divorces, family crises, and deaths and did not let us forget that we would still be good anthropologists once the dust settled. She recognized that there were times when priorities had to shift and that sometimes there were no easy ways out, but at the same time, she made sure that anthropology and our own research remained on the list of things that needed to be done. For at least several people, her faith in us was an important anchor when all else seemed in flux. At times it was also maddening as we listed the reasons certain suggestions were impossible because there was no time, or energy, or whatever was demanded. And, after listening patiently, there was always the quiet "yes, but you *need* to do this." And somehow the time, energy, and whatevers appeared, evolved, or were created.

While some of this may be attributed to the character of Bryn Mawr itself, Jane realized that her students often had complicated lives that made fieldwork tricky to coordinate. Furthermore, the non-Mafia had to make our own arrangements for entry into the field, not having Jane to point out appropriate contacts. Although in my case this was not too difficult, it did prove to be extremely time consuming. At least three of us had our daughters in the field and she correctly saw this as an advantage rather than a distraction. The fact that our field seasons were interrupted for months at a time allowed us time to reflect on our experiences and also made it easier to identify the changes that occurred when we were not physically present. Jane's own broad interests permitted her to make connections between our work and hers that raised questions that might not have occurred to someone working in our region and strengthened our research. As Julia Lydon phrased it, "She was always there."

Fourth, all of us have a strong interest in issues of *ethnicity and identity.* What does it mean to belong to a circumpolar culture divided between two nation-states? What is the relationship between shamanic revival and national identity for the Sakha? How do you exhibit your Kurdish or Lao heritage in Tennessee? When they take your land and burn your home, how is your Seneca identity affected? This is an issue that Jane raised in her own fieldwork, in her stress on the person as an individual within a society within a region. Related to this is an awareness of issues of land rights. When Jane was first elected to the Tiwi Land Council, I remember her telling me that it was time to "give something back." This was meant not in the context of reciprocity, although clearly it was reciprocal in nature, nor as an ethical requirement demanded by the profession, but as part of a personal moral commitment that obligated her to use the knowledge that the Tiwi had shared with her in a way that forwarded the goals that the Tiwi themselves had determined. The evolution from traditional ethnographer/ethnologist to applied anthropologist was a logical development for Jane and the two are part of the continuum that comprises the holistic approach of anthropology.

Although the non-Mafia infrequently had the opportunity to meet and interact with Ann Chowning, all of us were aware of the importance of the collaboration between her and Jane. Jane always stressed the value of a colleague in the field with whom we could compare data and experiences and who would serve as a check on our intellectual and emotional highs and lows. I did not have the opportunity to experience this until nearly a decade after my initial fieldwork, and, not surprisingly, it was Jane who was the source of the collaboration.

At the retirement party for Jane at Bryn Mawr,[4] she suggested to me that I speak with Glenn Sheehan and Ann Jensen about a potential project they were interested in that they found in a request for proposal (RFP) issued by the National Park Service concerning ethnographic research among Iroquois descendants of participants at the Revolutionary War battle of Oriskany in the Mohawk Valley of central New York. Both Glenn and Ann are archaeologists but they had worked closely with native peoples in their Alaskan research. Jane suggested that their experience in applied work and my experience with the Iroquois might be a useful combination. Later that evening over gin and tonics, we tentatively explored the possibility of a joint proposal under the auspices of their company. As I reviewed the RFP, it became clear to me that the intent of the research was not concordant with its scope. The National Park Service was interested in knowing whether there were oral histories among Iroquois people that related to this battle that would enhance and/or correct the presentations about the siege of Fort Stanwix and the Battle of Oriskany at Fort Stanwix National Monument. They also wanted research in the archival material. The outline of the desired ethnographic research was, however, limited to Iroquois people residing within the continental United States and reflected boundaries that did not exist at the time of the August 1777 battle. In order for the research to address the goals, it was critical that Iroquois people residing in what is now Canada be consulted. Jane's emphasis on doing research in ways that were academically and ethically appropriate as well as testing the (apparent) limitations reverberated as I called Trish Rae, one of Jane's master's students, a Canadian employed by the Mohawks of the Bay of Quinte. She confirmed that the majority of those who fought with the British at the battle were Indians (members of First Nations in Canadian terminology) and most of them had relocated to what became Canada at the conclusion of hostilities. We discussed the proposal requirements as outlined by the National Park Service and concluded that unless Canadian Iroquois were included, the intent of the proposal could not be addressed and we would not be willing to participate. Glenn suggested that we call the regional ethnographer, Dr. Rebecca Joseph, in Boston and explain our dilemma. Becky told us that a proposal that included research in Canada would not be excluded from consideration even though federal regulations required consultation only with groups resident within the current territorial boundaries of the United States. We decided to proceed with the proposal and were awarded the contract. I served as codirector with Glenn and lead ethnographer; Trish was lead ethnographer for the Canadian arm (Bilharz 1998b).

Working with Trish provided me (and, I hope, her) with the advantages that Jane and Ann had in their work. Frequent debates over the interpretation of various documents and interview data were a refreshing incentive for more in-depth research, and working together in the field was a welcome change from the isolation of my original work. When we encountered difficult situations in the field, it was good to have the support of a trusted colleague. Throughout, we had the unwavering support of the Applied Ethnography Program of the National Park Service as well as the park superintendent, Gary Warshefski. At a time when it was easy to dismiss concern with indigenous peoples as mere political correctness, it was indeed refreshing to find people in the government who were dedicated to doing a job properly. As Jane had always emphasized, government people can be the "good guys" as often as they are the "bad guys." When we learned from our research that there were natives who had come from the western Great Lakes region as well as others who were not Iroquois, we included in our final report a suggestion that an additional project be funded that would expand upon what we were increasingly viewing as a confluence of civil wars—between opposing Iroquois nations, German immigrants, and immigrants from the British Isles—as well as competing colonial class and religious interests.

By this time, Glenn and Ann had moved to Alaska and the second project was funded through the Research Foundation of the State University of New York at Fredonia. I served as project director and principal investigator and again Trish and I shared the archival and field research (Bilharz 2002). The two projects spanned nearly eight years from beginning to end. At the 1999 International Congress of Anthropological and Ethnological Sciences held in Williamsburg, Virginia, we, along with the National Park Service and representatives of the Iroquois Nations, presented a preliminary report on the project and its effects on the interpretation of the battle and the management of Fort Stanwix National Monument. I see this as a logical outgrowth of Jane's feeling that it is necessary to "give something back." While Trish had been involved in applied research since her graduation from Bryn Mawr, this was my first formal entrée into it, although I had previously done some informal and unpaid consulting work.

Five of the last six of Jane's doctoral students worked outside Oceania. In actuality, this should be five of five because Pam Rosi's graduation was delayed by ill health. Our subsequent careers have been very different from those of the Oceanists. I believe I am the only one with a tenured academic position in a traditional setting, although others work or have worked as adjunct professors. All of us are engaged in applied research, working for school districts (Barsness and Lydon), in gerontology (Pauline Johnsen), and in fostering communication between native Siberians and North Americans (Marjorie Balzer). Roark-Calnek, Balzer, and I are currently working with indigenous peoples on land rights issues.

What does this divergence from the Bryn Mawr Mafia, many of whom hold or have held traditional academic positions and may or may not be involved in applied research, mean? Does it reflect a changing job market? Is it related to Jane's increasing interest in these issues and the fact that we are her last students? Is the divergence more apparent than real? Does it reflect the different ages at which we completed our doctorates? I suspect that all of these are valid in some way for all of us.

There is one final note that I would like to add in relation to Jane's impact on us that I suspect is held by all those who have had the honor of being her students. It would be naive to assume that our paths were not sometimes rocky or that life at Bryn Mawr was idyllic. As many of us recall all too well, there were many very dark days and times of discord, culminating in the demise of the graduate program in anthropology (among others). Throughout these personally and professionally trying times that surely rivaled any she encountered in the field, Jane never lost her integrity or her dignity, never lashed out in anger or spite or pettiness. When I reflect on what Jane has brought to my life and career, this is what stands out. By her own example, she has shown us not only what it means to be a brilliant scholar, outstanding mentor, stern taskmaster, and (mostly) gentle critic, but also primarily a kind and decent human being. Because of Jane Goodale, we all sing better with pigs. As the Senecas say, "*Nya weh*, Jane!"

Notes

1. The Senecas of the Tonawanda Reservation remained in the confederacy and retained chiefs.

2. One can read this as an interesting parallel to the traditional government in which the contributions of women who could not be chiefs were instrumental

(if not critical) to the functioning of the system. If this is true, then the failure of Senecas to adopt women's suffrage earlier in the century might reflect this tradition.

3. He is unwilling to tell me about the other 5 percent!

4. A retirement, as we all know, only from her formal teaching and advising duties and not, thankfully, as a scholar.

WILLIAM W. DONNER

9. *Separation and Support,
Conflict and Romance in
Relations between Sikaiana
Men and Women*

As an ethnographer and teacher, Jane Goodale often discussed not only the importance of gender in shaping general social relations, but also the importance of examining the ways gender affects different relationships in different ways. When I was an undergraduate taking her course in social organization, Jane was finishing her book *Tiwi Wives*, and some of her lectures drew from that book. I was fascinated that Tiwi men and women could view the same activity and understand it in very different ways that were, nevertheless, mutually reinforcing. Jane also showed that whatever the usefulness of abstractions about male and female, men and women had very different interactions as parents and children, husbands and wives, brothers and sisters, and grandparents and grandchildren. The ways in which relationships can change in different contexts has affected much of my research about Sikaiana social relations, and the way in which men and women interact in different ways in different contexts informs much of what is written in this paper.

But there is a far more important and general inspiration from Jane that shaped my development as an ethnographer and the ideas in this paper. She impressed upon her students the importance of a holistic and sympathetic study of other cultures. Her analyses were integrative in developing interpretations based upon ethnographic descriptions that were rich in detail. She also stressed that anthropology was for the curious, and that intellectual progress was not so much in finding answers, but in asking better questions.

In this tribute to Jane's influence as a teacher and anthropologist, I want to examine issues about gender and sexuality in Sikaiana life that have always intrigued me, but also perplexed me as well. In writing this chapter, I realize that my contribution is somewhat different from the others in this book in being more ethnographic and less personal. That my contribution is so different is partly Jane's fault. In all my courses with her as a Haverford student majoring in anthropology at Bryn Mawr and as a graduate student at the University of Pennsylvania, she emphasized the role of ethnographic data in learning about human behavior and the sheer excitement of this learning. The varied sources of my data—Sikaiana terminology, quotations from songs, interviews, and observations of interactions—show her influence as a teacher who stressed the importance of ethnography. Moreover, the issues discussed in this paper include some that have intrigued and excited me for many years. If I have not, as the title of this volume so aptly puts it, found the "right thread" in my analysis, I hope that I can acknowledge Jane's influence by presenting some ethnographic material that raises questions about social relations, in this particular case, about how sexuality can affect the varied relations between men and women.

At the beginning of my stay on Sikaiana, a Polynesian outlier in the Solomon Islands, George Vanteiti, a young and recently married man, explained to me the meaning of the Sikaiana word *hakasaosao*, the term for a go-between in contemporary courtship. Courtship on Sikaiana must be conducted in secrecy and Sikaiana people often used a trusted person as a go-between to help arrange meetings. Vanteiti explained that the term *hakasaosao* was related to the term *hakasao* (which I later learned means literally to "make safe"). *Hakasao* describes the difficult maneuver of moving a canoe through a narrow passage between the lagoon and open ocean. Vanteiti said that just as there is a challenging separation between lagoon and ocean, so too there is a challenging public separation between young men and women that must be secretly bridged in romance and courtship. About two and half years later, toward the end of my stay on Sikaiana, I was checking some entries in my dictionary of the Sikaiana language with Christian Manakau, a man in his fifties who was the atoll's schoolteacher. Often, especially for terms concerning human motivations and relations, Manakau complained that my English explanations were not "strong" enough. He almost always suggested examples involving romance. At one point, after giving me several such examples, he paused, and then explained to me that he had to use these examples because Sikaiana was so small and had such limited resources that there was very little else to be concerned with besides romance.

Concepts of gender permeate every aspect of Sikaiana life. The Sikaiana often talk about *te kau haahine,* "the group or line of women," as distinct from *te kau taanata,* "the group or line of men." This division is evident in work roles, use of space, ceremonial events, and cultural expectations. But gender is manifested in different ways in different contexts. Although there is support and cooperation between men and women, there also is an undercurrent of opposition, which is often humorous. This humorous conflict finds a ceremonial expression in the *puina,* a traditional event in which men and women divide into separate groups and then compose songs that are critical of the opposite sex. The public separation of men and women makes it difficult for couples to meet in romance. But secret meetings do take place and develop into romantic relationships. In traditional society, before the conversion to Christianity, there were lifelong extramarital love affairs; in present-day Sikaiana, there are premarital romantic attachments that can lead to marriage. Although both the traditional adulterous relationships and the present-day premarital love affairs were deplored in public, they were widespread in private. Private intimacies overcome public separation and subvert public norms.

Background

Sikaiana is located about 100 miles east of Malaita Island in the Solomon Islands. The people speak a Polynesian language and are predominantly Polynesian in their cultural institutions. Although geographically isolated, Sikaiana has been greatly affected by global economic and social processes. In 1929, Anglican missionaries arrived on Sikaiana, and the island rapidly converted to Christianity in the 1930s. Following World War II, many Western institutions were introduced and incorporated into the daily life of the island. By the time of my first arrival in 1980, there was a school, cooperative store, council, and court on Sikaiana. Also following World War II, many Sikaiana people began permanently migrating away from Sikaiana. By the time of my stays in the 1980s, there were about 200 to 250 people living on Sikaiana with about as many Sikaiana people living in and around Honiara, the capital of the Solomon Islands.

I stayed with the Sikaiana, both on Sikaiana and in Honiara, for a total of about forty-one months in 1980–83, 1987, and 1993. This paper describes the situation on Sikaiana during this time period.

Gender in Daily Life: Separation and Support

The physical separation of men and women permeates the public life of Sikaiana. The inside of the church building is divided into a male side (left side facing the altar) and a female side (right side facing the altar). Before their confirmation, children sit in a center aisle. Men take Communion first, then women follow. The Sikaiana people often hold meetings to discuss projects and concerns, including their school, their cooperative store, and other community projects. At these meetings, men and women usually sit in separate areas. When visiting friends and relatives, men and women often divide into separate groups to talk and gossip. Men and women often drink alcohol in separate groups. At meal times, men eat first and women later. Many consider the heads of fish to be women's food and men usually leave them on their plate for the women to eat. In volleyball contests on Sikaiana, men and women often divide into separate single-sex teams that compete against each other. The men and women also form separate teams to play against one another in other games including a card game, *kaihulihuli,* and a traditional game somewhat similar to kick-the-can, *haiumu.*

The separation of men and women also reflects the assignment of different and complementary work roles to men and women. Men clear taro gardens; women plant, mulch, and harvest the taro. Women plait coconut-leaf mats that men use for constructing the walls and roofs of houses. Women plait the fine pandanus mats used for sleeping. Men make canoes. Men do all the work that involves climbing trees. They catch birds from treetops and harvest coconuts and other fruits from trees. They also cut and collect the coconut sap from coconut trees. The women cook some of the sap into a molasses, although much more of it is kept by the men to make fermented toddy. At sea, men and women engage in different activities. Men fish with both a line and net. Women collect shellfish and snails at sea, although men sometimes collect shellfish as part of fishing trips. Women do most of the cooking, washing, and housework, and women are usually responsible for the care of the children.

Men participate more than women in the political affairs of Sikaiana. In the past, most of the traditional ritual roles associated with Sikaiana's ritual life were held by men, including the *aliki* ("chief" or "priest"), *takala* (the "chief/priest's assistant" and successor), and other ritual assistants. There was one female ritual assistant, the *sapai ulu*, who was described as having a role in helping the *aliki* put on his ceremonial vestments in preparation for ritual activities. During my stays, men held most of the present-day offices that link the atoll with provincial and national administrative services. All the members of the local government council are male, as are the court justices, area constable, radio operator, provincial representative, and priests and catechists. Most of Sikaiana's public meetings are conducted by men, although women attend these meetings and their opinions are voiced.

Although they do not hold offices, Sikaiana women, nevertheless, are actively involved in the numerous groups and committees that shape and manage social life on the atoll. In the 1930s, some Sikaiana women suggested to the bishop of the Melanesian Mission that a "sisterhood" be formed that was modeled on Christian religious orders, in particular the Melanesian Brotherhood that was responsible for Sikaiana's conversion to Christianity. The Brotherhood was recruiting many young men from Sikaiana at that time (and still does). These Sikaiana women became the first female members of a Solomon Islands religious order. During my stays in the 1980s and early 1990s, there were several clubs and committees run by women, most notably the Mother's Union, a church-sponsored women's organization. In 1987, women migrants in Honiara founded a sports association that raised money to help pay for Sikaiana teams in the women's sports competitions in Honiara. The men soon copied the idea, forming their own sports association whose activities soon subsumed those of the women.

The most important resource on a small atoll is land. Land is held by patrilineages, which gives men more control over resources. Women belong to their father's lineage and they and their children have some rights to this land, although their rights within a lineage are conditional upon approval of the lineage's men. But women are often consulted about land issues. During my stays, the oldest living Sikaiana people were all women and their views on land use were seriously considered (see Donner 1992).

Ceremonial Conflict between Male and Female: The Puina

Relations between men and women are complementary and mutually supportive. But there is also an undercurrent of opposition between men and women, which is often expressed in humor. Men and women tease the opposite sex as they go about their chores. Indeed, much of the daily humor of Sikaiana is couched in playful banter between the genders. This humorous opposition was expressed in a traditional ceremony that is still performed occasionally, the *puina*. During the *puina*, men and women divided into separate groups for several days in order to compose songs that are critical of the opposite sex. One group went to the three smaller islets at the western end of the reef (Muli Akau) and composed songs in secret. When they returned to the main islet (Hale), they sang their songs to the opposite sex. All songs were composed in secret and then sung in public. The opposite sex would try to anticipate or learn the themes of the songs and have a reply ready. Many of the songs used figurative speech to both camouflage and enliven their meanings (see Donner 1987).

Many of the *puina* songs composed before the island's conversion to Christianity described the joys of adultery, mainly to antagonize the opposite sex. These songs praised a secret lover while taunting and criticizing a spouse by describing the joys of adultery or the special presents given between the lovers. In one song, a woman boasts that she has made a special rope for her lover, while giving her husband a rope that is not as strong. In another song, a woman boasts that her lover is very clever at arranging their secret meetings, never being found out by anyone else. A song composed by a man boasts about the beauty of his sweetheart's thigh tattoos, which in former times were considered very erotic and were kept covered except in intimacy. Another man's song laments that there is no place to escape with his lover. A woman's song taunts her husband that the tightness of her virginity was given to her secret lover, not him. Although these songs were sung in public, it was difficult to determine the specific individuals involved because only the composers knew for sure the specific targets of these songs, if indeed there were any. Regardless of their personal meanings, these songs were sung in public to taunt the opposite sex as a group.

After the conversion to Christianity, the missionaries and church leaders discouraged the performance of these song festivals because they viewed the content of these songs as lewd and hostile. A modified version of the *puina* continued after World War II during the school holidays, *uiki hakamalooloo* (literally "week of rest"). As in the *puina*, one sex would go to Muli Akau to compose while the other stayed on the main islet. Other competitive activities accompanied these festivities. Young men staying at Muli Akau planned raids onto the main islet in order to steal garden produce and even pigs. Young women were expected to guard against these incursions and "capture" any young man who landed.

The songs composed in the 1940s and 1950s continued the themes of taunting between the sexes but dropped the themes of adultery, which were discouraged by the newly adopted Christian teachings. The following songs were probably composed sometime in the 1940s. The women are taunting the young men's shyness in making advances, which had to be done in private. The song reminds them that the young women are working alone all day waiting to be approached by a bold young man.[1]

> To the false lust of the young men of my age.
> I walk alone in the interior, I collect food alone in the interior, I work alone in the interior. I don't see you. You wander around without purpose along the shore; you are always drinking fermented toddy; you sleep without purpose inside your house. You don't strive to meet me; you don't show any interest in me; you are mistakenly afraid of me.
> My beauty, My beauty.

The men composed the following reply asserting that they no longer have any place to meet in secret with the young girls.

> In reply to the speech of the women, I was not being hesitant in making advances. That is the truth. I always go to you; I am not hesitant; for you have grown into a beautiful woman.
> My heart yearns for you; you have grown into a beautiful woman.
> I search for you, I always move toward you; I make a play toward you; because we are good together. I made advances to you; but, there is no deserted place for us to meet together so that we can talk; there is no place for us to make plans in our happiness and desire.
> So, I am saying goodbye, this is the end for us—
> You can just keep waiting!

These song festivals became rarer in the 1950s and 1960s. In 1969, a song festival with a skit was performed at the time of the American landing on the moon. The men taunted the Sikaiana women by describing the great beauty of a woman living on the moon who was far prettier than any Sikaiana woman. The women composed a reply that included the taunt that this beautiful woman on the moon had no desire for the men of Sikaiana.

In late 1981, I participated in a simplified version of the *puina* as part of the Christmas celebrations. For several weeks in the evenings and on Sundays, the atoll's men and women gathered in separate places to compose and practice songs. The songs were composed in secrecy so that each sex could surprise the opposite sex with the critical content of their songs. I attended the men's composition sessions, which often lasted late into the night.

The themes of the songs composed in 1981 centered on the incidents of the Christmas holiday of the previous year when many of the atoll's young men and women were expelled from church for having sexual affairs. The Sikaiana church is against premarital sexual relations. Anyone engaging in these relations is expelled from Holy Communion and must make a public confession before being reinstated. In this small community, these public confessions can be very embarrassing. The women's song complained that someone, presumably a boasting young man, had told everyone about his affair when it should have been kept secret. In another song, the women lamented that the young men did not properly care for their bodies, never shaving or washing. Another song made fun of me for not being able to find a Sikaiana wife, comparing my (allegedly) unfavorable characteristics (stooped posture, body odor) with some of the atoll's older bachelors who also could not find a wife.

Although the songs are supposed to be composed in secret so that the opposite sex is surprised by the content, the men learned about the songs that were critical of the young men's neatness. The men prepared a reply boasting that in the present, things are different than they were in the past. In the past, a man had to be good-looking and hard working in order to find a woman who would marry him. But at present, the Sikaiana's young men only had to learn to play a guitar and the women would all come running to him.

The men also composed songs that teased specific women by name for their premarital affairs. Traditionally, songs do not mention specific personal names, but some of the songs composed in 1981 mentioned specific women by name. During the composition sessions, someone objected to these direct references to several young women, but he was told that this was justified because the songs served to instruct the young women in proper behavior. When one man objected that one song accusing a specific woman of stealing crops was untrue, several men replied that they did not care about the veracity of the songs because the songs were being composed simply to make the women angry. In traditional times, the songs about the joys of adultery were also sung to make the opposite sex angry.

During the days when the songs were still being composed and memorized, there were constant boasts between males and females about the effectiveness of their songs in criticizing the opposite sex. These boasts took place whenever groups of men and women passed each other: along the way to church in the morning, on the way to work, and in the evenings after meals. These boasts were often couched in metaphors of fighting, using both traditional idioms such as *hakamalo*, "tucking in a loincloth" (in former times a way of preparing for a spear fight), and more contemporary idioms such as shooting with a "gun" and throwing a "bomb."

Intimacy Between Men and Women:
Romance and Courtship

Although there is separation in daily work activities and mutual opposition in humor and song, there is also intimacy in romantic relationships.
As discussed above, much of the opposition in song composition derives
from commentaries on romance. Both in the past and at present, romantic
intimacy must be achieved by overcoming public separation.[2]

For the Sikaiana people, marriage is the most important relationship that they will establish. With marriage, a Sikaiana person achieves
a respectability that the unmarried never attain. I think that the song
composed in the 1981 *puina* ridiculing me played upon the importance
of marriage. Along with the older bachelors, I was being ridiculed for
not being married. Since the Sikaiana's conversion to Christianity, it is
the "work of a young man" to find a wife. Before the Sikaiana's conversion to Christianity, however, marriages were arranged by parents, foster
parents, or relatives when the children were quite young. In some cases,
these marriages were arranged to transfer rights to land between lineages.
But in most cases, people recalled that marriages were arranged simply
out of friendship. Before the conversion to Christianity, it was also very
common to have secret sweethearts or lovers, who were referred to as
the *hina*. The oldest Sikaiana people recall that almost everyone had at
least one such lover, and sometimes more than one. The three oldest
people on the island, all women, had specific lovers whose names were
remembered and consistently agreed upon (which suggests that the affairs could not have been all that secret). Older Sikaiana people also
agreed about the practices and terminology that refer to the activities
of secret lovers.

Romantic love and desire was felt for the secret sweetheart, not
for one's spouse. One elderly woman described herself as cringing with
disgust when she was brought to her husband on her wedding night.
She described her repulsion by using the same word, *"ita,"* that the Sikaiana use to describe the way some children cringe at being touched
by strangers.

In these secret *hina* liaisons, a man approached a woman in a secluded
place or used a go-between to help arrange meetings. If the woman agreed,
the couple began their affair, which might last for the rest of their lives.
Gifts were often exchanged as part of the relationship. A gift starting the
relationship was called the *hakatapu*, literally "to make forbidden."[3] In
continuing their affair, the couple used a go-between, *tama kai* (literally
"person food/eat"), to transfer gifts and help arrange secret meetings.

The go-between, often the man's sister, should be someone who could be seen in public both with him and with his lover without arousing suspicion.

One elderly woman described the importance of gift exchanges in the *hina* relationship.[4]

> You [the lover] try for me, you try sincerely. I know that you are sincerely interested in me. It will not end. Because you court me with gifts. Later we become lovers and have our opportunity. You send me things—the lovers today do not exchange gifts. The gift exchanges of the *hina* is different, it was really important.
>
> You the man, you have your go-between [*tama kai*]. You are afraid of your spouse [will find out] in your giving. You make clothes, you bless [*hakatapu*] our relationship. We call it *hakatapu*. You walk along. You say to your *tama kai*—the person knows what you want—to take your things. Me too. I give things to you. You give things to your *tama kai*, to hold, then when you come courting you know that the things are coming. I know that you gave things to that person to give to me. You say to me, at some time when we meet, you know, do you have the things I sent? I say yes. You say: they came to you? I say, yes I have them.
>
> We are very careful, so that no one knows about us. We want to meet again, but we must do it secretly.
>
> You leave the island for work—our men used to go away a lot [Sikaiana men left the island to work for wages]. The boat arrives back on Sikaiana. You buy me many things, fragrant body powder, everything. You arrive. You give the things to your *tama kai*. You come to tell me. Later, we are still lovers, we meet again in some deserted place.
>
> My things come for you, food, mats, loom cloth, the work of us women. I give them to my *tama kai*. And then when we meet, I ask if you got those things. How was that thing I gave you? Did you get that other thing? It keeps going on like that. It includes everything: food from the interior, the harvest, the cutnut, breadfruit, everything. You know my *tama kai*. You meet and talk [with the *tama kai*] and then when we meet, we can talk.
>
> It doesn't stop. It just keeps going.

Two elderly women I talked with felt that there would be one favored lover throughout a lifetime, although some people, especially males, might have several affairs. There is a widespread story that the last chief of Sikaiana, who lived to be very old, continued meeting his lover into their old age. The meetings included a meal and conversation.

The woman quoted above continues her description:

> Some longtime *hina* quarrel. You see that I have become lovers with someone else. You are angry and end our affair.

On the other hand, you do something [have another affair]. I know. I know. I am not angry, it is just the way men are.

Other women, they hear that you have taken a different lover, those women become angry, and end the relationship.

The woman can end a relationship too. But others are not angry about affairs. No matter you go to a different woman. And I know. Sometimes, you come and tell me. We are lovers and find each other to be our true love [*kalemata*, literally "eye"]. You come to tell me. You come and tell me that you went to another woman, I am not angry. It is not bad. Keep it beautiful. [But] If you hear about me, you are angry. I made a mistake. You are really angry. You turn and end our affair.

Other people get revenge. You go to another woman, then I will go to another man. I am going to trade [get even] with you. That's really bad. But in my time: no, your lover is your lover, your true desire. That's it. I am not angry that you went to another woman. You come to me, tell me that you were with another woman, I am not angry. . . .

Other women get revenge. It's really bad. Like, if I hear about you going to another woman, I will seek another man. Is that good? It's terrible. Terrible. It really depends upon the manner of behaving of the person [different people are different in their behavior].

Then this person added a comment that apparently was a disapproving referral to the premarital affairs of Sikaiana's present generation of young adults, although I think she is exaggerating the present-day situation on Sikaiana.

The present young generation is different. They keep going to new lovers, then go to other lovers.

This woman compared her lack of sexual interest in her husband with her desire for her secret *hina*.

In my young womanhood, you [the *hina* or lover] came to me. Oh that was really sweet! You really desired it because you were the first one to come to me. I didn't have any experience. I had not yet gone to my husband. I have a husband [to be given in arranged marriage]. It was really exciting that you came to me first. Really exciting. No one had come to me yet.

I really desire you, you were the first to come to me. I let you have my body. You were first; my husband came later.

Despite the expectation that everyone had a secret lover, older people remember that there was jealousy and hostility toward a spouse if the identity of the lover was discovered. If a husband learned that his wife had been unfaithful, he might beat her and in some cases challenge her sweetheart to a fight. He might try to keep a closer watch on his wife.

An adulterer who was discovered could lose rights to use the land of his lover's husband's lineage. Ancestral spirits might use illness and death to punish the people who had affairs with their descendants (the Sikaiana believed that punishment was given not only to the offender, but also to members of that person's family).

After the conversion to Christianity, church leaders discouraged arranged marriages and couples were encouraged to marry through their personal preferences. The traditional *hina* relationship was highly discouraged. Although there certainly were some adulterous relationships, they did not have the institutionalized and ceremonial form of the *hina* relationship. But many of the practices of the *hina* relationship were transferred to Sikaiana patterns of courtship and premarital sexual relationships, which, like the traditional *hina* relationships, are secret and widely practiced. Moreover, premarital affairs are condemned by the church and discouraged by many parents.

During my stays in the 1980s, almost all marriages were based upon the couples' preferences. Sometimes, young men approach parents about marriage before becoming involved with their daughter. Many parents consider this to be an ideal way to start a marriage. But more often, young men and women begin affairs without their parents' explicit approval or knowledge. A young man may ask another person, usually a closely related female, to act as a go-between (*hakasaosao*). The go-between will approach the desired woman, try to convince the woman of the man's sincerity, and, if successful, help arrange a secret meeting. All courtship should be conducted in secret, usually at night. In a society as small as Sikaiana, however, it is very difficult to keep a secret and the Sikaiana people seem to be very sensitive to the nuances in behavior of a couple who are romantically attracted. Family members and friends often suspect or know about these affairs. If knowledge of a sexual affair becomes public, representatives of the local church may act. The couple will be forbidden from taking Holy Communion for a period of time and then forced to go through the embarrassment of a public confession before the entire congregation. There is another important reason for secrecy. Other people with different marital plans for the couple may try to thwart the wedding through gossip or by helping a rival suitor.

In their initial courting, the couple is often described as being "embarrassed," "shy," or "ashamed" (*hakanapanapa*). Although they may be shy, men are expected to take the initiative in courtship. They approach their desired one, initiate the advances, and, if truly attracted to the woman, are expected to try hard (*hakammate*) to win her love even if initially rejected. Metaphors of hunting or fishing are used to describe their efforts. Young men sometimes joke that they are going to "shoot pigeon" (*hiti lupe*) when they are going to court a woman. The common term for successfully finding a spouse, for both men and women, is *sahe,* the same verb used for catching fish. Terminology describing "luck" or success at hunting and fishing, *maalama* and *laoina,* are also used to describe success in romance, usually a man's success with women. Finally, when advances are successful and someone does become involved in a romance, that person, most often the woman, is described as "dying," *mate.*

At their initial meetings, the couple discusses their feelings for one another and their future plans. People told me that women should resist a man's initial advances and test his sincerity by waiting to see if he continues his efforts. If the couple finds they are mutually attracted, they "promise' (*polopolo*) to remain faithful and eventually marry. Sometimes, as with the traditional *hina* relationships, the couple exchanges presents to symbolize their commitment and, whenever possible, they continue to meet secretly. It is assumed that a couple that is alone for any length of time will have sexual relations.

Women are often described as doubting a young man's sincerity when making initial advances because men sometimes falsely promise marriage in order to engage in sex, or change their minds about marriage after a sexual encounter. There is a widespread assumption that some people remain committed to former lovers even after marriage to a different person, and as a result there is a frequent worry that some people, especially husbands, will be jealous of their spouse's former lovers. There is an idiom, *lautona,* that is used to describe the feelings of jealousy that some people have toward their spouse's former lovers. People told me that the idiom derives from the core use of the term *lautona,* which refers to an organ or perhaps a parasite found inside a marlin that continues to vibrate long after the fish is dead. Young women are warned that if they have many lovers, their husbands will continually suspect them of still harboring desire for these former lovers. Such a woman, Sikaiana parents warn their daughters, will suffer beatings as a wife.

When ready to marry, a young man should approach the woman's parents and his own relatives in order to obtain their approval. If parents try to prevent a marriage and the couple is determined to marry, they might elope (*hulo,* literally "run away"). On Sikaiana, this may be done by secretly leaving the largest islet, Hale, and living on one of the other islets at the other end of the reef for about a week. When the couple returns, the marriage is usually accepted. Although relatives may be unhappy, they no longer try to prevent it. When a young unmarried woman becomes pregnant, there is an effort to determine the child's father and to put pressure on the couple to marry.

Many Sikaiana parents complain that in recent years there has been an increase in premarital sexual activity, something they view as bad. It is difficult to determine the accuracy of these statements about changes in sexual conduct. Many males have different standards for their own behavior as opposed to that of their sisters and daughters. My impression is that for a period following their arrival, the missionaries were successful in their efforts to limit premarital and extramarital sexual relationships. More recently, in the 1960s, '70s, and '80s, there seemed to have been some increase in the frequency of premarital affairs and public knowledge about them. Premarital affairs that become public knowledge will cause greater condemnation for women rather than men, if the couple does not end up getting married. Parents express their opposition to premarital affairs and lecture their children, especially daughters, about proper conduct. But parents also want to give their daughters enough leeway to meet a young man and eventually marry, and often look the other way if their daughter is having an affair with a potential marriage partner whom they consider to be acceptable. In the 1980s, many people associated the increase in premarital sexual affairs with a breakdown in traditional or customary practices, *kastom*, that was motivated by the influences from other cultures, including Western influences. The illicit adultery of the *hina* relationships was ignored or forgotten, and concepts of customary practices were derived from missionary teachings that were introduced to Sikaiana in the 1930s (see Donner 1993, 2002).

The present-day system of courtship continues many of the practices of the traditional *hina* secret love affairs, but also replaces others. Private and secret intimacy overcomes public separation. But these present-day courtship patterns often result in marriage and are therefore integrated into normative community life. Adultery has been transformed as well but in a different manner. During my stays in the 1980s, there was gossip about a few extramarital affairs, and some of this gossip was almost certainly grounded in truth. But extramarital affairs did not seem to be very frequent. Moreover, these affairs were not integrated into the atoll's social life. There was no expectation that married couples had lovers, or ritualized exchanges of gifts, or the composition of songs that boasted of the joys of sex with one's lover. Whereas the secret adultery of the *hina* relationships was ritualized and institutionalized, extramarital affairs on Sikaiana in the 1980s were not ceremonial, and although they took place, they were not expected. During my stays, adultery could cause quite serious problems between the people involved, made more serious because in this small society, people are constantly in each other's presence, enhancing the jealous feelings of some spouses. During my stays, adultery was private and personal, and, unlike the former *hina* relationship, without any expression in communal activities.

Public and Private, Conflict and Intimacy

For me, one of the most puzzling aspects of Sikaiana gender relations concerns the traditional practice of institutionalized adultery, the *hina*. How could such a practice function? Everyone is having an affair and yet everyone is concerned that their spouse is having an affair. Sikaiana is a very small community but these affairs must be conducted in secrecy and privacy. The public opposition and ridicule of men and women in the songs is directly related to the private intimacy of an individual man and woman as lovers. In public songs, groups of men and women taunt each other as spouses; in private, individual men and women have highly charged love affairs with someone other than their spouse. The private intimacy of secret romance between the lovers corresponds with, and is even fueled by, the public conflict and deceit toward the spouse.

Comparative cross-cultural studies find that adultery is common enough, as are efforts to restrict it. Such efforts are usually more restrictive toward women than men (Ford and Beach 1951: 11–118; Frayser 1985: 324–38; Stephens 1963: 251–56). There does not seem to be much comparative theorizing for interpreting adultery. Even Malinowski (1929) seems atypically brief in his discussions of Trobriand adultery, about which he describes the Trobrianders as surprisingly prudish. There is a considerable literature on Trukese extramarital affairs. Most of these studies were written in the 1950s when psychoanalytic theories were important and show that influence. Both Goodenough (1949) and Swartz (1958) emphasize the tensions and insecurity of Trukese men during adultery. Swartz argues that adultery allows for the release of aggression against the society and its norms (see also Gladwin and Sarason 1953: 229–30).

There can be something subversive in adultery, especially Sikaiana's system of institutionalized adultery, both in terms of a society's public norms and also in terms of male control and domination. In *Tiwi Wives*, Jane described adultery among the Tiwi. Young women, before they have children, have extramarital affairs with young men and also compose songs that praise their secret lovers. These affairs are highly desirable for young women who are married to older men and for younger men who do not yet have access to wives. The system is clearly subversive of the system of domination of marriage and sexuality by older males

(Goodale 1971: 130–36). Indeed, the *hina* system of adultery on Sikaiana seems to me to be more subversive of males and their authority, not only by allowing women to express their sexuality but also by undercutting the men's dominance of Sikaiana life. Both men and women worried about their spouses' fidelity. But the men, who have more control over the public institutions of Sikaiana life, including the ritual roles and the control of lineage land, seem to me to have more to lose in their authority and legitimacy. If the older women are to be believed (and their statements are consistent with present-day Sikaiana assumptions about men and women), husbands were far more concerned and jealous than wives about their spouses' affairs. The system operated with an ironic logic: the lust of the men for different partners results in their jealousy about the affairs of their own wives.[5]

In referring to the way that less powerful groups can use gossip and ridicule to challenge those in authority, Lincoln (1994) has developed the concept of "corrosive discourse." The songs, humor, and daily interactions of women on Sikaiana have this corrosive quality, with women often questioning the actions of males and their authority. The *hina* system of adultery takes this concept of corrosiveness further: corrosive sexuality.

The *hina* romances on Sikaiana also allowed intimacy and secrecy in a society that has few occasions for private moments and relationships. The fact that these relationships must be conducted in secrecy probably enhanced the excitement. Goffman (1961) has noted that social systems often have activities that form what he calls an "underlife." These activities are secret and ostensibly unacceptable, but people engage in them to make their lives more enjoyable or exciting. Goffman focuses his argument on prisons, asylums, and other "total institutions" in Western societies, where every aspect of a person is under scrutiny and control. But Goffman argues that even in more loosely structured social systems, one asserts a sense of "self" by doing things that are unacceptable. Goffman argues that the self is defined by society and public institutions, but it also maintains itself as a distinct entity by engaging in activities that separate it from those societal institutions. In some respects, Sikaiana social life is similar to a total institution in terms of being a contained environment (there is only about a square mile of land) with constant scrutiny. The relations of secret lovers in the *hina* can be seen as part of the atoll's underlife and as a way to develop a sense of distinctiveness and privacy in a very small and public society.

The *hina* relationship also carries an implicit critique of the normative expectations, at least in respect to marriage, and possibly in respect to male control. Perhaps the *hina* relationship can also be viewed as one of those mechanisms, found in other cultures, that offer a critique of, or distancing from, normal expectations. *Hina* relationships introduced, if not a dialectic, at least a dynamic that undercuts normative expectations and power relations, a kind of cultural critique.[6] But this corrosive dynamic was still in some sense a communal one. The *hina* was an activity that was highly ritualized and standardized, even though it was conducted in secrecy by individuals. The public displays of songs about the joys of adultery were community events. In contrast, present-day adultery is highly corrosive for specific marriages and perhaps the reputations of individual men and women who become subjects of gossip, but present-day affairs do not seem to have much impact or focus on the community as a whole, nor do they result in the taunting song composition that the *hina* relationships did. Unlike present-day adultery, *hina* affairs were widespread, ceremonialized, ritualized, and publicized in songs. The *hina* developed a sense of individual self that was still communal, a private encounter that was shared in public, a subversiveness that was also normative.

The present-day love affairs of young people seem to draw much of their organization from the traditional *hina* relationships. Like the *hina*, they are widespread and secret practices that challenge normative expectations: private intimacies overcome public separation and norms. But, unlike the *hina*, the present-day romantic relationships lead to marriage and become integrated into Sikaiana public life.

Gender and Intimacy in a Changing World

Jane Goodale was a pioneer in looking at the manner in which gender, like kinship and descent, structures social life. She never was pedantic or simplistic in her analysis of gender. She showed how gender can structure different relationships in different ways within the same society. She encouraged a curiosity that trusted ethnographic data and encouraged new questions. She also believed that cultures have some degree of symbolic integration and that understandings of gender should be integrated into broader understandings about personhood and culture (Goodale 1980, 1995; see also Zimmer-Tamakoshi's article in this volume).

As Jane would expect, present-day sexuality and gender on Sikaiana—like everything else in their lives—have to be understood in the broader context of changes in Sikaiana life and Sikaiana's increasing involvement in a larger region and world. During the time of arranged marriages and the adulterous *hina*, Sikaiana life was relatively isolated. There were occasional but sporadic contacts with other islands and, in the nineteenth and early twentieth centuries, with Europeans. The *hina* relationships created intimacy and challenged normative expectations in a relatively self-contained and isolated social world. But over the course of the past 100 years, Sikaiana has become heavily influenced by outside forces. Western institutions have been integrated into atoll life and Sikaiana people have migrated away from the atoll, so that by the 1980s there were more Sikaiana people living in other parts of the Solomon Islands than on Sikaiana. Most Sikaiana people now work away from Sikaiana, many in Western occupations. The subversive or corrosive effects of the *hina* relationship on the social order seem quite minor when compared with the systematic impact of contact with Western culture and global processes over the past 100 years.[7]

Struggling with limited economic opportunity and constantly changing social and economic conditions, the Sikaiana community in the 1980s still remained in large part a local one whose very fabric is constructed from the relations between men and women. The division of labor and separation of the genders remain important for daily life on Sikaiana and is part of their incorporation of many Western institutions. Men and women make fun of the opposite sex as they go about their chores, and they still occasionally perform ceremonial song festivals, the *puina*. Culture change is reformulated into local humor, providing much of the material for Sikaiana joking (for example, using images of modern warfare and space exploration to play out their opposition to each other in their daily joking and song composition). Men and women continue their complementary roles in the incorporation of new institutions and practices. The men often are more involved in the activities that take them away from Sikaiana, while the women often maintain and develop institutions that provide some stability and community. The pattern of institutionalized adultery that was found in the *hina* is no longer practiced, but the premarital romantic affairs of the young people have a similar pattern in which private intimacy must overcome public separation and opposition. Finally, Sikaiana often struck me during my stays in the 1980s as a place that has a very personal and close public life in relation to the much larger and more impersonal relations that took place away from the atoll. On Sikaiana, there was constant interaction with, participation in, and knowledge about one another's life. From the perspective of the outside world, the public life of Sikaiana was very close, personal, and intense. But embedded in that very personal, public community there were also spheres for private and secret relationships. Amid the challenges and problems that were part of its incorporation into a larger global system,

Sikaiana maintained its own distinctive public life from which young lovers must still escape in order to secretly meet in private.

Acknowledgments

I am indebted to the contributors to this book, in particular Jeanette Dickerson-Putman and Laura Zimmer-Tamakoshi, for suggestions and comments. I also received helpful suggestions from Kim Shively. Jane's support and mentoring are obvious. No one, except myself, is responsible for any of this paper's faults.

Notes

1. All quotes are translated from Sikaiana by the author.
2. This paper is concerned with the courtship and behaviors surrounding sex rather than the sex act itself, about which I have considerably less data.
3. *Hakatapu* is derived from *tapu*, which is the Sikaiana cognate of the common Polynesian term (borrowed into English as "taboo") meaning "forbidden." Missionaries used the term to refer to the "sacred," and now in most contexts, the term *hakatapu* means "to make sacred."
4. Translated from the Sikaiana recorded on a tape.
5. See Hrdy (1981) for a sociobiological perspective that argues that adultery is more subversive of male than female reproductive interests.
6. In some respects, this argument parallels that of Swartz (1958) for Truk, although Swartz is far more psychoanalytic in grounding his argument, and I ground my argument in social relationships. Gluckman's idea of "rituals of rebellion" (1963, 1970) and Turner's "anti-structure" (1969, 1975) have some relevance. But Gluckman's and Turner's concepts were developed to show how conflict supported the normative order. I find something more subversive about the *hina* relationship.
7. Zimmer-Tamakoshi's essay discusses this aspect of gender and culture change. The romance and secrecy of the *hina* relationship has been transferred to premarital relationships between young people. But present-day patterns of courtship seem far less subverting of the general social order than the traditional *hina* relationship. There is a new area of corrosiveness that is perhaps even more subverting of social relations, both traditional and modern—drinking. Sikaiana people drink frequently, and the drinking patterns, which can be violent and unpredictable, also challenge the accepted social order, both modern and traditional. Drinking is a far more powerful challenge than adultery to modern authority systems, which are very complex and extend far beyond the life of the atoll (see Donner 1994).

10. *Indigenous Religion in an Intercultural Space*

Measles or Magic?

In 1913, medical officer H. K. Fry was sent to Melville and Bathurst islands off the Australian north coast to investigate an epidemic. Fry found that about 200 people, from an estimated total of 650 to 700 islanders, had died as a result of the disease in two weeks' time. During his travels of about six weeks in the islands, Fry not only collected mortality statistics but also sought to establish the nature of the disease. His instructors believed measles to be the most likely candidate, but the medical practitioner wrote: "The extremely low number of infant deaths was entirely against measles being the cause of the holocaust, and supports the native diagnosis of magic" (Fry 1949: 80). The tragedy was still within living memory when Jane Goodale conducted fieldwork on Melville Island in 1954.

She attended a ceremony in which the men "discussed the fact that the people of the islands were now few because the white people had brought other tribesmen into their land who sang magic songs of poison that caused the tribe to dwindle" (Goodale 1971: 224). Jane has been concerned with the impact of the epidemic on Tiwi society, particularly in relation to a certain sickness (called *tarni*) and the *kulama* (yam) ceremony (see also Goodale 1963, 1970, 1982). Moreover, she called for the need for "further investigation" (Goodale 1971: 225). What was the cause of the epidemic: measles or magic? And what can we say about its cultural ramifications?

Ethnographic Fieldwork

Before entering into a discussion of the epidemic, its cause, and its consequences, I would like to draw attention to another type of magic; namely,
the "ethnographer's magic" (for a discussion of the continued relevance of
Malinowski's metaphor, see Otto 1997). Michele Dominy and Debbie Rose
(this volume) stress the importance that fieldwork and cultural sensitivity
have for Jane. Her love for both ethnography and for Tiwi people has been
an important ingredient in the performance of her ethnographer's magic.
"Fieldwork is what anthropology is all about," according to Jane (in Dickerson-Putman, this volume). Furthermore, Jane's earlier interest in medicine and detective stories (Dickerson-Putman, this volume) may have been
formative in the development of her ethnographic approach (cf. Ginzburg
1988; Venbrux 1995: vi–vii, 14–15). Jane's support and encouragement as
a mentor have been invaluable to all of the anthropologists who worked
with the Tiwi in the past three to four decades (including Andree Grau,
Gary Robinson, and myself). During my own fieldwork, I learned how the
biographies of both Jane and the Tiwi have become interwoven.

"We miss Jane," Rachel Puruntatameri told me on a recent visit
to Melville Island. "She minded me as a kid," Rachel added. When she
was still a toddler, in 1954, Jane had looked after her.[1] In 1980–81, Jane
frequently took Rachel and her husband Paddy Puruntatameri out hunting in the mangroves (Goodale 1988: 139–40). According to Rachel and
Paddy, she continued to do so on regular visits to Snake Bay in 1986–87
and in the 1990s. Obviously, Rachel and Paddy kept warm memories of
her and also cherished the photographs that she took of them.

Jane had demonstrated so often that she took care of her Tiwi family.
I saw Paddy for the last time in 1998. Although he was ill, he was very
interested to hear news of his "daughter" Tutangantilauwayu. Over the
years, Rachel and Paddy had proudly told me time and again that Paddy
had bestowed this personal name, meaning "female spear," on Jane. Since
Paddy was Jane's "father," he was entitled to give her a name (cf. Hart
1931; Goodale 1971: 29–33). When Rachel became a widow, her memories of her kind old husband were so painful she decided to move from
Snake Bay to another community on Melville Island. In August 2002 and
September 2006, Rachel asked me to tell Jane that she was all right.[2]

"The old man" (Goodale 1971: 224), named Kerbo by Fry (1949), who
sang about mainland magic being the cause of the epidemic was Paddy
Puruntatameri's father's father, Korupu. He can thus be identified as Jane's
great-grandfather. Alongside her venerable American ancestors, she may
take pride in this connection to a truly legendary Aboriginal man.

In recent years, Jane has focused her analysis on biography and history as a way to contextualize the ethnographic legacy that will be inherited by future Tiwi generations. The following work contributes to these analyses and is also inspired by Jane's analysis of "variation" (Goodale 1988: 128) and the creativity of the Tiwi people (Goodale and Koss 1971; see also Rosi, this volume). I examine the historical epidemic and its ramifications and consider how early-twentieth-century Tiwi cultural production in relation to the epidemic was sited in an "intercultural space" (Merlan 1998; Myers 2002).

A Watershed in Tiwi History

Around the turn of the twentieth century, there was a dramatic shift in the orientation of the Tiwi to the outside world. Prior to that time, the Tiwi was "the one tribe which offered consistent, uncompromising resistance to European intrusion" (Reid 1990: 97; but see Venbrux 2003). Pilling has portrayed this opening up to the outside world as a watershed in Tiwi history (Hart and Pilling 1960: 97, 100–101). To date, an adequate explanation for this remarkable change in attitude has not been forthcoming, and neither Pilling (1958; Hart and Pilling 1960) nor former lay missionary Morris (2001) takes the Tiwi holocaust—the epidemic—really into account. For Australian Aborigines, "perhaps the most dramatic consequence of European invasion" was epidemic disease (Reynolds 1990: 56; see also Campbell 2002). I propose that the epidemic under discussion has been decisive in the "pacification" of the Tiwi Islands and only after the tragic occurrence did Europeans dare to go about the islands unarmed (Venbrux 2001a).

What is to be foregrounded here, however, are the "hidden histories" (Rose 1991) that reflect the ways in which the Tiwi adapted to the epidemic (see Inhorn and Brown 1990). How did the Tiwi come to terms with a newly introduced disease that had tremendously weakened their ranks? Two of Jane's works provide separate but complementary answers. In 1970 she argues that the Tiwi adapted to the disease by changing some of the ritual associated with the *kulama* ceremony. Later, in 1982, she shows that the *kulama* yam has to be seen as a "key symbol." In the following I will synthesize the approaches she takes in these works to show how the dynamics of Tiwi religion allowed them to modify and accommodate their worldview to a changing intercultural space.

When I first met Jane at a conference in Darwin in 1988, she was arguing with the late Arnold Pilling about certain events in Tiwi history. At issue was when and why carvings of human figures had been made for the first time. I have come to regard them as props (equivalent to the statues of saints) in an interreligious dialogue that the Tiwi had with a Catholic missionary (Venbrux 2000). Jane might feel that in doing so I am more or less taking sides with Pilling, but hopefully we will be able to discuss it further in the near future.

In the past few years, we had several interesting conversations at ASAO meetings. Jane provided me with excellent advice before I went into the field. In many ways she has continued to give me encouragement. Nowadays, however, the mentor (if I may say so) has also become an informant. My current research interest concerns the interrelationship between Tiwi material culture and the wider world over time. Because of her personal and professional involvement with the Tiwi, spanning half a century, and great experience in Tiwi material culture, not in the least as a collector, Jane made a superb informant, or, as she would prefer, "guide." In her guidance, and also in her work as mentioned, she has made clear to me how important it is to recognize "variation" (a point also taken up by Fred Myers; see Myers 2002). The emergence of a "little tradition" (concerning the spirit *jamparipari*) of the Tiwi patrilineage to which Jane belongs is a case in point. I shall discuss it further below in relation to the epidemic. First I outline the historical interaction of the Europeans and mainland Aborigines in the islands, highlighting the 1912 outbreak of measles.

An Outbreak of Measles

In 1905, buffalo hunters Joe and Harry Cooper (after an earlier failure) established themselves on Melville Island. An armed workforce of Aborigines from the vicinity of Port Essington on the Cobourg Peninsula accompanied them. Since 1909, Sam Green, a white sawmiller, was also based on Melville Island. And Father Gsell, a French missionary of the Sacred Heart order, established a small mission station on the southeastern point of Bathurst Island, in June 1911. Cooper's and Green's camps on Melville Island, and also the mission station on Bathurst Island, were sources of European food rations and goods. In 1911, Herbert Basedow, an anthropologist with a medical training, reported, "It is perhaps on account of their isolation from civilisation that I found the blacks comparatively free from any serious disease" (1913: 293).[3] The Tiwi, however, were vulnerable to a so-called virgin soil epidemic because of their recent exposure to the outside world (Crosby 1976).[4]

In early December 1912, a party, including anthropologist Baldwin Spencer and medical officer Mervyn Holmes, visited Bathurst Island.

A large crowd of Tiwi people from all over the islands had gathered in the environs of the new mission station. Spencer and his companions witnessed and documented a two-day performance of postfuneral rites.[5] Dr. Holmes, who made still photographs on this occasion, was soon to examine a number of Tiwi people who had apparently contracted measles (Breinl and Holmes 1915: 3). The disease had spread to the islands from the mainland city of Darwin, where it had been recorded somewhat earlier (Hargrave 1993: 11).

Mainland Magic

Some three months later, Fry had no doubt "that an outbreak of measles occurred at the mission just before Christmas." He noted "that a sickness spread amongst the blacks about the same time."[6] Observation and interaction with the Tiwi between March 2 and April 19, 1913, afforded Fry the opportunity to learn that the Tiwi "explained" the occurrence of the epidemic through a "native diagnosis of magic."[7]

On March 10, Fry arrived at a Tiwi camp at Marinalampi in the north of Bathurst Island. A yam ritual (*kulama*), led by an old man named Kerbo (Korupu by his descendants), was in progress.[8] Fry managed to obtain translations of some of the lyrics that had been composed and sung in the yam ritual by Korupu. One song dealt with the epidemic. "While cooking yams [Korupu] sang of Tarula [mainland Aborigines] planting magic a week after Spencer's visit. Three along coast. Just after wet season started sickness. String bag buried. Sun makes hot and whoof up go smoke, and wind blow all about. Magic starts with feeling like snake walking up legs, the stomach and bloody diarrhoea, when reaches heart, no more eat, die."[9]

Next, Fry received "a similar account of the sickness" at a camp located in southeastern Melville Island. Later, in April, when visiting the camp of the white sawmiller Sam Green in northern Melville Island, he got "the same vague account of the sickness which had finished."[10] Fry concluded that it was on "Melville Island [the] same story as on Bathurst. Magic begins like pricking in big toe, like snake going up the legs. Reaches stomach, bloody stools. When reaches heart, short of bre[a]th, die."[11]

The epidemic must have had a devastating impact on the survivors since numerous people in this small-scale society passed away in a short span of time (see table 10.1). "All died in a fortnight," Fry was told.[12] The fact that the death rate was higher for Tiwi than for the mainland Aboriginal population undoubtedly raised Tiwi suspicions.

Fry noted that Tiwi people named the mainlanders with the Tiwi

Table 10.1. Summary of the death returns on Bathurst Island

Tribe	Approx. Present Population	Men	Women	Boys	Girls	Male Infants	Female Infants	Total
				Bathurst Island				
Mulauola	70	8	19	0	0	0	0	27
Migula								
(Ullankula)	60	4	8	0	0	0	0	12
Tiklauola	120	12	7	5	4	1	1	30
				Melville Island				
Mandibula	70	28	36	0	17	0	0	81
Yaimpe	?			—Plenty—				
Turubulla	?	0	0	0	0	0	0	0
Paluiana	?			—Plenty—				
Oleankola	?	0	10	7	0			17
Muanabulla	?	4	7	5	4			20

Note: Total Present Population of Melville is about 200.
Total Present Population of Aboriginals of Melville and Bathurst islands is about 450.
Known mortality 187.
Population Previous to Epidemic about 650.
Total mortality about 200.
Source: H. K. Fry's draft of his letter to Administrator of the Northern Territory, reporting on his visit to Bathurst and Melville Islands. Pine Creek, May 15, 1913. (Held in the Anthropology Archives of the South Australian Museum in Adelaide.)

word for "shotgun," *tarula.* Cooper allowed his buffalo-shooters to carry rifles. From 1905 until August 1911, these mainland Aborigines (Iwaidja from the Cobourg Peninsula) used violence, their gun power in particular, to abduct Tiwi women.[13] The era of raiding with guns and rifles, however, had come to an end. A cosmological war now waged in the islands.

A few mainland youths had become "very interested" upon hearing about magical practices and been shown objects and photographs by Baldwin Spencer (Spencer 1928: 657), who stayed at Cooper's camp in 1911 and in 1912. Spencer's talk about secret/sacred objects and magical practices from the mainland (Spencer 1914: x, 91–92) may have been a lesson for them about what they now could use, as well as a lesson for the Tiwi about what they had to fear. The arrival of other mainland Aborigines may have provided an opportunity for putting it into practice. When Spencer took up the position of chief protector for the year 1912, he ordered the deportation of Aboriginal offenders from Darwin to Cooper's camp, where they were added to the workforce as part of their "reformation."[14] The newcomers originated from Arnhem Land and other areas in the Darwin hinterland, and probably included experts in magic. Spencer made a short and final visit to the islands in December 1912.

A week after he left, according to Korupu, mainland Aborigines (*Tarula*) buried magical objects in the form of "'sung' stringbags with kapok" in three different spots on the beach in the north of Bathurst Island. Fry's other Tiwi informants at various places in the islands also believed this had been the cause of the epidemic. In spite of repetitive questioning, Spencer had failed to get evidence that the Tiwi had sacred or magical objects (Spencer 1914: 23).[15] But it is certain that the magical objects existed in the islands, because an acquaintance of Cooper, trader D. M. Sayers, collected a number of them around this time (these are kept in the South Australian Museum in Adelaide; see figure 10.1). Sayers obtained the stringbags from either the Aboriginal deportees from Darwin or other mainland Aborigines in Cooper's workforce.[16] Unlike Spencer, Fry did not get assistance from Cooper's employees. Cooper's mainlanders, according to Fry, were "non-cooperative because they had worked the fatal magic."[17]

Poisoning

In 1954, as mentioned, Tiwi people still had remembrances of the lethal feat. It needs to be stressed, however, that there was talk of mainland Aborigines' "magic songs of *poison*" (Goodale 1970: 358, 1971: 224, my emphasis). In other words, the men in question associated the use of magic with poisoning. This raises the question of whether the historical epidemic and its fatalities could have been due to poisoning or not. I want to make clear that the symptoms of the disease and other circumstantial evidence do indeed suggest that poisoning caused the tragedy.

According to Stephen Rothmann, a German medical student at the

Figure 10.1. "Sung" stringbags with kapok, collected in the islands by D. M. Sayers, on display in the Southern Australian Museum, Adelaide (photo: Eric Venbrux; courtesy of the South Australia Museum).

University of Heidelberg, the symptoms of the disease point in the direction of poisoning. The description, recorded by Fry, of "a feeling like snake walking up the legs" is similar to descriptions of tingling or numbness that are found in cases of poisoning. Other symptoms of poisoning are the "stomach problems and bloody diarrhea." These symptoms, according to epidemiologist Dr. John Condon of the Menzies School of Health in Darwin, "could be caused by an inert toxin but are also quite consistent with several infectious organisms" (personal communication 2006). The one or the other, so it seems, was ingested; indeed, the stomach and especially the bowel are the first organs to be severely affected by the toxin. Next, in the last stages of the disease, the cardiovascular and respiratory systems would be involved as well; this was symptomatically expressed in the Tiwi account to Fry that "when reaches heart, shortness of breath, no more eat." Fry heard the same story time and again.

Other features also suggest that an ingested toxin may have been the cause of the illness. The symptoms described above are consistent with a brief period before the onset of symptoms or signs of illness of up to a few days time that is often associated with poisonings. The occurrence of only a single burst or peak in the epidemic disease (rather than recurrent, but decreasing, outbreaks)[18] is also a common outcome of poisoning. The ingestion of an inert toxin from a single source at one point in time, followed by a very brief period that allowed for the dispersal of poisoned people elsewhere in the islands, tends to further support this argument.

The scenario of poisoning leads us back to the big Tiwi gathering near the mission station in December 1912. Although this was not a favorite area for the Tiwi (Gsell 1956: 45–46), the presence of the new mission station may have been a major reason for the island-wide gathering of people.[19] The small creek near the mission station was most likely the source of both the water and the fish needed to support the large number of people present for the ceremonial gathering. A particular technique used to catch large quantities of fish involved the use of a fish poison from a plant that would have caused a serious health risk for those who made use of the water afterward:

> The tubers of *Tephrosia remotiflora* (perennial form), called *Matajama* in Tiwi, are dug up and collected in a basket made from bark. When a creek or water body with a lot of fish is located the tubers are pounded and then someone who carries the basket swims through the water. The swimmer must keep his eyes shut and leave the water as soon as possible. The *Matajama* causes the fish to float to the surface of the water as if the water has been dynamited. Crocodiles are also stunned or killed

and the water cannot be used for drinking or washing until it is flushed out again by rain. In the past four or five [baskets] of *Matajama* would be collected and large amounts of fish could be caught for ceremonial gatherings. However the *Matajama* can not be used regularly as it depletes the fish resource and renders the water unusable. (Puruntatameri et al. 2001: 84–85)

Because the water in the creek was brackish (versus fresh), accidental poisoning could easily have occurred: the water or fish being poisoned without people knowing this was the case.[20] It is also possible that some Tiwi had only recently been introduced to the technique by mainland Aborigines, or that the latter, camping on the opposite side of the sea strait, had used the poisonous plant in the creek themselves.[21]

The mission staff and white visitors were not affected because they drank water from Father Gsell's well.[22] The majority of infants and children also survived the epidemic (Fry 1949: 80). Why? It was not the time of the year for extended households to travel over longer distances (cf. Hart and Pilling 1960: 45). Consequently, only a small number of infants and children attended the near-Christmas meeting in the environs of the mission station. Most of them thus escaped from being poisoned.

The sequence of events described above suggests that the poisoned creek was a possible source of the "epidemic disease." If so, however, it still allowed people to return home after the gathering, and so the disease "spread" to various parts of the islands.[23] Within a fortnight, a great many Tiwi died.

Lifting the Alien Magic Spell

Grief, grievances, blaming, and revenge were, among other things, the subject matter of songs composed for the forthcoming *kulama*, a seasonal yam ritual (Venbrux 1995: 119–49). As we have seen, in that ritual Korupu blamed the mainlanders for having planted the magic that caused the epidemic among the islanders. Goodale (1971: 225) suspected that this disease was *tarni*, since it was later given attention in the yam ritual.

Baldwin Spencer observed a *kulama* ceremony in March 1912. It appears that at that point in time (before the epidemic occurred), disease was not really a focus in the *kulama* (Goodale 1971: 224). A true concern with sickness in the ceremony was first recorded in 1913 after the epidemic had taken place. Fry writes that the Tiwi "seemed to distinguish two maladies, a cough sickness, & an abdominal sickness. The latter they ascribed to magic on the part of other blacks, *the poisoness* [sic] *influence* creeping up the leg to the abdomen" (my emphasis).[24] Anita Pangiramini, an expert in Tiwi medicine who had experienced presettlement life as a child, also makes this distinction between chest infections and a sickness concerning the belly, called *tiukuputji* and *tarni* respectively (Pangiramini, personal communication 1988). The additional evidence provided by Fry and Pangiramini confirms Jane's hypothesis (Goodale 1971: 225) that Tiwi equated the magic-induced, epidemic disease with *tarni*.

If *tarni* was a newly introduced disease caused by poisoning, as Jane (Goodale 1971: 224–25) suggests, one wonders why the Tiwi did not utilize the culturally accepted methods for avoiding poisoning that were available to them at the time. This knowledge was available in the seasonal yam ritual in which the poison was removed from a type of toxic yam (called *kulama*).[25] The treatment in the *kulama* ceremony made the round yams that normally could not be eaten, and were taboo, edible. Jane noted that the *kulama* she observed in 1954—in contrast to the one seen by Spencer in 1912—had "the prevention of sickness as a rationalization for the ceremony" (Goodale 1971: 224). This sickness, called *tarni*, was "counteracted by ceremonial means" (Goodale 1971: 225). According to Jane, "The yams were by some devious thought processes, made the seat of one of the new forms of illness, and the ritual that centred around the toxic variety became, in itself, the means by which the poison was seasonally removed" (Goodale 1970: 365). She characterizes this shift as an instance of "ritual change" (Goodale 1970). The change came about as a Tiwi response to the actions, as perceived and experienced, of the mainlanders. Herewith, Jane makes an important contribution to the understanding of the dynamics of an indigenous religion in an intercultural space.

The only thing that is left unclear in Jane's reasoning is the character of the "devious thought processes" (Goodale 1970). In the remainder of this section I am concerned with a further interpretation of what went on. I try to show, in particular, that the Tiwi concerned might have been less erratic in their thinking than it seems. In a later publication (Goodale 1982), Jane convincingly demonstrates that the *kulama* yam can be seen as a key symbol. The notion of the yam as a key symbol helps to explain the rationale for the procedure, especially its symbolic efficacy.

We have seen that contemporary Tiwi attributed the epidemic disease not to "natural" causes but to human agency: mainland Aborigines had worked magic on them. The business of the epidemic, from a Tiwi perspective, was clothed in the language of magic. This local understanding is critical to the choice of appropriate counter-magic. The clearest statement of how the mainlanders had employed magic came from Korupu. Extraordinary and magical powers were attributed to him.[26] Furthermore, he dominated the people in the north of Bathurst Island, where mainland Aborigines were supposed to have launched their attack by planting magic in the beaches. The magical objects (round stringbags filled with kapok) buried by the mainlanders resemble *kulama* yams both in size and shape.

Jane found that it had become common belief among the Tiwi that the resulting sickness (*tarni*) was "permeating all yams during the rainy season" (Goodale 1971: 225). The poisonous *kulama* yams, however, stood out as a potent symbol of sickness and danger. They were circumvented with taboos and could only be consumed after complex ritual treatment realized their detoxification (Goodale 1970, 1982). The striking resemblance of these objects to the yams and the contamination of the yams in the earth suggests that this is a classic case of sympathetic magic. James Frazer's laws of similarity and contact or contagion seem to apply (cf. Carucci 1993). The capacity to ritually process the toxic yams was Tiwi people's forte. Although not "a rationalization for the ceremony," the processed yams were, as Jane (Goodale 1970: 359) attests, already known for their health-giving properties.[27]

The common "individual treatment" of sickness did not provide an effective cure for the devastating epidemic. According to Jane, "The Tiwi did find a way to counteract the impersonal nature of this illness by means of the *kulama* ceremony which, in effect, personalized the illness in a form they could treat through a proper ritual observance that had always been health-giving" (Goodale 1970: 358–59; cf. Weiner 1983). In the ceremony, the yams are the main symbolic vehicle for quite a number of transformations (see Venbrux 1995: 143). Spencer notes, "The island natives evidently regard the *kolamma*, probably because it has to be specially treated before being safe to eat, as a superior kind of yam, endowed with properties such as ordinary yams do not possess" (1914: 103). Jane (Goodale 1982), following Sherry Ortner, regards the *kulama* yam as a "key symbol" which links the resources of food and people together. Inspired by Jane's 1982 article, I have demonstrated elsewhere (Venbrux 1995) how the ritual treatment of the yam both structures and ties together many things and generates new meanings. Jane (Goodale 1970) identified a similar process of ritual change in the *kulama*. It may have been Jane's great-grandfather Korupu who initiated this change.

In his ceremony, Korupu's lyrics charged the poisonous yam with new meaning, turning it into a medium for counter-magic. He thus inverted the "magic songs of poison" performed by the mainlanders. The magical poisoning could be undone by means of a ritual detoxification of the symbolically potent and sacred yams. Furthermore, the "planting" of the stringbags seems an inversion of the digging out of the round *kulama* yams. Korupu sang about this process when the yams were cooking in his 1913 *kulama* ceremony. In his song, Korupu sought to lift the alien magic spell through the equation of the interred stringbags and yams.

A Spirit Came Out of the Jungle

Korupu's singing did not exhaust his people's ritual treatment of mainland magic. When the fire in the *kulama* oven is burning, the male descendants of Korupu's father Puruntatameri have to perform a song about *jamparipari*, a major dreaming of this patrilineage. During initiation, the first song to be performed in the *kulama* by a young man of the Puruntatameri patrilineage has to be about *jamparipari*. This underscores its importance for the members of this group.

Tractor Joe Puruntatameri (a classificatory father of Jane) once performed his first *kulama* song for me. The song, which he had composed for his initiation in 1942, dealt with *jamparipari*. My "grandfather" Tractor Joe explained that the spirit manifested itself as a lighthouse. When the Tarula or mainland Aborigines came to the islands, according to his cousin Justin Puruntatameri, the spirit had come out of the jungle. He punished the mainland wrongdoers. Jamparipari moved through the air "like a rocket," chucking its victims into the sea west of Bathurst Island, another senior man named Francis Borgia Tipaklippa added (Tipaklippa, personal communication 1989). Justin Puruntatameri, who identified himself with his grandfather Korupu, told me that he had encountered *jamparipari* once. The spirit blocked him the road: a huge and tall white shape (marking with his hands the contours of a gigantic "tree trunk") with light. He was unable to circumvent or pass it. The imagery of the lighthouse is also part and parcel of the *jamparipari* dance: a dance performed in mortuary ritual by patrilineal descendants of Puruntatameri.

In this dance representing the lighthouse, the dancer carries two armrings woven from pandanus leaves. These armrings have a small double strip of the leaves or string ending with feathers attached to it. The armbands hang at the dancer's elbows when he spreads out both arms vertically to the height of his shoulders. He moves around with the body bended, accelerating pace so that the feathers are at the same level as the expanded arms. Next, moving the body to an upright position but the arms still stretched outward, he holds an armring in each hand. Meanwhile, the dancer produces the sound: "whhhuuuuhh." He lets his body spin, concluding the dance in a sudden standstill. In the final step, both arms rise. They go straight up in the air, the fingers stretched and the armrings held with the thumbs. The lighthouse had come to rest, standing, with the two rings as "eyes" or lamps. The sound produced had an unmistakable likeness to the one of a lighthouse. Also, the dance movements and the armrings evoked the image of a lighthouse: beams or rays of light going round in the night. During my fieldwork in the late 1980s, every time when Justin or Tractor Joe Puruntatameri performed the dance, the Tiwi audience responded with awe.

Fry's field notes contain a description of mortuary rites that took place in the aftermath of Korupu's *kulama* ceremony in March 1913. Korupu's eldest son led the postfuneral rituals for his deceased daughter (probably a victim of the epidemic). Obviously, the man in question performed the *jamparipari* dance. He went around, wearing the armrings, and produced the characteristic sound. He had red rags tied to his elbows. Of particular interest are the armrings worn by Korupu's eldest son in his dance, because these ornaments contain strips of red cloth, and so do hair skeins worn on the occasion. Korupu's son donated the body ornaments to Fry at the conclusion of the ceremony. (These are kept in the Pitt Rivers Museum in Oxford.)[28] The use of introduced materials in the ornaments struck me, because other descendants of Puruntatameri, such as Justin and Tractor Joe Puruntatameri, were wearing similar "hybrid" objects in their *jamparipari* dance in the late 1980s. Their armrings and girdle had not small strips of red calico, but colored woolen threads. At the time, these rather exceptional artifacts puzzled me. The armrings (*pamanjini*) did not seem "traditional," unlike most of the bangles employed in ritual. Simultaneously, a greater significance appeared to be attributed to them.

This raises the question if the incorporation of the introduced fabric material by the artifact-producers was intentional. Both the strips of red cloth and the colored woolen threads being attached to, or worked into, the Tiwi ornaments entail an "indigenous appropriation of European things" (Thomas 1991).[29] In colonial times, red cloth was one of the most popular goods for trade of Europeans with indigenous peoples in the Pacific and elsewhere (see also Taussig 1993: 93–99).[30] Spencer notes that the material was in demand by the Tiwi (1928: 652, 686–687). According to Markus Schindlbeck, the incorporation of new materials in traditional objects in the Pacific expressed people's dealing with a new world. In many instances, goods introduced by Europeans, such as red calico, obtained an almost magical meaning. By making these things part of their own material culture and thought, indigenous peoples sought to bridge the gap with an alien world, especially by means of a partial appropriation (Schindlbeck 1993: 9). Jane's Tiwi ancestors did so with the strange light of the lighthouse, captured by the incorporation of introduced materials in their ornaments, in the *jamparipari* dance. They were symbolically appropriating the power of whites in order to counteract the fatal magic employed by mainland Aborigines.

It is no coincidence that armrings and other ornaments employed in Tiwi mortuary ritual are made of pandanus leaves. Pandanus (*miarti*) offers protection against dangerous or evil spirits (cf. Spencer 1914: 106), such as those of the deceased (*mopadruwi*), the Rainbow Serpent (*amputji*), and, ultimately, *jamparipari*. Its efficacy in Tiwi perception has to do with an avoidance relationship: all males, including a male spirit like *jamparipari*, have to avoid their mother-in-law. Anita Pangiramini explained to me that *miarti* (pandanus) is the mother-in-law of *jamparipari*, and, therefore, the latter cannot come near pandanus. The cottonwood tree, called *tawari*, wherein the spirit (*jamparipari*) stays, is never found in the vicinity of a pandanus. This observable fact provided clear evidence. The next step, following this line of reasoning, is the incorporation of introduced materials, such as red calico and colored wool, in the ornaments for the *jamparipari* dance. Connecting pandanus with the imagery of *jamparipari* kept the spirit in check. The performers demonstrated they were able to control it.

The spirit can cause sickness, death, and other evil. Sometimes *jamparipari* is associated with a comet or a shooting star. Some describe him as a "vampire" with red eyes (Winnifred Puruntatameri, personal communication 1989). Harney and Elkin discuss *jamparipari* in terms of magic: "[T]he idea is to bring the destroyer, Lamparipari, upon the victim. This is done by burning a piece of blood—a hard piece which has dried up—and letting the wind carry the smell to the victim. The latter becomes affected because Lamparipari is attracted to this smell and sucks out his blood" (1943: 232). Justin Puruntatameri told me that the victims of a then recently occurred car accident had crashed when they turned their heads upon hearing the whistle of *jamparipari*. The sound of the spirit, he had warned them, had to be ignored.[31] In the late 1980s, variants of the tales about *jamparipari* also belonged to Tiwi children's folklore. Korupu's great-great-grandchildren, in particular, related stories about having seen the red-eyed spirit after sunset.

In the beginning of the twentieth century, when the islanders got into serious conflict with the invading mainlanders, *jamparipari* first came to the scene. The spirit, however, was not created *ex nihilo*. We can trace *jamparipari*'s antecedents to an earlier representation. In March 1912, witnessing a *kulama* ceremony, Spencer heard that "one man 'sang' the *Mabanuri*, or shooting star, which is supposed to be an evil spirit" (1914: 106). Furthermore, the armlets (*pamajini*) were the subject matter of another song and "supposed to aid in protecting him [a third-grade initiate] against any shooting star" (Spencer 1914: 106). As mentioned, the spirit is still sometimes associated with a shooting star. It happened to be a dreaming of Puruntatameri (born in the late eighteenth century), who lived in the southwest of Bathurst Island. Shooting stars, a premonition of a death, could be frequently observed there; and these are dealt with in a dreaming dance of the Puruntatameri patrilineage (Grau 1983: 236). The area (Tikelaru) was also the homeland of Puruntatameri's son Korupu. The latter inherited his father's dreaming. He grew into prominence as a major leader with many wives in the second half of the nineteenth century.

With the encroachment of the Europeans, things were changing. Consequently, the dreaming and its dance were transformed. In the early twentieth century, Darwin was the principal port in northern Australia. The main shipping route westward went along Cape Fourcroy, the south-west point of Bathurst Island (Searcy 1905: 47). Puruntatameri dreamings such as boats and ship masts are reminders of the incorporation of the new phenomena in Tiwi cosmology. At Cape Fourcroy a lighthouse was established, assumingly when the shipping route became significant (Port Darwin was founded in 1869). The appropriation of the lighthouse fits in with the complex of Puruntatameri dreamings dealing with ships.

In the *jamparipari* dance, this became an embodied practice for Puruntatameri's descendants.[32] The bad omen of the shooting star in conjunction with an appropriation of the power of Europeans, derived from both the introduced fabric material and the lighthouse, made the *jamparipari* dreaming for the Tiwi concerned a powerful protective measure against what they perceived as the malignant powers of mainland Aborigines. In the context of mortuary ritual and considering the traumatic consequences of the epidemic or holocaust, this must also have given the survivors some consolation.

Conclusion

Jane Goodale's long-lasting and ongoing relationship with the Tiwi people allowed her to immerse herself in the local experience of the postcontact period. I have taken up some themes in her work such as the issues of variation, creativity, ritual change, and the adaptation to introduced disease. Regarding the *kulama* ceremony, I have also tried to highlight the convergence of Jane's 1970 and 1982 analyses of the *kulama* ceremony. She writes, "I wish to draw attention to the *kulama* in the hope of provoking comments from all who have seen or studied this Tiwi ritual, and thereby elevate the position of the *kulama* to its rightful position as a rather unique Australian Aboriginal ceremony" (Goodale 1970: 350).[33] I have applied Jane's integrative methodology to better understand the initial phase of Tiwi people's sustained contact with Europeans. The Tiwi were not passive victims of the tragic epidemic and subsequent depopulation or the encroachment of Europeans and mainland Aborigines. Tiwi people believed that the epidemic had been caused by mainland magic. Whether the epidemic was caused by magic, measles, or poisoning, the important point is that Tiwi people made sense of it in terms of their interactions and communication with other cultures. They creatively resisted and protected themselves against the threats of mainland magic and epidemic disease in the *kulama* ceremony and with the *jamparipari* dreaming.

Notes

1. Jane published a photograph of Rachel as a child in *Tiwi Wives* (Goodale 1971: 166).

2. Of course, Jane has been closely involved with a great many other Tiwi people in a period of time spanning nearly half a century. Paddy's sister Polly Miller, Happy Cook (Jane's "sister"; see Goodale 1988: 127, 129), and Mary Elizabeth Moreen should certainly be mentioned.

3. In March 1912, Baldwin Spencer was to make a stay of three weeks on Melville Island: "[T]he inhabitants of which he is particularly anxious to study, as they are hitherto practically uncontaminated by European influence" (Frazer 1912: 73).

4. "Virgin soil epidemics are those in which the population at risk have had no previous contact with the diseases that strike them and are therefore immunologically almost defenseless" (Crosby 1976: 289). Crosby further stresses that these "epidemics are different from others in the age incidence of those they kill, as well in quantity of their victims" (1976: 293). Fry's findings (Fry 1949) are in accordance with these two characteristics of a virgin soil epidemic.

5. See also Mulvaney and Calaby (1985: 294) and Spencer (1914: 23). The occasion might have been the first large gathering of Tiwi people at the mission station. "For quite a time," writes Gsell about the start of his mission station, "my only native visitors were Boolak and Tokoopa, the hunchback and the one-eyed man" (1956: 51).

6. H. K. Fry to the Administrator of the Northern Territory [J. Gilruth], Pine Creek, 15 May 1913. Anthropology Archives, South Australian Museum, Adelaide (henceforth AA/SAM).

7. H. K. Fry, Fieldnotes 1913, AA/SAM.

8. Korupu had white hair and a beard. His face and body, however, were smeared with red ochre. Fry observed the proceedings. He remained with a group of about thirty islanders for a few days, learning more about the epidemic and its fatalities. H.K. Fry, Fieldnotes 1913, entry 10 March 1913, AA/SAM. For more information on Korupu, see also Pilling (1970: 268–69) and Gsell (1956: 58).

9. H. K. Fry, Fieldnotes 1913, entry 11 March 1913, AA/SAM.

10. H. K. Fry to the Administrator of the Northern Territory, 15 May 1913, AA/SAM.

11. H. K. Fry, "Gleanings from Scattered Notes, 12.5.59, and Outstanding Memories," AA/SAM.

12. H. K. Fry, Fieldnotes 1913, entry 11 March 1913, AA/SAM.

13. A raid with firearms on a Tiwi camp on Bathurst Island had just occurred, according to Gsell, when he arrived to establish a mission station in June 1911 (1956: 47–48). When Baldwin Spencer took up the position of chief protector for the year 1912, he appointed Cooper subprotector of the Aborigines of the islands. Spencer also ordered the deportation of Aboriginal offenders from Darwin to Cooper's camp, where they were added to the workforce as part of their "reformation." Sam Green in turn, employed workers provided by Cooper for obtaining timber. Tensions between Green and Cooper arose. Green objected to the maltreatment of Tiwi people by Cooper's mainland employees, and also to their lethal violence in the recent past. Green's complaints to the commonwealth minister in Melbourne led to an inquiry and eventually to the removal of Cooper's mainland employees from the islands. See Melville Island Inquiry, (CRS) A3, N.T. 1916/245, Australian Archives, Canberra. Fry recorded that Green was "hot on C. [Cooper's] niggers." H. K. Fry, Fieldnotes 1913, entry 15 April 1913, AA/SAM.

14. At that time, Korupu's son Cabbagee was one of the Tiwi youths added to Cooper's workforce. Cabbagee knew Spencer as Mr. Pantja. He told Pilling (1958: 54) that Mr. Pantja introduced the term *dreaming* to the Tiwi as the English equivalent for *irumwa*, a "totemic" affiliation.

15. Spencer, however, did not exclude the possibility they would have. After all, his experience with the Larrakia of the Darwin area had shown him that such a fact could remain hidden for researchers for a considerable period of time (Spencer 1914: 91–92). Like Spencer had done before him, Fry showed a bullroarer to some islanders in order to find out if they knew about the object. In his field notes, Fry makes mention of having brought up the topic on the evening of March 11: "Casually demonstrated a roughly-made bull roarer, but taken to be a fishing line by an old man." He adds that "Cabbagee [Korupu's son] did not recognise it earlier in the day," AA/SAM.

16. The ornament to a certain extent resembles the Tiwi *tokwainga*, a goose-feather ball on a string that is also worn around the neck (the ball being taken in the mouth and bitten as a sign of aggression). In later years, some Tiwi men adopted the stringbag, substituting their *tokwainga*. I became acquainted with one of these men in 1988–89; he had relatives on the mainland whose application of magic was feared by other Tiwi people.

17. H. K. Fry to the Secretary of the Royal Geographical Society, Adelaide, 1 June 1959, AA/SAM.

18. This singular peak is characteristic for epidemics that are caused by intoxications. Other forms of infection would show recurrent, but decreasing second, third, or more outbreaks (cf. Rose 1991: 5). Normally, this process leads to a population's development of immunity to the pathogen in question, resulting in a situation that strikes a balance between reinfection and healing.

19. Probably, many of their young children stayed back home; hence, they survived the epidemic, as reflected in Fry's mortality statistics. The available data

do not tell us why the meeting took place. It may have been the first so-called Christmas gathering, organized by the missionaries to establish their presence. Dignitaries had been invited, including John Gilruth (the administrator of the Northern Territory), Baldwin Spencer (chief protector of the Aborigines), and Mervyn Holmes (the chief medical officer). The postfuneral rites may have been staged by the Tiwi for them in exchange for tobacco or some other material compensation (see also Venbrux 2000, 2001a). "Death corroboree seen by Spencer was not well done," Fry jotted down in his small notebook on 17 April 1913, AA/SAM.

20. Even more so, because the water in the creek tended to be at a low point at that time of the year (see Pye 1985: 31), increasing the likelihood that the poison would be insufficiently "flushed out." It would not affect the mission staff and the European visitors as they relied on the water from the well dug by Father Gsell and his Filipino employees. Father Gsell also failed to get fish (Gsell 1956: 55).

21. Jane Goodale suggested to me that the mainland Aborigines may have been responsible for the poisoning (personal communication 2003). As the knowledge is rare among even elderly Tiwi today, the technique may have had its origin on the mainland indeed.

22. If Tiwi people were allowed to use it, they would have been reluctant to do so; Gsell (1956: 52–53) reports a fear for the Rainbow serpent (*amputji*) in relation to the well that had been dug.

23. The mortality statistics (see table 10.1) and accounts collected by Fry, who traveled from the mission station as his base to the various dwellings in the islands to be reached from this focal point, reflect this spreading. The mortality rate in the various territorial groupings decreased with geographical distance and being more difficult to reach from the mission station. Recently, Mow-Be, an Amerindian leader of the Nukak-Makú in the rain forest of Columbia, committed suicide by taking the roots of a plant used to poison fish; it took him two days to die (Schulz 2006).

24. H. K. Fry to the Administrator of the Northern Territory, 15 May 1913, AA/SAM.

25. The yam is known to botanists as *Dioscorea bulbifera*: see Puruntatameri et al. (2001: 43–44).

26. Justin Puruntatameri described his grandfather Korupu to me as a "doctor" and "magic man." He could look through people's bodies, was a clairvoyant, and was the only one who dared to go into the jungle at night.

27. Indeed, rubbing the body with a mixture of yam mash and red ochre was (Spencer 1914), and is (Venbrux 1995: 138, 121), considered an effective prophylactic and healing act.

28. Strips of red fabric material have been worked into a number of armrings (PRM 1917.6.7–.9) and attached to hair skeins (PRM 1917.6.4–,6) that were acquired by Fry on the occasion of his visit to Korupu's camp. Fry donated them to the Pitt Rivers Museum a few years later.

29. Recently, Thomas has argued that such an appropriation not necessarily means that indigenous peoples' "strategies were conservative, in the sense that they attempted to preserve a prior order rather than create a novel one" (1999: 18). Having considered the case of introduced cloth in Polynesia, he concludes:

"More often than not we have acknowledged the indigenous peoples of the [Pacific] region have been concerned not to 'contextualize things,' but to use things to change contexts" (1999: 19).

30. "What they liked most, apart from tobacco, was red-turkey-twill" (Spencer 1928: 652). Mainland Aborigines, according to Anita Pangiramini and other senior women, used pieces of red calico or red handkerchiefs with a round stone wrapped in them in love magic to attract Tiwi women. (A few named Tiwi men adopted this technique.)

31. It must be noted that the car accident occurred while they were passing Justin's "country." Justin Puruntatameri made the point that he thus could not be blamed. Simultaneously, he stressed the powers of the spirit; that is, his dreaming *jamparipari*.

32. As Paul Stoller (1995) has argued, such mimicry is a strategy to gain power over it that subsequently can be used to deal with local problems. Important to note is also the role of dance and song in the management of emotions in mortuary ritual (Hart, cited in Seligman 1932: 198, note 1; Venbrux 1993).

33. See also Venbrux (1995: 119–49) and Hiatt (1996: 165–82).

11. *Food and Ghosts:*
     Dance in the Context
     of Baining Life

I was an impressionable undergraduate when I first studied
Melanesian ethnography with Jane Goodale at Bryn Mawr College. The
exoticism of the subject matter was tempered by the personalities of the
people who transmitted it to me. In particular, although New Guinea
lurked on the fringes of my experience as an alien and fantasy world, it
was, nevertheless, one that was mediated through a cohort of familiar and
female acquaintances: Jane Goodale, Annette Weiner, and Ann Chowning. In retrospect, I am sure that I felt enabled to contemplate research
in Papua New Guinea because I could project myself into the footsteps
of these powerful female role models.

When I first studied Melanesia, however, I had no intention of becoming an anthropologist, let alone a Melanesianist. This vocation grew
gradually as I found my niche in the Bryn Mawr Anthropology Department. In particular, I was allowed to socialize with graduate students and
faculty on what was at the time as close as I came to an equal footing. I
was jealous of the interesting projects and material each was pursuing.

Even when I decided to pursue graduate studies in anthropology, I
was not committed to Melanesia as a subject area. But once again, I was
seduced by a cohort of peers, this time through ASAO. My ties with Jane
Goodale served as an introduction to what was, at the time, a small and
intimate group. Oceania became as attractive as the people who worked

there. I was still relatively unaware of the strong forces that held me in thrall until I realized that I was preparing to do research in New Britain. This was getting pretty close to my Bryn Mawr roots, and I thought I had it made. In anticipation of my own research, I familiarized myself with the ethnography on Melanesia, particularly the studies on exchange, gender, and ritual. Although I knew very little about the group I decided to study, the Baining, I felt prepared through osmosis. Imagine my surprise when I found myself in a community that seemed to have so little elaboration in ritual, gender, exchange, and all the other attributes I had expected in a Melanesian society. In particular, the Baining appeared very different from the Kaulong of New Britain, who had formed my earliest impressions of New Britain societies. True to my anthropological training under Jane and others, I committed myself to doing as thorough an ethnographic study as I could. I had learned from her that ethnography was a journey of discovery and we might not recognize our destination until we arrived. In this sense, the title of this book, *Pulling the Right Threads*, describes an involuted but ultimately satisfying process. For me, the thread was the word *play*, the word the Baining used to describe their dances. On the most basic linguistic level, Baining play and English play appear remarkably congruent. Play is both what children do and a performance or spectacle performed for pleasure or enjoyment. I had learned about these dances through the only published material I could find about the Baining before I arrived. Three articles, by three different authors, and totaling a mere twelve pages, described the "Snake Dance" of the Baining (Bateson 1932; Poole 1941; Read 1931). My early queries on these dances had been deflected with the remark, "They're just play" (Baining *atalak*). What I had failed to consider when hearing this comment was what the Baining really meant by *play*. It took me several years to realize that *play* was a fraught activity that breached the boundaries of social life. For this reason, children were not encouraged to play. In addition, dances and dancers mediated the boundaries of society. In this chapter, I describe one Baining danced called *Amambua*.

Preparations

Amambua is a ritual within which there are a series of named stages. *Amambua* refers to the whole event as well as to the songs that are sung during it. This dance can only be performed during the pitpit season (wild sugar cane), which runs from about Christmas to Easter, although it need not be performed for years on end.[1] The reason for this seasonal restriction is that *Amambua* involves a large-scale food display called *arltulki.* This display is built on a large stage, containing two carefully arranged mounds of food, composed of taro, pitpit,[2] and coconuts. These food structures are called *akarum*. The scaffolding behind the *akarum* is hung with a variety of foodstuffs: bananas, yams, taros, coconuts, bunches of betel nut, and packages of pepper leaf. The posts themselves were flanked by bundles of pitpit and sugar cane stalks.

Each family in the community is expected to contribute to the display. On the appointed day, everybody went to the gardens to gather food. People returned from their gardens and gathered at a meeting point where they proceeded to make special bundles of the foodstuffs. When these preparations were completed, they marched en masse to the yard outside the church and school, where the display and dance were to be held. The group proceeded to the display platform and deposited the food on the ground in front, separating the different foodstuffs into different piles. After unloading their contributions, the women retired some distance back from the platform, where they watched the proceedings. From this point, I was told, women should keep their distance from the food display lest the *aios* (spirits, ghosts) who come to inhabit it should inflict some damage on their reproductive powers.

Meanwhile, the men began to construct the display. At each end of the platform, they piled taro around an upright pole. The taros were arranged in concentric circles around the pole, and then built up until they formed a cylinder. Over the top of this heap, they attached layers of pitpit. In my field notes, I described the effect as looking like "a tutu on top of a heap of cannon balls." At the apex of this cone of pitpit, two or three coconuts were tied to the pole. These coconuts represented the hat or headdress of the mound. The mound as a whole is called *akarumgi* (*akarum,* plural).

The *akarum* are said to represent chickens, *andurek;* thus, the display resembles a hen sitting on her eggs. The taros are the eggs, the pitpit are the wings and feathers of the bird, and the pitpit husks are the neck. The whole thing is topped off by the coconuts, which are described as the headdress of the chicken; that is, the crest.[3] In any case, the identification of the display with poultry seemed to bear no symbolic meaning. I learned nothing about what chickens brought to the event, or why it was important to have "chickens" there. This lack of symbolic referent was in keeping with most of the ornaments and regalia I observed in Baining dances. They occasionally used metaphors to describe the pieces they constructed but shied away from actually attributing meaning to these images.

On the scaffolding behind the heaps was hung an assortment of prized and useful foodstuffs. These included yams, which are not a common crop among the Baining; coconuts of a special orange color that the Baining call sun; taros like Siamese twins in which two tubers have grown together; large bunches of bananas; large bunches of *areca* nut; and wrapped bundles of pepper vines. These foodstuffs are referred to as the decorations of the *akarum;* they are not individually significant but are there for their visual effect and beauty and because the Baining take pride in their abundant productive powers.

While the food display was being constructed, parties of men made masks and ornaments in the bush to be worn by particular sets of dancers during the dance. The *Amambua* performed in April 1977 consisted of three separate corps of dancers who punctuated the rhythm of the nightlong dance with special activities. These three events were *aioski* (ghosts), then *alamsaka* (coconuts), and finally *asingal* (not translatable). Since *aioski* and *alamsaka* are virtually identical in structure, I will only describe *aioski* here. Each of these dances entailed separate preparations and decorations. On this occasion, the preparations were not particularly extended. *Aioski* demanded the most preparation, roughly four or five days. I was not permitted access to the *aioski* preparations because in principle the bush preparations are forbidden to women, but these restrictions were enforced only by the *aioski* group, and I was allowed to visit the bush sites where preparations for *alamsaka* and *asingal* were being made. From informants' statements and my own observations, the procedures for *aioski* resembled the others.

Preparations in the bush are similar for all Baining dances, although each group had a separate preparation site. The men first picked a site where they built or used an existing hut. This was followed by a trek into the bush to collect the raw materials for their regalia; for example, headdresses, whips, and body paint. The remaining days were spent in the *akusak,* or bush house, fabricating these ornaments in secret. Traditionally one person, who was called *ambarta,* or older brother, was recognized as leader in the bush preparations.

The Dance

CHASING OFF THE *AIOS*

In the late afternoon, shortly before the dance was to start, a group of men gathered to rid the food display of the *aios* (or spirits) who had infested it. On a signal from their leaders, they swept out of the bush behind the dance ground, shouting, whooping, and throwing sticks toward the food platform. They charged toward the platform, but then held back while a senior man climbed up alone. Holding a leafy branch, he ran across the platform slapping and brushing the *akarum* heaps, the upright stalks of pitpit, the sugar cane, and the low rungs of the scaffolding. The act of chasing off the *aios* is called *haputki andalaingi*, and can be interpreted as sweeping away the *aios* (*haputki* is a broom). The tree branch used to hit the food display symbolizes the broom. The first stage of the process, that of charging the platform and shouting, was said to chase off the *aios*. The second stage, when someone goes up onto the platform and breaks up some of the food, is said to release the "wind" from the food. This wind is associated with heaviness that infects the food.[4] When the men broke and smashed some of the food, this heaviness rose like a wind or breath from the display and left the food.

AMAMBUA

The actual singing and dancing began at seven o'clock, when it was truly dark. The first women began dancing in the middle of the second song. The women all danced in a single file around in a circle, holding their hands up toward their heads as if to balance a heavy load, often with a child on their shoulders. The step was a very simple shuffle step, 1–2–3– pause, 1–2–3–pause, and was performed relatively slowly and sedately.

The men and boys gradually joined the circle. They carried their co-conut plaited baskets with the handle pushed up into the crook of their elbows or higher and held their arms in a "running" position. They tended to dance with more energy; instead of shuffling, they turned the same basic step into a sort of jaunty skip. Occasionally the young boys would let out a loud whoop, which was said to be an expression of pleasure and excitement.

New groups of dancers approached shyly, holding cut branches to shield their faces. They would hover at the edge of the clearing and call out until they were invited into the circle by the chorus. As latecomers they would frequently dance around the outside of the circle for one or two revolutions before throwing away their branches and fully joining in.

After several hours, the circle became too big and crowded to accommodate all the dancers comfortably. At this point, the women broke off and formed their own circle inside the men's. As the number of dancers waxed and waned, the dancers would divide or merge back into a single circle. The flux of dancers was a result of a number of factors. From time to time, people dropped out to rest, eat, or chew betel. The earliest and most persistent dancers tended to be mature women. A number of women danced virtually all night, whereas the men danced for a while when they first arrived and then frequently retired to the sidelines. Many of these men would have supplementary dance roles later on when *asingal*, *alamsaka* and *aioski* were performed. The young men and boys were by far the most determined dancers among the men, and although they came and went, they often formed a significant segment of the circle. Despite the simplicity of the dance step, many of the younger women felt shy about getting up and dancing. They said they were ashamed because they did not know how to dance but most eventually joined in. The experience of shame in this public context is in keeping with the pervasive nonassertiveness of Baining personality.

The songs are sung in a relatively unmelodic wail. The pace varies in different songs from a relatively slow, undulating wail to a faster and more staccato chant. The chorus accompanies itself with a percussion instrument made out of a length of bamboo. The bamboo is cut so that a bottom is formed by the internal membrane between the sections, and the top is open. It is held vertically and pounded against a hard surface such as a log, plank, or stone. The sound of the vibration of bamboo against board is amplified in the bamboo hollow, and people experiment with bamboos of different lengths to get a good sound.

The pattern of singing and dancing proceeded almost continuously through the night. At about 11:00 p.m., the dancers and assistants for the *asingal* group quietly disappeared. They went to decorate themselves and prepare for their performance

ASINGAL

The name *asingal* has no known meaning, nor is the dance seen as ritual or symbolic in any way. The Baining say that it is just a "decoration" of *Amambua*, in the same way the hanging food decorates the food platform. *Asingal* is not essential to the performance of *Amambua*. It is a frill and its presence depends on the scale, time, and energy being invested in the dance.

At about 12:30, the *asingal* dancers arrived. They had their own chorus of about half a dozen men, who positioned themselves about twenty yards from the *Amambua* chorus. This song differed from the *Amambua* songs in form and performance; the fact that it was sung by this all-male chorus and that it was the only song that most of these youths knew emphasized these differences. The singers played a slit drum. The singing and dancing of *Amambua* ebbed but did not disappear during this performance.

The *asingal* dancers were wearing straw helmetlike headdresses and banana-leaf skirts. Their bodies were covered with zebralike white stripes that glowed against their dark skin. The rock or soil from which the white paint was made might possibly have had some phosphorescent character- istics because it glowed eerily in the slight illumination of several fires and a few kerosene lamps. The wooden rod carried by the dancers was also painted with zebra stripes.

The dancers entered in two lines and danced forward. The dance step was a sort of hop from leg to leg that could be done either as a forward movement or in place in front of the chorus. When the dancers reached the chorus, they danced somewhat sedately in front of it until a certain point in the music. At this point, all order and sedateness was flung off and the dancers started careening backward, arms and legs flailing and moving in every direction. This free-for-all evoked hysterical laughter from the audience, who laughed, shouted, and jeered. Just as suddenly, at another point in the song, the dancers stopped where they were and again started to dance sedately toward the chorus, forming a double line as they came. These two phases alternated with one another throughout the dance, which lasted about fifteen minutes.

The dance was obviously seen as entertainment by the audience, who howled with delight. They manifested no sense of awe or ritual potency connected with it, and no pushing of sick children under the dancers' legs, which as we shall see, occurs with *Aioski*. People were reluctant to make any interpretations of the dance, its costumes, or its meaning, although somebody said that they laughed so hard because the dancers looked like crabs scurrying along the beach. When *asingal* was finished, *Amambua* became the focus of attention once again, and people gradually returned to the dance circle. A number of the *asingal* dancers came and joined the circle. They had removed their masks but were still wearing their paint. They danced around with a certain air of pride.

MUD MEN

At about two in the morning, the active participants had somewhat di- minished, the circle of dancers was at a low ebb, and many of the spec- tators had stretched out for a nap along the sidelines. At this point, the serenity was shattered by a loud war whoop and five or six men came tearing into the dance ground. They were covered with mud from head to toe and wore banana leaves over their faces. Each man carried a bark container filled with mud. They proceeded to swoop through the crowd and smear mud over everyone present. Lots of people tried to run away or duck, but most were attacked; those sitting down were hardest hit since some of the mud men rolled over and over on top of them.

These mud smearers are called *awusein put ta,* which means "mud-on-them." They are supposed to arrive in the middle of the night when people are getting tired and want to sleep. When the actors designated for this role saw this, they stealthily tapped one another and went off to prepare. They used taps as a signal so that no one else would hear or notice. Secrecy is important because they are supposed to sweep down and take people by surprise, so that although people knew in the abstract that they would be coming, they had no time to get away. Everyone had to submit to this treatment.

I believe that this mud-slinging episode was originally part of a larger series of events. According to informants (and Rascher 1909), in the past there would have been several groups. One group would have flamboyantly eaten feces.[5] Another group would have eaten raw taro. Since raw taro burns the throat and stomach and causes them to itch, these participants would begin to go wild with pain and run around as if crazy for several hours. Apparently this wild behavior was an expected part of the scenario. They would do this on the fringe of the dance ground. People suggested that there were *aios* inside uncooked food, but the connection between the *aios* and this wild behavior was unspecified.

After the dramatic interlude of the mud men, the monotonous singing and dancing of *Amambua* continued until dawn. The mud men disposed of their bark mud pails and banana leaves and joined the circle. Sometime before dawn, the dancers and assistants for *aioski* and *alamsaka* quietly drifted off into the bush. On the occasion described here, the whole performance was stopped temporarily around sunrise while the priest, who had come up the mountain to watch the dance, conducted an early morning mass. After the mass, singers and dancers again took up their stations and the dance continued. If there had been no interruption, they would have just kept going until the dance line arrived.

AIOSKI

The *aioski* dancers arrived in a double line led by two guardians who were not decorated. The lead dancer was not only decorated but carried a traditional war club as well. His partner was supposed to carry a traditional catapult, but on this occasion I did not see one. The rest of the dancers carried bundles of ginger sticks. As they approached the grounds, they shouted. When the dancers first enter the dance ground, women are advised not to look at them. They should turn around or hide their faces in a cloth. If they do not, they might faint and a pregnant woman might lose her baby. Older women, apparently past menopause (although this criterion was never explicitly mentioned), are allowed to watch. After a few moments, everyone can look. If a child or woman has been particularly sickly or cranky, the parents or grandparents might push him or her under the legs of the lead dancers as they enter the dance ground. There were six children pushed under during the big *Amambua* performance. The power of the *aioski* dancers is said to rid them of their sickness.

They entered in a double line and started to dance in a circle outside the women's circle. The *aios* dancers are said to be "pulled" onto the dance grounds by the singing of the chorus. There is a special song that is said to do this. They danced around the circle three times, after which undecorated men from the audience and sidelines began to join them. Each *aioski* dancer was paired with a secular dancer. Ideally, these partnerships are enduring, and people pair up with the same partner dance after dance. In Lan, these partnerships had not really developed, so the pairing operation took some time. The only restriction on partners was a taboo on in-laws pairing up. The undecorated dancer took the *aioski* by the wrist and they proceeded around the circle several times. After these dancers joined, there was a quadruple line of men dancing around the women's circle. At the end of the song, the circle broke up and these pairs moved away; there were couples scattered across the dance ground. Each couple then divided the bundle of ginger sticks carried by the masked dancer. Each man took two sticks. The partners then fought with these sticks, flicking them like whips across the chest or upper arms of their opponent (the areas painted black). As the sticks struck the flesh, they made a loud cracking noise, like a firecracker explosion, and they left a streak across the skin that often turned into a welt. During or just after this fight, the *alamsaka* dancer threw off his headdress. The two men then returned to the circle and everyone danced around in a single file. Amid this climactic event, a group of women had maintained their dancing. When the men returned to the circle, men and women all formed a single line. As soon as the fighting finished, one man collected all the dance paraphernalia, the headdresses and sticks, and threw them away in a special heap just below, and out of sight of, the dance ground. This place was now called *amungom*, the ritual rubbish heap.

BETEL THROWING

The dancing continued for about ten minutes, the duration of two songs, during which time the circle reversed its direction a number of times.

At the end of the second song, a senior man stood up and joined the dancers; during the third and last song, he led them to stand in front of the chorus. They danced here, hopping up and down in place until the end of the song, at which time they suddenly stopped and hurled a torrent of betel nut husks into the seated chorus. The chorus and audience discharged a round of betel nut skins back into the crowd of dancers. *Amambua* was now finished.

FOOD DISTRIBUTION

After a rest and respite, including, of course, a betel nut chew, the men began to distribute the food from the display. A portion was given to every woman and single man in the community. Had neighboring communities been invited, they would each have been given a whole *akarum*, food mound, to divide among themselves, but as it was only an in-house event, the two *akarumbim* were divided among all the participants. People made special requests for some of the food items hanging on the scaffolding, and these requests seemed to be readily granted. At about 10:30 in the morning, people gathered up their food shares and left for home.

Framing the Event

Amambua exhibits the clearest ritual structure of any Baining dance. Only *Amambua* seemed to have an external temporal referent in the aboriginal context, as it is associated with the pitpit season.

Pitpit season is seen as an annual marker both because it is a seasonal crop and because it takes a full "year" to grow. The several words for pitpit are synonyms for year: *araik, atavut.* The season extends over several months that coincide well with the Christian calendar, so that if you ask when the pitpit season is, the answer is invariably "from Christmas to Easter." This period also coincides with the onset and duration of the heaviest monsoon season, making a doubly marked period. Pitpit is a valued foodstuff. Although not considered a staple because it does not substitute for taro, Hong Kong taro, tapioca, or sweet potato, it is, nevertheless, considered an excellent accompaniment. Because it is very plentiful during the season, people eat a more varied diet (a staple and a side dish) than they consistently do at other times. Because pitpit substitutes for all other side dishes when it is available, the food display does not include these foodstuffs. I have heard people comment that people get fat during the pitpit season. The food display and construction of the *Amambua* constitute an appreciation of pitpit.

In this ritual, all the food is raw. The display emphasizes its natural state: the taro stalks and leaves are left on the tubers; much of the pitpit is still on its stalk, as is the sugar cane; the yams are unwashed; and the betel nut is still on its branches. None of the food has been transformed into cooked food. While in this form, it may be inhabited by *aios*, who are the natural counterparts of humans in the same way that the food exhibited here is the natural counterpart of cooked food. The difference is that whereas humans eat food and internalize it, *aios* are internalized by the food that they enter. These inverted relationships initiate the dance, but in the course of the dance, the *aios* are transformed into social actors. Only after the dance is the food distributed and transformed into social artifacts.

THE PROCESS

The dance begins when the *aios* are chased off from the food display and dance grounds. This rite of separation is also inverted in the course of the dance because the *aios* later return in the form of dancers. The *aios* abandon the dance area to the humans. The *aios'* counterpart, the wild natural attributes of the food, is symbolically destroyed by smashing some food.

The main phase of *Amambua* is not in any classical sense a period of liminality in Van Gennep's sense (1960). Although opposed to secular events in several ways (e.g., it occurs at night, in a communal place where people sing and dance), the themes of *Amambua* are far from being an-tistructural. In fact, I show that what is enacted represents the patterns and processes of Baining life. Although these patterns and processes are manifested in the idioms of dance, music, and masks, the values they represent are intrinsic to secular as well as ritual life.

The principal phase of *Amambua* is the repetitive dancing in a cir-cle. Even here, however, there is a subtle alternation between uniform dancing around the circle with men and women interspersed in a single line doing the same dance, reversing direction in tandem, and so on, and periods when the sexes form two separate circles and might even be dancing in opposite directions. This pattern seems to parallel the daily life and routine of the Baining; everyday life is represented by a single dance line, while occasions or phases when the division of labor is more marked are represented by the double set of circles, with women and children inside and men on the periphery. Women dance with their arms in a position reminiscent of carrying heavy loads (including children) back from the gardens. The men's position gives them greater freedom of movement, perhaps an indication of their greater movement away from the "place" (village). Women and men equally participate and contribute to the singing.

I have mentioned that newcomers to the dance circle make their entrance behind tree boughs. I was intrigued by this procedure, which called up for me Shakespearean associations of Burnham Wood coming to Dunsinane. Because it was an action ascribed to visitors from other communities, I thought it might well have reference to the mode by which raiding parties approached their targets. Informants denied any such association, however; in fact, they were unable to account for this custom in any other way than by saying it was tradition.

I suggest that this act encapsulates underlying concerns in Baining life, especially that of nature penetrating society. People coming from another community, or coming from the bush rather than the hamlets or gardens are, at least temporarily, outside the social network, and thus not fully social beings. Their marginality is symbolized by branches and boughs from the bush. At first they maintain their separateness as they dance around holding their boughs, but they are gradually assimilated into the social milieu and they throw away the branches and merge with the other dancers.

If the form of *Amambua* represents basic Baining patterns, then the disruptions to the dance suggest intrusions on daily life. *Asingal* may be interpreted in this light. This dance has no overt symbolism; neither its costume, song, nor dance seems representative of any specific belief or idea. Its significance derives from its contrast to the surrounding dance. It is said to "decorate" or dress up *Amambua*. It contrasts with *Amambua* in several ways: it is danced just by men; the men are masked; the dance is done in two lines or scattered about; and only men sing. In all these ways, it embodies a dimension of gender differentiation in Baining life. The relation of *asingal* to *Amambua* is analogous to the relation *Amambua* has to daily life. The performance and preparations for *asingal*, *aioski* and *alamsaka* are done only by the men. While the men engage in *asingal*, the women maintain their steady *Amambua* dancing. This pattern is analogous to the way women continue daily routines while the men make the bush preparations for these dances.

The choreography of the dance contrasts orderly dancing in a double line and sprawling, flailing dance steps scattering the dancers across the dance ground. This mirrors the alternation between patterned social life and more erratic forays into nature or the bush. The song that accompanies the dance recounts the composer's experience of coming upon a place in the bush where a pig had been wallowing in the mud.

Like *asingal*, the other intrusions—mud smearing, feces throwing, and taro eating—all flaunt natural materials untransformed by social actions and behaviors that flout the standard practices and values held by the Baining. The Baining believe that playing in the mud is reminiscent of pig's behavior and they punish children for imitating them (Fajans 1997). Dirt, in general, is associated with nature, cold, and dark. When the mud men smear mud over the dance participants in the middle of the night, nature impinges on each person and encroaches on society.

While only a few people engage in eating feces or raw taro, these acts challenge the basic values of Baining life, which arise from the way food exchange, cooking, and the consumption of food create social bonds. As a medium for social transformations, cooked food is ingested and incorporated into the transforming individual. The practice of eating raw taro and feces inverts this metaphor. Rather than ingesting sociality, the participants are ingesting the obverse.

These middle-of-the-night interruptions represent a cluster of associations (pigs, raw taro, feces, dogs) that are at the margins of society. They occur on the periphery of the dance ground, which evokes their marginal, extrasocial qualities. These liminal and antisocial activities punctuate the relatively mundane, continuous dancing of the women, which occurs in the center of the dance plaza (itself a symbol of the hamlet) and evokes normal, ongoing social life.

Asingal embodies another theme significant among the Baining: the opposition between free-ranging movement and the attraction of the "place." Youths and young married people are those most likely to roam and wander in the bush, while the elders remain in the hamlets. In social terms, these young people are pivoting between two family and domestic groups. They are separating from their old groups, but their new social attachments are not yet fixed. Their capacity for the formation of families and local ties of their own is still in a fluid, potential state, symbolically embodied in their capacity for dynamic, kinetic movement. The transition to full adulthood takes the form of the conversion of this dynamic potential into the fixed attachments to family and "place," on the one hand, and the conversion of the kinetic energy of youthful movement into a magnetic force, as it were, which attracts the less socialized energy of youth to itself, on the other. In the dance, the dance ground appears as a magnetic center that actively attracts elements from the bush (men, *aios*, mud, raw food, feces, etc.) into the "place." The dancers all go out into the bush, and are then "pulled" back to the place by the songs, sung by a stationary chorus of predominantly older people.

This dynamic balance, mimicked in the dance, is threatened when the *aios* dancers arrive in the morning.[6] The term *aios* has many referents: corpses, ghosts, fireflies, lianas, food-inhabiting spirits, and, lastly, dancers. In the dance context, the term *aios* was not associated with deceased ancestors or ghosts, but with a nonhuman agent. This alterity is both produced and represented by the mask and headdress they wear. When the dancers put on this headdress, they either become or are possessed by *aios*. I am not clear which they believe happens because I elicited both answers. When the dancers throw down their headdresses after the fight with ginger whips, they revert to their normal selves. While they are *aios*, they are invested with extraordinary powers such as the ability to cure sickly children.

This power is not only beneficial; in its raw, unchanneled form, it is also dangerous. Those who encounter the *aios* in uncontrolled settings, such as the bush, are subject to serious illness or injury. Some of the power of the *aios* can be harnessed as they enter the dance grounds. Here on the margins between nature and society, their potency can be transformed, controlled, and appropriated. Instead of causing illness, it can be made to cure it. In the interstices between bush and place, the wild, dangerous power becomes metamorphosed into harnessed, beneficial power.

The Baining believe the *aios'* power is contained in their ginger whips. That these sticks embody transformative energy is evidenced by the attribution of hot and cold characteristics to them. For the Baining, heat (e.g., fire) is the transformative agent par excellence. The Baining see mature social actors as people with stores of internal heat (manifested in their ability to sweat), who use this power to transform natural things into social ones (e.g., forests into food or children into social beings). The *aios'* power, their heat, is external to themselves, carried in these ginger whips. As such, it is especially potent because it can be alienated from its possessor. For this reason, it is especially efficacious in curing people.[7] Its alienable quality is even more important during the fight. Here the *aios* fight with mature, social males whose power is internal. When they hit these men, the heat from the sticks leaves the sticks and enters the men. The sticks become cold and the men carry their welts proudly. In exchange, the men also hit the *aios*, and suddenly the *aios'* external heat is internalized. They are no longer natural, cold creatures, but social beings. They throw off their headdresses and become men. Natural beings are transformed into social beings while the men from the place have harnessed additional amounts of natural energy through this fight and are, in turn, socially renewed.

The *aios* arrive spoiling for a fight. The two leaders carry the main Baining aboriginal weapons, the war club and the catapult. The rest of the dancers are armed with ginger sticks. These powerful bush creatures are definitely threatening to society at large. They are met by men, the traditional warriors of Baining society. *Aioski* dancers are thought to be courageous; a number of youths told me they had not performed it because they were scared of the whips. These youths were also not yet full adults.

The idea of renewal emerges in several ways. Although the dance is an enactment of social reproduction, human reproductive powers are in jeopardy during *aioski*. The dance presents an inversion of secular processes. Normally, men use their transformative powers of fire and sweat to transform the bush and other natural things. In the ritual, men harness transformative power from the forest in the form of the ginger sticks. These sticks contain natural heat, symbolized by their explosive properties. When found in the bush and hidden from women, they are hot. Exposure to women makes them cold, which inverts the usual pattern in which women are the guardians of social heat in their role as cooks and reproducers. Women and ginger sticks are antithetical to each other. Each causes the other to lose its power. The *aios* can usurp women's power by "giving birth" not in a natural way as women do, but in a social sense as when ill people are pushed through the legs of the *aios*. Thus, the overlapping roles of women and *aios* are segregated spatially, visually, and sexually, but the processes are analogous. *Aios* and women are incompatible until after the *aios* throw off their masks. The act of whipping serves not only to transform the *aios* into men, but to integrate them with the women.

The *aios* are drawn to the dance plaza by one of the songs. The magnetic, attractive power of society "pulls them." When they reach the margins of the dance ground, they pause and form a double line that metaphorically bridges the bush that they have just left with the place they are entering while embodying the ambiguous duality of their medial position between bush and "place." Here, at the transition between bush and place, the children are pushed under the dancer's legs. The connotation of a new start at this point seems evident, if implicit.[8]

When *aios* enter the dance grounds, they do not join the circle of women already dancing there; rather, they begin their own double circles outside. This spatial pattern emphasizes the structural relationships of inner/outer and center/periphery in a way that a single line, with its connotation of integrated wholeness, would not. Shortly after the *aios* form this double circle, however, unmasked dancers from the audience come up and join them. By pairing one by one with an *aioski*, they produce a quadruple line or circle as they dance around. In effect, the men from the place encompass those from the bush by forming circles both inside and outside of them. These ordered relations become randomized during the fight. Each couple uses the same weapons and the battle alternates back and forth between the two opponents. The outcome is determined, however, and the men unmask the *aios*.

The opposition between *aios* and the undecorated dancers is multiply layered. It encompasses bush and "place," and female and male. The *aios* are referred to in the singular as *aioski*, the feminine version of that word, and the dancers from the place are males.[9] The battle mediates all these oppositions. The *aios* bring out the natural in men by forcing them to fight, but the men conquer nature through this battle and unmask the *aios*, who are thereby transformed into men. The power of the *aios* no longer threatens society but is absorbed by the now socialized dancers. The power that resided in the ginger whips is internalized through the fight and the dancers carry the marks of this transformation in the form of the welts on their skin. After the fight, the *aios* transform from potent, natural creatures to Baining men just like their partners. The men who "tame" the *aios* must be strong social actors. A weak person, one who is sick or too young, may not participate in the fight.

Belief in the potency of the battle was made evident in the discussions surrounding Dauwit's death. Dauwit died quite suddenly a week after he had participated in the dance. Nobody thought that the fight itself had caused his death; rather, they believed that Dauwit had some sort of latent illness or weakness. The *aios'* potency had awoken this sickness when he was whipped, and had caused his death. Only the most fit, mature, socialized people can confront this power. I interpret this to mean either that Dauwit had been unable to "socialize" his natural partner, or he may have been too weak to transform its natural heat into social strength. In any case, he succumbed to natural power.

Aioski enacts a reversal of the life cycle, which progresses from living being to *aioska* (dead person) through a set of transformations that I have described elsewhere (Fajans 1997). In the dance, *aios* are transformed into their full opposites: mature, socialized, male adults. The battle transforms the *aios*, who are cold, natural creatures, into social persons, who are hot and powerful in themselves.

CLOSING THE DANCE

The finale of the dance inverts the rites of separation at the beginning of the event. Throughout, the dance roles and statuses are progressively fragmented: first men are separated from women into different dance circles;

then the *aios* are separated from the village people (the *aios* dancers are part of the group until the early hours of the morning when they go off to change). Only after the *aioski* fight does everybody come together and dance in a single circle. A single circle overcomes the divisions, epitomizing social unity in which everybody is in the same position relative to everyone else, and space is divided into only two domains: inside social space and outside it. The dancers have reconstituted the spatial coordinates of their cultural order; the inside representing the "place," the locus of the socially transformed, and the outside representing the bush. The margins between the two are demarcated by social beings who contain within themselves the power to create these transformations. They create them in daily life by socializing children and in ritual life by socializing ghosts.

This act of integration achieved, the dance has returned to its point of origin and it is time to close. The rite of closure is apt, since it is a symbolic reversal of the normal act of social greeting: betel nut exchange.[10] During the last song, the circle breaks up and all of the dancers gather in front of the chorus, shifting from foot to foot to the music. On the last note, they throw betel nut husks (which they have surreptitiously gathered and secreted prior to the end) into the seated chorus. The singers respond by also hurling them. Betel nut is usually exchanged in a relatively formal way, governed by rules of politeness and respect. One must offer betel in a gentle and respectful way from one person to another. To invert this process by (1) exchanging husks and not whole nuts (the residue and not the substance), (2) doing it en masse and not individually, and (3) hurling them and not handing them gently constitute the inversions of this rite. That the exchange comes at the end of the dance and not at the beginning of a social encounter further inverts its meaning.

Amambua conforms to the classic pattern of rituals of passage (Van Gennep 1960). It is set off from profane time by the chasing off of the *aios* to open the dance and the throwing of betel husks to close it. These acts can be interpreted respectively as rites of separation and reintegration. The act of chasing off the *aios* initiates a whole string of events that ultimately results in the *aios*, with their connotations of ghosts, spirits, and extrasocial power, being incorporated into society. The completion of this process is signaled by inverted greeting behavior. By inverting the ritual to initiate a social relationship, the dancers are symbolizing its opposite, the closing of relations with asocial, natural beings and powers. This rude farewell to the defeated and co-opted *aios* marks the point at which the ritual celebrants, newly empowered with the force they have transferred to themselves from the *aios*, return to normal daily life.

Aios are an important category for the Baining. *Aios* are corpses, ghosts, fireflies, bush spirits, lianas, creatures that inhabit food displays, and dancers. They represent, in effect, not a single entity but a category of beings opposed in specific ways to fully social persons. As such, they are a residual category. In this dance, we have seen several types of *aios* and several beings who, although not designated as *aios*, are structurally similar to them as inversions of normal social beings; for example, mud men and those who eat raw taro and feces. The *aios* first appear as inhabitants of the food display from which they are expelled, and later reappear as dancers. The Baining deny any equation of the two, but we can see that they fill similar symbolic roles. The food-inhabiting *aios* are opposed to their human counterparts in two ways. The first is that they "go inside" the food displays, instead of the food going inside them. Human agents do not share substance with raw food at all, but rather act upon it and transform it by harvesting and cooking it prior to taking it inside themselves. The second way is that in which the substance is shared. The food displays seem to retain their form and substance despite the incorporation of the *aios*, whereas human beings incorporate food but retain their own size and shape. Humans act on and transform their food internally while the *aios* cannot do this. The *aios* can also be separated (expelled) from their food homes, whereas once people have eaten the food, it becomes inseparable from themselves except when eliminated in the form of feces, which may be another association between the events. After the *aios* are expelled, they are relegated to the bush. But this exile occurs just before nightfall during which time the boundaries between bush and place are most permeable. The performance of the dance at night inverts the normal cycle of Baining activity. In this inverted time, people also act in inverted ways; they wallow in mud or eat raw taro and feces, behavior we have seen previously to be suggestive of pigs, madmen, and dogs. The patterns of inversion and reversal bind all of these aspects.

DISTRIBUTION AND DISPERSION

After audience and participants have reacclimated themselves to normal time through conversation and betel nut chewing, the food distribution, the final act of the dance, takes place. The food, all raw garden produce, is from the food display. A portion of food is given to every family (in care of the wife/mother) and to every unmarried adult old enough to be able to transform it from its raw to its cooked state (i.e., everyone above puberty). The food, however, is not cooked or eaten collectively, but instead is carried back to households and consumed by individual social units. This way of distributing the food parallels and underscores the normative, processes through which adolescents and adults transform natural into social products by their own labor. In *Amambua,* the food is contributed by family units and is returned to family units; in the interim, however, it shares in a collective display. It thus mirrors the activities of the people themselves. The food was not only publicly assembled, it was elaborately displayed and then exchanged during the distribution. Just as people do not take home what they had brought, they do not themselves go home just as they came. Because food giving and taking is at the heart of Baining sociality, as the process by which the social household unit is created, the final ritual food exchange, is, in a sense, the constitution of society at an even more encompassing level. *Amambua* is one of the very few communitywide activities, and even here relations are mediated by food bonds. The creation of the food display and its final dispersion brackets the period in which broad social cooperation occurs. Food once again frames social relationships, in this instance on a communitywide basis. The distribution of the food into individual packets signals the return to the household level of organization at the end of communal ritual.

Conclusion

Jane Goodale concludes *To Sing With Pigs Is Human* with the remark, "[T]he task I set for myself in writing this book was to convey the complexity and meaning of the symbols with which the Kaulong communicate to each other the essence of meaningful, human life in the forests and clearings of this world" (1995: 246). In a different part of New Britain, with a different set of rituals, I too found myself seeking to interpret and make accessible the meaning of Baining activities and symbols. This task was difficult because the Baining do not use words to explicate the values of their cultures and social relations. The Baining enact their social values and cosmological principles in symbolic ritual acts for which they are unable to provide verbal exegesis. Only by viewing the ritual in conjunction with the activities of everyday life can the meanings of these dances become apparent. The dance may be set apart from everyday life, but it is not conceptually isolated. Rather, it is a time when the fundamental structuring principles of the social order are manipulated, jeopardized, and renewed. The Baining conceptualize the life cycle as a process from natural being to social actor and then back to nature again. This progression, especially the latter half, manifests itself as an entropic process because the Baining do not have overt beliefs about reversing the process of aging and dying. The dances, however, introduce the possibility of reversal, as *aios* are transformed back into living social beings. The dances thus represent the perpetuation of social life through constant renewal.

At the beginning of my fieldwork among the Baining, I felt bereft of models for interpreting their culture and social organization. They did not seem to fit within the Melanesian complex of gender, exchange, initiation, or leadership. Only by looking beyond the concrete models of Melanesian societies to the themes that impelled and motivated the various practices I had read about could I find resources for understanding my own material. The ethnographic and analytical examples that I first learned from Jane at Bryn Mawr became the principles that guided me through my own initiation into the ranks of Melanesian specialists. I am deeply aware of this debt.

Notes

1. Although parts of *Amambua* have been performed intermittently over the last couple of decades in Lan, the full ceremony had not been done for years. People in their mid-thirties in 1977 had never seen the food display constructed, nor had they seen the mud throwers participate in the event. The last major performance (without the food display) had been in 1960 (dated by a man who had gone into the police force just afterwards). The performance I witnessed in 1977 was undoubtedly catalyzed by my presence and inquiries about the custom, but it was quickly seized upon by several elders in the community as an important occasion at which the younger members of the community could learn their own traditions. On account of this increasing enthusiasm, the performance grew and more aspects were included than had originally been planned. According to my informants in 1991 this was also the last major performance of *Amambua*. By 1991 many of the elders who directed the activities I include here had died, and others did not feel comfortable enough to perpetuate them.

2. Pitpit is grown from a segment of stalk of a mature plant. When a plant is harvested, the stalk is immediately replanted in a new garden where it bears fruit the following year. There are numerous varieties of pitpit, some maturing earlier, in December, and others successively coming into fruit until the season ends in the middle of April. The *Amambua* performance I saw was done in late April.

3. While the *akarum* is thought to be like a chicken and share its attributes, it should be pointed out that chickens are not indigenous to the area, so it seems possible that the form of the *akarum* was reinterpreted in light of the new referent of chickens. Such an explanation would explain how the image of a hen sitting on her eggs could be juxtaposed with the distinction between the male and female heaps (since roosters do not sit on eggs). Perhaps the visual metaphor has taken predominance over whatever indigenous symbolism there might have been.

4. The heaviness is related to that of *awumbuk*, a sense of lassitude experienced

by people who have been left behind by those they have been living and socializing with. Here, it is said to be left behind by the *aios* who have departed.

5. Informants argued among themselves as to whether this had in fact occurred; no one had seen it, but the more enthusiastic informants said it had been done, and they are supported by Rascher. Neither the mud smearing nor the fecal acts had been performed by recent generations until this episode of mud smearing which was stimulated by my inquiries.

6. The description of the chorus "pulling" the *aios* to the dance ground reminded me of informants' descriptions of domesticated pigs in heat "pulling" wild male pigs to the hamlets. I think there is an analogy here between domesticated and wild creatures but it is one that I doubt any Baining would have formulated by his or her self.

7. It can be detached from one agent and affixed to another.

8. The only other instance where I heard of an analogous behavior to that of pushing children under the dancers' legs was when informants described the remedy for an infant who cries incessantly. In this case, the child is pushed through a hole in the bamboo matting of a house wall. This act is clearly symbolic of rebirth since the house is analogous to the womb (the womb is called "the house of the child"). When the child emerges from the house it is like being reborn. Passing through the dancers' legs is also symbolic of birth.

9. Most Baining words have arbitrary gender endings, but those which refer to people or animals take either the masculine or the feminine ending depending on whether they have a male or female referent. Thus, *aioski* refers to a female corpse, for instance, while *aioska* refers to a male one. The fact that this dance is called *aioski* does not appear arbitrary.

10. The Baining exchange betel nut and pepper as a form of handshake or greeting. Whenever people encounter each other on the path, in the gardens, at a meeting or when visiting, they formally give and receive betel.

JANE C. GOODALE

Conclusion: What Is
Ethnography? Is It Real?

An aboriginal artist standing behind a potential buyer
of his work answered her question "Is it real Aboriginal
art?" with a question of his own: "Am I real?" It is in this
context that I speak to you tonight.

A few years ago, as Ward Goodenough and I stood watching
people in the lobby of the anonymous hotel chosen by the American
Anthropological Association for its annual meetings, I turned to Ward
and remarked, "It's funny, but I don't see any of the Old Guard here.
Where are they all?" Ward turned to me and dryly remarked, "You and
I, Jane, are the Old Guard." I was shocked and inwardly rejected this
characterization, but I find my sense of historical perspective causes my
blood pressure to rise and a protest also to rise in my throat when someone pronounces: "Ethnography is not real. There is no such thing as an
ethnographic fact!"—a dismissal of all who not only practice but value
it, as a personal and professional worldview or cultural charter. Indeed,
I wonder whether these disclaimers understand that many of us believe
there is a culture of ethnography. And history has shown us that cultures
are notoriously hard to get rid of except by genocide.

It was at the annual ASAO meetings in Asilomar, California (in the
'70s), that I first came to hear that some at the meeting were contending
that ethnography was old fashioned or worse. My students, not yet labeled

*[Editors' note: This concluding chapter was first presented as a Distinguished
Lecture at the 1994 annual ASAO meetings. Jane has partially edited this
talk and updated it with a postscript.]*

as members of the Bryn Mawr Mafia, told me that they were getting negative vibes when they told people that they were going into the field to *do*
ethnography. I advised them to forget what others said, that for at least
as long as I lived, ethnography was not obsolete or dead. Many of these
former students are now tenured professors who continue to demonstrate
the validity of my words while they make ever more significant advances
in the practice and teaching of ethnography. Long live the Mafia!

After a lecture on mission contact in the Pacific, a student asked me
why I was down on missionaries, when I had been preaching all semester
about a new religion called anthropology? He was right, of course; I do
believe, and I sometimes preach. I am very well aware that I may be seen
to preach here tonight to a room already filled with many believers.

The Association for Social Anthropology in Oceania was founded
on the principle that description and comparison is as much a conjoined
pair as is participant observation. Comparison is, I am sure we all agree,
only as good as the description, and that comparison is better served by
controlling the parameters—in our case, limiting our data and comparisons to Pacific cultures.

In the early years of ASAO, a recurrent protest was that it took too
long to go through the association's ideal three-year plan of *informal*
topical roundtable discussions followed in the second year by *working*
discussions, where analysis of data was presented and compared, and
finally, in the third year, followed by a *formal symposium* in which an
increasing theoretical refinement of topic is worked out prior to publication. I shall not reiterate the arguments—suffice it to say that there was
a feeling among the junior members that the ASAO process of comparison just took too long and some among the participants felt that their
data and its interpretation stood better alone than among others and
perhaps also that comparative ethnography is worthless, or even that it
is impossible to do.

I suggested at some point in this multiyear debate that perhaps we
should publish our data separately and then come together to nut out the
interesting points for comparison and by doing so attempt to further the
understanding of the particular topic in more general and theoretical terms.
Needless to say, this was not taken up as an agreed-upon procedure.

However, like the successfully plodding tortoise, ASAO and I have
maintained our faith in the ethnographic process of description and comparison. Long live ASAO!

In presenting my thoughts today, I have been stimulated by nonbe-
lievers who write statements such as the following:

[This work] is . . . not an ethnography. One of its major premises is that the ethnographic era of anthropology, an era marked by the excision of Societies from their historical contexts, is behind us—we may hope never to return. . . . [The author goes on to define ethnography]: Ethnographic practice provides empirical support for the theoretical justification of ideologies that tolerate—while claiming not to advocate—segregation of that "Other" world. This is accomplished through Ethnography's pre-figured finding that "other" peoples lie at some point several degrees removed from a Euro-American standard." (Wilmsen 1989: xiii)

Raising my voice I yell, "That's not me at all!"

Close to this (in my book of horrors) is the postmodernist habit of dedicating the first half of a talk, paper, or chapter of a book to burying all who disagree with their approach, which is followed by a lauding of the Politically Correct Guru with whom they studied or wish they had. Only after this exorcism and name-dropping do we come to the presentation of data and its analysis. This is a habit based, I am sure, on the erroneous assumption that there are only a few sacred texts written by even fewer high priests who will damn you to the underworld if you don't mention their name(s) and latest works.

I was recently told by a young colleague that while my forthcoming Kaulong monograph (*To Sing With Pigs Is Human*, 1995) was very interesting, I hadn't mentioned Foucault, even in a footnote. Having read Foucault and found nothing pertinent to the analysis at hand, I asked, "Why should I?" and was told that no one will read my work if I didn't. Sometimes these erroneous names and comments escape to the footnotes. I wonder if Ward remembers telling me that I couldn't write a whole dissertation with absolutely no footnotes. That's right: 350 pages without a footnote. I felt that everything that needed saying was in the text and things not worth saying shouldn't be—and furthermore, since I hate interrupting my reading of texts to hunt for nonessential name-dropping, I would spare others this annoyance. When Ward said he would write some for me, I (still the student) said "thank you very much," and so the three footnotes in the original *Tiwi Wives* came into being.

I have never really figured out to whom footnotes are addressed. I think perhaps that many of them are only of interest to those whose names are mentioned there. When I find myself relegated to a footnote, I do not feel very honored.

A friend of mine has written a poetic-pair of what she calls "foot-notes." The first, written in 1947, is entitled *A Metaphysical Plea to My Illustrious Mentors* (Hatcher 1972) and goes:

> I know I must follow your footsteps
> Before I can stand on your shoulders—
> But must you tread such a tortuous path
> Through the brush and the mud and the boulders?

In 1970, in *To Students of a Later Day*, she asks (Hatcher 1972: 293):

> You reach demanding for the stars
> Standing on others' shoulders
> Scorning the effort to follow the path
> Through the brush and the mud and the boulders
> You may have superior insight
> You may have superior wit
> But when you stand on the shoulders of others
> The least you can do is not shit!

I couldn't have said it better myself!

In approaching this talk I am following the advice of others and talking about what I know best. I begin by discussing what I see in *my* mirror—how I came to be the kind of ethnographer that I am. I follow with an example of ethnographic insight that I believe is a light which, if not at the end of the tunnel, at least lights a possible entrance. In the concluding section, I throw out a challenge which has fascinated me for a number of years as perhaps an idea good to think with.

I will state at the outset that I believe ethnography is as relevant to anthropology as the biologist's microscope or the astronomer's telescope. Increasing refinement of technology is, of course, as necessary and as impossible to halt as phonetic drift. But let us not throw out the baby even when the bathwater is muddy with multiple use and the baby has become a politically incorrect dinosaur. Can we not use an evolutionary model of theoretical change rather than a catastrophic one? Or perhaps chaos is the name of culture.

What I See in My Mirror

I began my training as an ethnographer under C. S. Coon, who not only coauthored our introductory text book *Principles of Anthropology* (Chapple and Coon 1942) but vividly lectured us about other peoples and other times and also about ourselves. We studied simple and complex cultures. Once he and Patrick Putnam, visiting from researching the Ituri Pigmy, led us as we participated in an elephant hunt down the halls of Radcliffe. Picture, if you will, Coon, the trumpeting elephant, being chased by forty Pigmy women screaming in culturally correct accent and volume to where Patrick Putnam lay in wait with his spears hidden under his very long beard. I remember hearing how cold-adapted Yaghan women had to swim the chilly waters of the Cape of Good Hope because their men couldn't cope with the cold. We also learned that Yaghans have type B blood rather than type O (because it came from the missionary Bridges?). Coon lectured from his analysis of the Bible as a model of culture change, describing a Near Eastern herding peoples as they evolved to become the commercial producers and traders of the Near East. We learned that the Rif of North Africa have blue eyes and the Tuareg, blue veils. We studied bodily mutilation around the world together with coiled basket types and modes of processing food, including cooking without matches or pots. This is, of course, anthropological trivia and I am sure we could all contribute to a challenging trivia game. But more important, these were data and facts. They didn't need interpretation. They didn't need a reality check.

My whole undergraduate experience with anthropology between 1944 and 1948 was filled with a dedication to the accumulation of data: data which does not go out of style or become post- or pre- something other than Neolithic, or horse. We received much of it in lectures, rather more than we did in the hours spent in the reserve rooms of libraries reading assignments from large hardbacked monographs. Outside of class, I spent two years as an honors tutee under Coon and read one classic monograph after another. This was the prepaperback period of ethnography. Monographs were far too expensive for any mere student to buy. Because we couldn't buy, we couldn't underline or highlight (even if the means had been invented). This was the take-your-own notes-or-suffer period of ethnographic learning.

In particular I remember People of Siberia taught by Dimitri Shimkin. In lecture, and reading, we spent seven weeks learning about reindeer physiology, salmon mating cycles, movement of ice flows, ranges of lemmings, rabbits, bears, etc., and their position in the food chain. These were facts gathered from a diversity of scientific sources. How important they were became known to us after the midterm quiz, when we first met the people and learned how they fit into, adapted, and altered their Arctic world.

This was also the A.P.E. period of anthropology at Harvard. Archaeology, Physical, and Ethnography went together, very often in the same course and taught by the same professor, and intended to give us data pertinent to our common inquiry: Who are these people, from where did they come, to whom are they related, and how have they adapted or changed over the period for which we have data?

While we lived, breathed, and studied facts, data, we were encouraged to speculate where there were no facts Often this challenge came in final examinations when we were not told *how* to speculate, or—in today's terms—what was legitimate or politically correct, only that we should *try*. We were even told that our speculation might well be better than the professors. How refreshing!

We were of course expected to know the difference between fact and speculation. This attitude toward anthropological education was one which I welcomed with open arms. I constructed humongous charts where millenniums of time met unbounded geographical space, in which I placed all my known facts color-coded for numerous factors; I had fun as I walked the length of the chart and speculated on questions which might be asked. The very process of chart construction on many feet of shelf paper had the desired effect of ordering my mental processes as facts became detached and reattached from time and space and recombined with each new line of thought I conceived. Sometimes I had success in meeting an examination question with a bit of scientific fiction to avoid terminal boredom with only facts. It seem to be a more interesting way to combine facts with speculation. It was later when Freddy de Laguna told me how she decides what to put in her field notes—"everything I need in order to write a novel"—that I felt legitimated.

The year after I graduated from Harvard, I attended my first AAA meeting in New York where G. P. Murdock defended his discussion of the *deme* [editors' note: the term refers to an endogamous local kin group] to a general session audience. *Social Structure* (1949) had just been published and was presented to me as the first attempt to scientifically (read quantitatively) compare societies and by doing so to advance our knowledge about the nature of human society. Some days now I recall the misery this book gave to me as a graduate student by telling my own students how I achieved mastery of his classification of societies on the basis of descent, cousin terminology, and residence—reciting the key: *Every happy young fox goes down south or never is cold* [editors' note: the key refers to Murdock's classification of different types of social organization such as "Eskimo," "Hawaiian," "Yuman," and "Fox"]. Of course, no one has ever asked me a question to which this is the answer, but I find it usually gets a laugh from the class; perhaps someday a pertinent question will present itself.

In the '80s, Murdock spoke at a meeting of the Philadelphia Anthropological Society and touched us all when he said he thought his life's work had been in vain and that the future was in better descriptive ethnography. I believe that it was because Murdock *tried* to compare societies scientifically that the descriptions were ultimately found to be inadequate or incomplete and ethnography was thus advanced into a new level of descriptive precision.

Murdock realized that one of the problems with descriptions up to that time was the lack of uniformity in use of social organization terminology. Thus in the first part of his *Social Structure* he attempted to standardize this terminology. It pains me to find that few modern ethnographers even think this is still a problem and gaily go on using terms without definition. Some, I feel, consider definition to be only a theoretical problem rather than an indispensable tool for description and comparison.

My problem with Murdock's standardization crept up on me without my conscious knowledge. It is so simplistic today that it is hard to realize how odd it was in the late fifties.

As students, we are required to be original preferably both in data acquisition and in its presentation. It took me more than two years after I returned from the Tiwi to hit on the cute if experimental approach of using a female ego through which I would describe Tiwi society. I did not fully realize the impact that this little twist of the kaleidoscope would make.

One of the big issues of the day in the early 1960s was cross-cousin marriage and the hunt for patrilateral marriage (male ego). (The question of course changes with a female ego). Tiwi women told me they could marry anyone, meaning either type of cross cousin and from any descent group other than their own, but it was better to marry FZS. What does "better" mean? I found that it didn't mean preferential.

Tiwi women married men at least twenty years their senior in their first prepubescent marriage. I asked myself, what does a twenty-year age difference mean? Without going into the formula at this time, take it from me, that it meant that her FZS-husband would be twenty years older than his MBD-wife, while her MBS-husband would be twenty years younger than his FZD-wife. Naturally, I reasoned, she had to marry a FZS-husband first as her MBS would not yet be born. At the other end of her life, her last husband would likely be a MBS since her all her FZS would likely be dead.

But more interesting pictures came into view. For example, why did Tiwi continually refer to "father's father" as "my dead FF"? Were there no living FF? When I calculated that a FF would likely be eighty years senior to ego, the picture became clearer and much more interesting analytically.

One continually fascinating question remaining in my mind is: What are the ramifications of the fact that within the same historic time frame in Aboriginal society, women will cycle through four generations (twenty years each) while men will cycle through only two generations (forty years each)? This occurs whether there are two, four, or eight categories, sections, divisions. Aboriginal social structure still presents fascinating and empirical challenges to those who will be challenged. In 1986, when I was last in Australia, I had the opportunity of meeting Frederick Rose, who "discovered" the age-difference factor among the Groote Eylande Aboriginal society and published it just as I was presenting my thesis. We both felt that there were many fascinating, important, and as-yet unexplored issues resulting from this age difference. Perhaps someone besides me will rediscover the significance of the age-difference factor in human society. Perhaps it is already here as just the other day the media was full of the news that postmenopausal Euro-American women are becoming first-time mothers and speculated on the cultural and social implications. A few pointed out that when elderly men become first-time fathers, no one thinks it newsworthy.

Who Is Watching Whom in Participant Observation.

An African American freshman student told me a few weeks into the fall semester many years ago that her mother and aunties had taught her that whenever she moved into another culture, the very first things she must do is to observe and learn who is friends with who, who is the leader, and who the follower. In other words, learn the covert social structure. This information her family mentors told her was essential to her survival. While this girl never took an anthropology course, she was unconsciously using participant observation and had in short order acquired an understanding of the social structure of her college universe, which amazed me.

I have come to realize that participant observation can be—and perhaps always is—a two-way street. In a hunter-gatherer symposium attended by both observed and observers, I suggested that our informants were probably doing ethnography among us as we did our study of them. In the back of the room I saw the whole row of Prominent Aboriginal Observers all vigorously nodding their heads.

A good proof of this is the movement of Aboriginal people into the business and management world of whites. While the whites were for decades training them to be blue-collar workers, the Aboriginals were learning how to behave like white managers from both honest and dishonest models. With some degree of self-determination, now they have set up businesses where they hire whites to do the work (reasoning that they already know how) while the ownership and profits remain in Aboriginal hands and in a business relationship where if they wish they can go fishing.

While these examples show that it can be done, I think we are wrong to consider that the method of participant observation can best be used without prior instruction. Teaching participant observation requires that one can objectify it, and this is indeed difficult but not impossible. When I was setting off into my first fieldwork, I was told by all that I should already know what to do with all that ethnography I had studied in the classroom.

I had, in fact, only learned one useful lesson in the classroom. After working with a Navajo linguistic informant for many hours, I exclaimed in proud discovery, "I think Navajo language has only four vowels!" Surprised, my informant said, "Is that what you wanted to know? Why didn't you just ask me? I learned that in grammar school." The lesson—informants know more than you. When in doubt, ask.

Before going to Melville Island, I had occasion to visit Stanner in Canberra, who asked me what I planned to study. I truthfully answered, "I have no idea." If he was justifiably shocked and horrified, he didn't shove me out the door but patiently over the next two days took pains to tell me what to look for, how to ask questions, and how to recognize and recover from culture shock. He also cautioned me to dress properly. As I said good-bye, he said, "You know, you really are well trained."

"But my trainers couldn't or wouldn't tell me what you just have," I said as I thanked him.

Strangely, he denied giving me this valuable advice many years later, claiming that he strongly held the belief that no one can teach another how to do ethnography—you just have to go do it.

In many respects, I agree with Stanner. You cannot ride a bicycle or swim by reading a book. My real instruction came in the field under the tutelage of the remarkable Australian legendary man of the Bush—Bill Harney (Bilarny to his friends). Bill was hired to help the NGS Expedition led by C. P. Mountford. He had spent his lifetime living with Aboriginal peoples. I'll never forget how he got the Tiwi to discuss totemic sibs with us by spinning a tale about his own totem, the bilarny stone, and that mine was a keg of grog, filled with very good ale. The Aborigines laughed and thought it a great joke and then proceeded to tell us theirs but made pains to tell us theirs were real. But the real benefit was that I, like Bill, was now considered as a human being, as an equal and as one who had a sense of humor. I also began looking into my own culture for other perhaps more real parallels.

For more than twenty years at Bryn Mawr College I have been teaching field methods as a requirement for senior majors. It is a full-year
course. Originally it was conceived as an opportunity for them to use
what they had learned of other cultures in studying their own.

Each student begins in September by finding a site and informants, in
observing and interviewing—and participating as much as other school
obligations will permit. They design a research proposal complete with
topic, theoretical focus, citing pertinent literature, and including appropriate methods and strategies by Christmas break. This is followed by
more intensive gathering of data, its analysis and presentation in April as
an original contribution to anthropology and a senior thesis with honors
if meriting a 4.0.

My colleague Phil Kilbride and I find ourselves continually challenged
by the task. We have learned that not all majors can do ethnographic
fieldwork, but not why this is so. We are quite sure, however, that grades
alone will not predict success. What prepares one student to succeed and
another to fail at the gate? I think it is safe to say that not all graduate
students can do ethnographic field research even when they excel in the
classroom.

For some the test comes in the field, and perhaps the most obvious
problem is a cultural mismatch, such as sending a gregarious city dweller
to live with isolated small groups and vice versa. I know I would never
survive in an urban study in the USA.

But let us take this a step further. What is a match? I surely do not
mean that only a woman can study women, gay or lesbian only gay or
lesbian, an African another African culture. I remember hearing someone
ask a feminist, "Do you want sympathy or objectivity by proscribing the
study of your culture by others?" I am afraid that this self-serving attitude
is prevailing more and more in the field of anthropology. In a course on
the Anthropology and Biology of Gender Difference which I cotaught with
a biologist, a student accused me, I think rightly, of being antifeminist
because I included very little feminist literature in the reading.

I believe that a certain amount of sympathetic empathy must exist
in order to carry out an ethnographic study. Cultural empathy has, I
believe, little to do with similarity of cultural background—bur rather
with the ability to connect on some level of human understanding.

Once while hunting with my thirty-year-old Tiwi son Albert, we
(he) killed a mother possum in whose pouch was a hairless marsupial
fetus. Albert refused to kill the orphaned fetus when I, feeling sorry for
its plight, demanded that he do it. He answered that he could not. When
I finally asked him why not, he replied, "Because I am too sorry for it." I

have frequently returned to this exchange over the years as debates over rights to life and death occupy us in our own culture.

Empathy is needed in the analysis and description as well as field-work. We all know the moment when we returned from our first field-work and said, to ourselves at least, now what do I do with all this data, even when I know it is not complete?

My technique, which I have passed on to students, is to begin typing and adding to the field notes what Sanjek calls headnotes, being all those items lodged in the mind, but never written down (Sanjek 1990).

I tell my students to begin to classify them and if necessary re-sort notes into these categories and to keep devising new categories. What I suggest is exactly how I learned to handle cultural data as an undergradu-ate, but I had to relearn it as a graduate student. I also tell my students that I bet they will never finish the task because they will find "their thesis" in this process. "If you have enough data, let your mind go free (of preconceived models) to do the analysis." It is clear that I believe in and teach the primacy of the inductive method, considering deduction a device to prove what induction has revealed to you.

A former student, in presenting as a term paper a structural analysis of a myth published by L. L. Warner, concluded with the statement that the Murngin (an Australian Aboriginal group) believe they are yams and seagulls. This was long after I had published *Tiwi Wives* (1971) and in fact when my mind was fully engaged in analysis of my Kaulong data. But her conclusion resonated with me and I told her I believe the Tiwi also think they are yams, but I don't know why, and I am not quite sure about the seagulls.

I first saw a *kulama* ceremony in 1954 shortly after our arrival on Melville Island. This is an annual three-day ritual during which a toxic yam called *kulama* is dug, soaked, cooked, mashed, soaked, and finally eaten. During these three days, initiated men and their wives and children are engaged in the singing as composers, helpers, listeners. My original description showed that there was little variation in the ritual from one described by Baldwin Spencer fifty years previously. Spencer thought that it was an initiation ceremony and that there was obviously a connec-tion between initiate and yam. In 1954, I wrote that I thought that the *kulama* ceremony was also a health-giving ritual, perhaps related to the toxic yam as a famine food. All other observers of this ritual have writ-ten that it was their feeling that there was much more to this ceremony than just initiation.

In 1980, just prior to returning to the Tiwi, I wrote a paper for a sym-posium on resource management and quite unwittingly found myself reconceptualizing the *kulama* ceremony and I followed an apparently random path of data recombination that astonished me. The pattern of reasoning was regenerative in that I was constantly led into new areas whose connectedness was only at that moment revealed. What my mind was able to do was to re-sort my headnotes, field notes, and published notes into some very new combinations.

This successful process is one which I often compare to finding the right thread when undoing a hem: The right thread frees the entire hem while the wrong allows only snippets of thread to come free.

In this particular instance, my new description of the *kulama* showed the ceremony to be of even greater importance than any observer had expected. The information-rich performance with its key symbol the *kulama* yam symbolically encoded the complex Tiwi dreaming, giving meaning to progression from unborn to living to deceased, and showing the complex complementary gendered responsibility for this maintaining this law.

I was excited with my new understanding, but quite reasonably wondered if I had not rendered my own reality rather than that of the Tiwi. Fortunately, I shortly returned to Tiwi land. While en route I gave a talk at the Aboriginal Institute in Canberra. Afterwards, an Aboriginal woman came to thank me for the talk, and I pressed on her my question, "Did what I say sound Aboriginal?" "Oh yes," she replied, "Give this talk to the Tiwi and I am sure they will tell you, 'That's what we've been trying to tell you all along' or perhaps they will say, 'That's what Tiwi is all about.'"

I did present my exegesis to the Tiwi in due course. In the morning after my discussion with a group of Tiwi men and women, a delegation of women came to me and told me that I had kept them awake all night. "Why?" I asked. "Well, we were talking about you. We decided that you were a very wise woman." They clearly indicated that I had put into words that which they only ritually express. But just so I didn't get a big head, they said that I didn't have it all right—and we then went on discussing a few of the peripheral arguments.

If my understanding of the *kulama* is right (and I am persuaded that it is), then how did I do it? For years I periodically asked myself why should hunting and gathering Tiwi see themselves as yams. (I even briefly thought that perhaps they were displaced Melanesianists!) I can now argue that they are not only yams but also seabirds and that this whole is encoded in the *kulama* rituals. What I had done was not reduce the complex to the simple, but I found a logical path through the complexity.

Could I replicate the process with different data in different contexts?

With the Kaulong of West New Britain, first cultural principles eluded me from the beginning. Like playing *Jeopardy*, I struggled to find the right questions to their cultural solutions to life. At times, finding cultural empathy seemed very far away, while at the same time, a challenge. Ann Chowning and I often thanked our lucky stars that our Passismanua [Census Division] fieldwork among the Sengseng and Kaulong of West New Britain was not our first fieldwork, or we might have fled.

My paternal grandfather taught me the game of poker when I was aged eight or ten with the excuse to my mother that it might be useful to me someday. It was! Kaulong seemed to be a society in which total anarchy prevailed, where gossip and lies were expected and sanctioned, where nothing was as it seemed, and where people preferred to live alone in peace, or at the most in the company of one or two others. Kaulong compete with shells, song, and spears; sex is lethal for men; and women are strangled by their brothers when their husbands die. I finally concluded they played life like a game of poker.

With a model I gained some degree of understanding, but I do not think I have yet pulled the right thread. In press is a monograph (1995) which combines prior analyses I have worked out over the past twenty years in various ASAO symposia, and others in different venues, and some newly formatted. I have hung it all on a clothesline of Kaulong concepts of humanness, since I believe being human is the winning poker hand. It looks pretty good. It compares well with other monographs of Melanesian cultures. I think I have come to describe Kaulong culture with data which is comparable to other cultures. But I am not convinced that I have captured Kaulong culture the way I was able to do with Tiwi.

On the other hand, I believe, I may yet be able to find the right thread as I *continue* to twist the kaleidoscope (and mix metaphors) using my field notes and headnotes, stimulated by analyses and data from cognate cultures.

Of course, I don't have all the facts on Kaulong. With four visits within twelve years I have gained an information-rich picture within a bounded time period. With the Tiwi, I have also made four visits but over a thirty-five-year time span, which gives me also an information-rich body of data but different in nature from that I have of Kaulong. Is it necessary, or even possible, to know another culture fully? I don't believe it is, but I do believe there is a critical mass of data which is necessary before description can have intrinsic validity and usefulness—by which I mean the description would be verified by more than a few members of that culture as being in empathy with their understanding.

And Finally—Chaos

The first time I met chaos theory, I felt a strong if strange attraction. In the hard sciences, the theory has had an uphill battle for acceptance but I realize I am not alone in attempting to find a fit with anthropology. The science of Culture (capital C) has been out of vogue throughout the most recent modern and postmodern period. But if each formulation was lacking in supplying answers, they have all, in their time, posed important new questions.

Sometime during the '80s, the television series *Nova* had a program on chaos theory. It twanged a chord deep within me which has resonated ever since. Two years ago, a mathematical friend loaned me John Gleick's book *Chaos* (1987) which she insisted I would understand. Like many books, it sat at the edge of my desk with many others waiting for me to pick it up and read it. When I was approached with the request to give this talk, I opened it. After only one reading in the short period available, I cannot say that I fully comprehend nonlinear models and fractals, but I remain intrigued. I have also learned that at the AAA meetings in San Francisco, there was a symposium applying chaos to anthropology and two papers were given by Melanesianists. I have heard that it has been applied to Aboriginal concepts of dreaming (by Nugget Coombs), and a colleague in archaeology interested in the history of food is also attracted to chaos. We agreed that one of the most compelling aspects of chaos is its requirement for enormous amounts of data: "Fractal processes [those beautiful spirals within spirals] are information rich" (Gleick 1987: 293).

Perhaps the difficulty we have had in linking theory to data is that the data we have been collecting just cannot be compared using lineal models. Are cultures nonlinear systems? According to Gleick, "Nonlinear systems, unlike linear systems, seem beyond classification . . . each different from every other. . . . Scientists might begin to suspect that they shared common properties, but when it came to make measurements and perform calculations each non-linear system was a world unto itself" (Gleick 1987: 153).

When we compare cultures, our comparison is most often focused on one or a few related aspects arguing that whole cultures are not comparable. However, Gleick says, "Non-linear systems cannot be taken apart and put together again. They cannot be solved, they cannot be added together. In fluid and mechanical systems the non-linear terms tend to be the features that people want to leave out when they try to get a good, simple understanding" (Gleick 1987: 23–24).

In anthropology we have discovered that the so-called simple hunter-gatherer societies are not necessarily less complex than highly industrialized societies. I once reviewed a proposal which wished to study a computer-simulated society because real ones were, the author said, too complex. In science, Gleick tells us, "Before chaos (theory) simple systems behaved in simple ways, complex behavior implied complex causes, and different systems behaved differently. After chaos simple systems gave rise to complex behavior, complex systems give rise to simple behavior. Laws of complexity hold universally caring not at all for details of a system's constituent atoms" (Gleick 1987: 304).

Does chaos hold any promise for understanding culture? We have dealt with cultural processes for many decades. In chaos there are phenomena or principles (I'm not sure which) that they call strange attractors.

> Strange attractors in nature (according to Gleick 1987: 140) are points around which random lines return. . . . But an attractor could never intersect itself, because if it did, returning to a point already visited, from then the motion would repeat itself in a periodic loop. That never happened. That was the beauty. Those loops and spirals were indefinitely deep and never quite joining, never intersecting. Yet they stayed inside a finite space confined by a box; how could that be? How could infinitely many paths lie in a finite space? (140)

If I follow this line any further than I have tonight, I will do so as an experimenter (read ethnographer) rather than a theorist. Gleick makes the distinction:

> Theorists conduct experiments with their brains.
> Experimenters have to use their hands, too.
> Theorists are thinkers,
> Experimenters are craftsmen.
> The theorist needs no accomplice.
> The experimenter has to marshall graduate students, cajole machinists, and flatter lab assistants.
> The Theorist operates in a pristine place free of noise, of vibration, of dirt.
> The experimenter develops an intimacy with matter as a sculptor does with clay, battling it, shaping it and engaging it.
> The theorist invents his companions, as a Naive Romeo invents his ideal Juliet.
> The Experimenter's lovers sweat, complain, and fart.
> (Gleick 1987: 125)

I am humble before those of you who have greater knowledge of chaos theory than I. I know I have not done it justice. Little did I realize a very early high school interest in physics and a postbaccalaureate year working on three variable stars in the Milky Way at Harvard would combine with my anthropological training to result in a fascination with strange attractors and fractals.

Culture and chaos are indeed complex. If we take complexity to mean information-rich, then we should welcome opportunities to enhance that richness with increasingly full ethnographic descriptions. I believe we do not yet have enough data to consider ethnography obsolete.

Several times tonight I have used a view through a kaleidoscope to describe my shape-shifting analysis of data. Are the patterns made by the tumbling pieces of colored glass nonlinear? Can only one twist of the kaleidoscope give insight into a cultural complexity? Or does each twist give us an alternative view, equally valid, but perhaps not equally useful for every comparison?

Coon once told me never to hold back an idea but to toss it out for others to destroy and then cheerily go on to the next one. So I make a plea for ethnography as the experimental arm of the continuing science of anthropology. Let us not overlook the complexity and the seemingly unrelated facts. Let us rather consider whether each culture is a nonlineal world of its own yet its similarity to others is in its nonlineal behavior.

Let us be challenged by chaos and continue as experimenters. Long live ethnography!

Postscript (2006)

I retired in January 1996 having spent the first of four additional visits to the Tiwi, the last of which was in 2002. I have been working on a history of the Milikapiti community which is, in many ways, different from that of the more Catholic-influenced communities of Nguiu on Bathurst Island and Pirliangimpi on Melville Island. In 1996 I brought with me copies of the records (government communications and reports) dating from 1955–77, from which I had a chance to take notes during my 1980–81 visit. As much of this material was sensitive to individuals, I allowed these people (and anybody else who wished) to read the report notes. I was concerned whether to include episodes, names, and other identifying information. No one objected; rather, they emphasized that I should include *everything* as this was *their own history*. I had hoped to return with this history of Milikapiti on the fiftieth anniversary of my first visit (2004). But such was not in the cards.

Retirement, as retirees had warned me, is the busiest time of one's life! I don't know where the time went. I did some traveling, writing some papers, editing others. I taught a course on Australian Aboriginal Culture at Bryn Mawr one semester. I visited the Tiwi in 1995, 1996–97, 1999, and 2002 following the ASAO meeting in Auckland.

Finally, in late 2002 and 2003, parts of my body began to rebel: first the knees and then the back, resulting in three major operations and rehabbing taking up most of my time and energy. On Valentine's Day 2004, I moved from my condo in Pennsylvania to a cottage in a retirement village (Carleton-Willard) in Bedford, Massachusetts. I no longer have the long summer migrations north to my home in Ipswich, Massachusetts, and then back south to Rosemont, Pennsylvania, in the fall. Now it is only an hour's travel, but still an emotionally important event. In Ipswich I am close to my beloved saltwater marshland, a lovely beach, and some of my childhood friends and newcomers who have become friends. I am still working on the history of Milikapiti and involved in the history and care of the original (1669) Goodale house, which, in 1929, my parents moved from a part of Old Salem to Ipswich on land given to them by my grandfather. I am getting used to everything taking twice the time it formally did, but content to be still alive and mostly intact.

In conclusion, I must remark on the initial and following impact the two symposia honoring my teaching by the students included in this volume had on me. The first hearing of the papers astounded me by the fact that what I had passed on to my students was my style of mentoring. I had imagined that I was teaching them various aspects and data of anthropology, but this was clearly secondary to the passing remarks I made as I lectured on the assigned topic.

"Pulling the right thread," in the margin notes in a lecture, came after I tried to undo a skirt hem the night before. (I doubt that men fully understand the context). But it also came after I wrote a paper on Tiwi management of resources, mentioned above, when I suddenly saw the gendered division of labor of the Tiwi reflected a gendered worldview, expressed most symbolically and emotionally in an important ritual. Somehow, some twenty years after I witnessed the ritual, I pulled the right thread and the meaning of the ceremony became clear to me. Later, I summarized my understanding of the ritual to some women who told me "I was indeed a wise woman," that I did understand their world. I still remember how wonderful it felt to know that I had achieved such knowledge.

In attending the symposia and reading the papers in this volume, I am enriched and find it hard to find the words to express how wonderful it feels also to know that I have made such a rich and important impact on both former students and the other anthropological colleagues represented in this volume! I am also grateful to Laura and Jeanette for organizing the two symposia and for their efforts in pulling together this volume. All of these individuals honor and instruct me as they continue to explore new ethnographic ideas and fields. I am impressed and pleased that they also carry on my tradition of mentoring as they teach yet another generation. Ethnography survives.

REFERENCES

Abu-Lughod, Lila. 1991. "Writing Against Culture." In *Recapturing Anthropology: Working in the Present,* edited by Richard G. Fox, 137–62. Santa Fe, NM: School of American Research Press.

———. 1993. *Writing Women's Worlds: Bedouin Stories.* Berkeley: University of California Press.

Anderson, Benedict. 1991. *Imagined Communities: Reflections on the Origin and Spread of Nationalism.* London: Verso.

Basedow, Herbert. 1913. "Notes on the Natives of Bathurst Island, North Australia." *Journal of the Royal Anthropological Institute* 43: 291–323.

Bashkow, Ira. 2004. "Neo-Boasian Conception of Cultural Boundaries." *American Anthropologist* 106 (3): 443–58.

———, Matti Bunzl, Richard Handler, Andrew Orta, and Daniel Rosenblatt. 2004. "Introduction to In Focus: A New Boasian Anthropology: Theory for the 21st Century." *American Anthropologist* 106 (3): 433–34.

Bateson, Gregory. 1932. "Further Notes on a Snake Dance of the Baining." *Oceania* 2: 334–41.

———. 1958. *Naven.* Stanford, CA: Stanford University Press. (Originally published in 1938)

———. 1972. *Steps to an Ecology of the Mind.* New York: Ballantine Books.

Behar, Ruth. 1995. "Introduction: Out of Exile." In *Women Writing Culture,* edited by Ruth Behar and Deborah A. Gordon, 1–29. Berkeley: University of California Press.

———, and Deborah A. Gordon, eds. 1995. *Women Writing Culture.* Berkeley: University of California Press.

Bell, Diane, Pat Caplan, and Jahan Karim, eds. 1993. *Gendered Fields: Women, Men and Ethnography.* London: Routledge.

Berman, Marsha. 1990. "*Samting tru or Samting nating?* What Is Contemporary Melanesian Art?" In *Luk Luk Gen: Contemporary Art from Papua New Guinea,* edited by Susan Cochrane Simons and Hugh Stevenson, 59–63. Townsville, Australia: Perc Tucker Regional Gallery.

Berndt, R. M., and Peter Lawrence, eds. 1971. *Politics in New Guinea: Traditional and in the Context of Change: Some Anthropological Perspectives.* Nedlands, Western Australia: University of Western Australia.

Bilharz, Joy A. 1995. "First Among Equals? The Changing Status of Seneca Women." In *Women and Power in Native North America,* edited by Lillian Ackerman and Laura Klein, 101–12. Norman: University of Oklahoma Press.

———. 1998a. *The Allegany Senecas and Kinzua Dam: Forced Relocation through Two Generations.* Lincoln: University of Nebraska Press.

———. 1998b. *A Place of Great Sadness: Mohawk Valley Battlefield Ethnography.* Final Report to the U.S. Department of the Interior, National Park Service.

———. 2002. *Mohawk Valley Battlefield Ethnography, Phase II: The "Western Indians" and the Mississaugas.* Final Report to the U.S. Department of the Interior, National Park Service.

———, and Thomas Abler. 1999. "L'heritage de Kinzua: La reconquete du pouvoir chez les femmes senecas." *Recherches amerindiennes au Quebec* 29 (2): 51–62.

Boas, Franz. 1940. "The Limitations of the Comparative Method of Anthropology." In *Race, Language and Culture,* 270–80. New York: Macmillan. (Originally published in 1896)

———. 1940. *Race, Language, and Culture.* New York: Macmillan.

Boserup, Ester. 1970. *Women's Role in Economic Development.* New York: St. Martin's Press.

Brash, Nora Vargi. 1987. "Which Way Big Man?" In *Through Melanesian Eyes: An Anthology of Papua New Guinea Writing,* compiled by Ganga Powell, 170–87. Melbourne: McMillan.

Breinl, A., and M. J. Holmes. 1915. "Medical Report on the Data Collected during a Journey through Districts of the Northern Territory." *Bulletin of the Northern Territory,* No. 15.

Brettell, Caroline B., and Carolyn F. Sargent, eds. 2001. *Gender in Cross-Cultural Perspective.* Upper Saddle River, NJ: Prentice Hall.

Briggs, Jean. 1970. *Never in Anger.* Cambridge, MA: Harvard University Press.

Brown, Judith, and V. Kerns, eds. 1985. *In Her Prime: A New View of Middle-Aged Women.* South Hadley, MA: Bergin and Garvey.

Brown, Paula. 1972. *The Chimbu: A Study of Change in the New Guinea Highlands.* Cambridge, MA: Schenkman.

———. 1978. *Highland Peoples of New Guinea.* Cambridge: Cambridge University Press.

———. 1988. "Gender and Social Change: New Forms of Independence for Simbu Women." *Oceania* 59: 123–42.

———, and Georgeda Buchbinder, eds. 1976. *Man and Woman in the New Guinea Highlands.* Special Publication Number 8. Washington, DC: American Anthropological Association.

Bunzl, Matti. 2004. "Boas, Foucault, and the 'Native Anthropologist': Notes Toward a Neo-Boasian Anthropology." *American Anthropologist* 106 (3): 435–42.

Burbank, Victoria K. 1989. "Gender and the Anthropology Curriculum: Aboriginal Australia." In *Gender and Anthropology: Critical Reviews for Research and Teaching,* edited by Sandra Morgen, 116–31. Washington, DC: American Anthropological Association.

Burridge, K. 1960. *Mambu: A Study of Melanesian Cargo Movements and Their Ideological Background.* New York: Harper & Rose.

Campbell, Judy. 2002. *Invisible Invaders: Smallpox and Other Diseases in Aboriginal Australia, 1780–1880.* Carlton South, Victoria: Melbourne University Press.

Carroll, Raymonde. 1988. *Cultural Misunderstanding: The French-American Experience.* Chicago: University of Chicago Press.

Carroll, Vern. 1977. "Communities and Non-Communities: The Nukuoro on Ponape." In *Exiles and Migrants in Oceania,* edited by Michael D. Lieber. ASAO Monograph No. 5. Honolulu: University Press of Hawaii.

Carucci, Laurence M. 1993. "Medical Magic and Medicinal Cure: Manipulating Meanings with Ease of Disease." *Current Anthropology* 8: 157–68.

Carsten, Janet. 2001. "Substantivism, Anti-Substantivism, and Anti-anti-substantivism." In *Relative Values: Reconfiguring Kinship Studies,* edited by Sarah Franklin and Susan McKinon, 29–53. Durham, NC: Duke University Press.

Chapple, Elliot D., and Carlton S. Coon. 1942. *Principles of Anthropology.* New York: H. Holt.

Charlton, Sue. 1984. *Women in Third World Development.* Boulder, CO: Westview Press.

Choulai, Wendy. 1996. "Art and Ritual." *Aina Asi A Mavaru Kavamu. Artlink* 16 (4): 46.

Chowning, Ann, and Jane C. Goodale. 1971. "The Contaminating Woman." Paper presented at the American Anthropological Association annual meeting, November, Washington DC.

———, and Jane C. Goodale. 1965. "The Passimanua Census Division, West New Britain Open Electorate." In *The Papua New Guinea Election, 1964,* edited by D. G. Bettison, C. A. Hughes, and P. W. Van de Veur, 264–78. Canberra: Australian National University Press.

———, Jane C. Goodale, T. Scarlett Epstein, and Ian Grosart. 1971. "Under the Volcano." In *The Politics of Independence, Papua New Guinea, 1968,* edited by A. L. Epstein, R. S. Parker, and Marie Reay, 48–90. Canberra: Australian National University Press.

Clifford, James. 1997. "Spatial Practices: Fieldwork, Travel and the Disciplining of Anthropology." In *Routes: Travel and Translation in the Late Twentieth Century,* 52–91. Cambridge, MA: Harvard University Press.

———, and George Marcus, eds. 1986. *Writing Culture: The Poetics and Politics of Ethnography.* Berkeley: University of California Press.

Cochrane, Susan. 1997. *Contemporary Art in Papua New Guinea.* Sydney: Craftsman House.

Cole, R. V., et al. 1985. *Women and Development in the South Pacific: Barriers and Opportunities.* Canberra: Development Studies Centre, Australian National University.

Cole, Sally. 1995. "Ruth Landes and the Early Ethnography of Race and Gender." In *Women Writing Culture,* edited by Ruth Behar and Deborah A. Gordon, 166–85. Berkeley: University of California Press.

Comaroff, John, and Jean Comaroff. 1992. *Ethnography and the Historical Imagination.* Boulder, CO: Westview Press.

Counts, Dorothy. 1985. "Tamparonga: The Big Women of Kaliai." In *In Her Prime,* edited by Judith Brown and V. Kerns, 49–64. South Hadley, MA: Bergin and Garvey.

———, and David Counts, eds. 1985. *Aging and Its Transformations.* Lanham, MD: University Press of America.

Crosby, A. W. Jr. 1976. "Virgin Soil Epidemics as a Factor in the Aboriginal Depopulation in America." *William and Mary Quarterly* 33: 289–99.

Davison, Jean. 1996. *Voices From Mutira*, 2nd edition. Boulder, CO: Lynne Rienner.

Dickerson-Putman, Jeanette. 1986. *Finding a Road in the Modern World: The Different Effects of Culture Change and Development on the Men and Women of an Eastern Highlands Community.* Ph.D. dissertation, Bryn Mawr College.

———. 1992. "Age and Gender Stratification in the Highlands of Papua New Guinea: Implications for Participation in Economic Development." *Human Organization* 51 (2): 109–22.

———, ed. 1996. *Women, Age, and Power*, Special Issue. *Pacific Studies* 19 (4).

———. 1998. Life History Interviews with Jane Goodale. June. Ipswich, MA.

———, and Laura Zimmer-Tamakoshi, eds. 1994. *Women and Development in the Pacific*, Special Issue. *Urban Anthropology and Studies of Cultural Systems and World Economic Development* 23 (1).

Dominy, Michèle D. 1990. "Maori Sovereignty: A Feminist Invention of Tradition." In *Cultural and Ethnic Identity in the Pacific*, edited by Jocelyn Linnekin and Lynette Poyer, 237–58. Honolulu: University of Hawaii Press.

———. 2001. *Calling the Station Home: Place and Identity in New Zealand's High Country.* Lanham, MD: Rowman & Littlefield.

Donner, William W. 1987. "'Don't Shoot the Guitar Player': Tradition, Assimilation and Change in Sikaiana Song Composition." *Journal of the Polynesian Society* 96: 201–21.

———. 1989. "'Far-Away' and 'Close-Up': World War II and Sikaiana Perceptions of Their Place in the World." In *The Pacific Theater: Islander Representations of World War II*, edited by G. White and L. Lindstrom, 149–65. Honolulu: University of Hawaii Press.

———. 1992. "Lineages and Court Disputes on a Polynesian Outlier." *Man* 27: 319–39.

———. 1993. "*Kastom* and Modernisation on Sikaiana." *Custom Today*, Special Issue, edited by Lamont Lindstrom and Geoffrey White. *Anthropological Forum* 7 (4): 541–56.,

———. 1994. "Alcohol, Community and Modernity: The Social Organization of Toddy Drinking in a Polynesian Society." *Ethnology* 33 (3): 145–260.

———. 1999. "Sharing and Compassion: Fosterage in a Polynesian Society." *Journal of Comparative Family Studies* 30 (4): 703–22.

———. 2002. "Rice and Tea, Fish and Taro: Sikaiana Migration to Honiara." *Pacific Studies* 25 (1–2): 23–44.

Dumont, Jean-Paul. 1978. *The Headman and I.* Austin: University of Texas Press.

Estioko-Griffin, Agnes, and P. Bion Griffin. 1981. "Woman the Hunter: The Agta." In *Woman the Gatherer*, edited by Frances Dahlberg, 121–40. New Haven, CT: Yale University Press.

Etienne, Mona, and Eleanor Leacock, eds. 1980. *Women and Colonization: Anthropological Perspectives.* New York: Praeger.

Fabian, J. 1983. *Time and the Other: How Anthropology Makes Its Object.* New York: Columbia University Press.

———. 1991. "Ethnographic Objectivity Revisited: From Rigor to Vigor." *Annals of Scholarship* 8: 381–408.

Fackenheim, Emil. 1994. *To Mend the World: Foundations of Post-Holocaust Jewish Thought.* Bloomington: Indiana University Press. (Originally published in 1982)

Faithorn, Elizabeth. 1976. "Women as Persons: Aspects of Female Life and Male-Female Relations Among the Kafe." In *Man and Woman in the New Guinea Highlands,* edited by P. Brown and G. Buchbinder, 86–95. Special Publication Number 8. Washington, DC: American Anthropological Association.

———. 1986. "Gender Bias and Sex Bias: Removing Our Cultural Blinders in the Field." In *Self, Sex, and Gender in Cross-Cultural Fieldwork,* edited by Tony Whitehead and M. E. Conaway, 275–88. Urbana: University of Illinois Press.

Fajans, Jane. 1997. *They Make Themselves: Work and Play Among the Baining of Papua New Guinea.* Chicago: University of Chicago Press.

———. 1993. "Allmentary Structures of Kinship: Food and Exchange among the Baining of Papua, New Guinea." In *Exchanging Products: Producing Exchange.* 43: 59–75.

Falgout, Susanne. 1986. Persons and Knowledge on Ponape. Ph.D. dissertation. Department of Anthropology, University of Oregon.

Feinberg, Richard, and Laura Zimmer-Tamakoshi, eds. 1995. *Politics of Culture in the Pacific Islands,* Special Issue. *Ethnology: An Intercultural Journal of Cultural and Social Anthropology,* 34 (2–3).

Finney, Ben. 1973. *Big-Men and Business: Entrepreneurship and Economic Growth in the New Guinea Highlands.* Honolulu: University of Hawaii Press.

———. 1993. "From the Stone Age to the Age of Corporate Takeovers." In *Contemporary Pacific Societies: Studies in Development and Change,* edited by V. Lockwood, T. G. Harding, and B. J. Wallace, 102–16. Englewood Cliffs, NJ: Prentice Hall.

Ford, Clellan S., and Frank A. Beach. 1951. *Patterns of Sexual Behavior.* New York: Harper and Row.

Fortes, Meyer. 1968. *Kinship and the Social Order: The Legacy of L. H. Morgan.* Chicago: Aldine.

Fortune, Reo. 1932. *Sorcerers of Dobu.* New York: E. P. Dutton.

Foster, Robert J., ed. 1995. *Nation-Making: Emergent Identities in Post-Colonial Melanesia.* Ann Arbor: University of Michigan Press.

———. 2002. *Materializing the Nation: Commodities, Consumption, and Media in Papua New Guinea.* Bloomington: University of Indiana Press.

Frayser, Suzanne G. 1985. *Varieties of Sexual Experience: An Anthropological Perspective on Human Sexuality.* New Haven, CT: HRAF Press.

Frazer, James G. 1912. "Anthropological Research in Northern Australia." *Man* 12: 72–73.

Fry, H. K. 1949. "A Bathurst Island Mourning Rite." *Mankind* 4: 79–80.

———. 1950. "A Bathurst Island Initiation Rite." *Mankind* 4: 167–68.

Ganguly, Debjani. 2002. "History's Implosions: A Benjaminian Reading of Ambedkar." *Journal of Narrative Theory* 32 (3): 326–47.

Gathercole, Peter, Adrienne Kaeppler, and Douglas Newton. 1979. *The Art of the Pacific Islands.* Washington, DC: National Gallery of Art.

Geertz, Clifford. 2002. "An Inconstant Profession: An Anthropological Life in Interesting Times." *Annual Review of Anthropology* 31: 1–19.

Gewertz, Deborah, and Frederick Errington. 1999. *Emerging Class in Papua New Guinea: The Telling of Difference.* Cambridge: Cambridge University Press.

Gilmore, David D. 1990. *Manhood in the Making.* New Haven, CT: Yale University Press.

Ginzburg, Carlo. 1988. "Morelli, Freud, and Sherlock Holmes: Clues and Scientific Method." In *The Sign of Three: Dupin, Holmes, Peirce,* edited by Umberto Eco and Thomas A. Sebeok. Bloomington: Indiana University Press.

Gladwin, Thomas, and Seymour B. Sarason. 1953. *Truk: Man in Paradise.* New York: Wenner Gren Foundation for Anthropological Research. (Reprinted in 1966, Johns Reprint Corporation)

Glasse, R. M., and M. J. Meggitt, eds. 1969. *Pigs, Pearlshells and Women.* Englewood Cliffs, NJ: Prentice Hall.

Gleick, John. 1987. *Chaos.* New York: Viking Penguin.

Gluckman, Max. 1963. *Order and Rebellion in Tribal Africa.* New York: Free Press of Glencoe.

———. 1970. *Custom and Conflict in Africa.* Oxford: Basil Blackwell.

Goffman, Erving. 1961. *Asylums: Essays on the Social Situation of Mental Patients and Other Inmates.* New York: Anchor Books.

Golde, Peggy, ed. 1970. *Women in the Field: Anthropological Experiences.* Chicago: Aldine.

Goodale, Jane C. 1960. "Tiwi of North Australia." In *Funeral Customs the World Over,* edited by R. W. Habenstein and W. M. Lamers, 36–47. Milwaukee, WI: Bulfin Printers.

———. 1962. "Marriage Contracts Among the Tiwi." *Ethnology* 1 (4): 452–66.

———. 1963. "Qualifications for Adulthood: Tiwi Invoke the Power of a Yam." *Natural History* 72 (4): 10–17.

———. 1967. "The Cultural Context of Creativity Among the Tiwi." In *Essays on the Verbal and Visual Arts.* Proceedings of the 1966 Annual Spring Meeting of the American Ethnological Society.

———. 1970. "An Example of Ritual Change Among the Tiwi of Melville Island." In *Diprotodon to Detribalization, Studies in Change Among Australian Aborigines,* edited by A. R. Pilling and R. A. Waterman, 350–66. East Lansing: Michigan State University Press.

———. 1971. *Tiwi Wives: A Study of the Women of Melville Island, North Australia.* Seattle: University of Washington Press.

———. 1976. "Big-Men and Big-Women: The Elite in Melanesian Society." Paper presented at the American Anthropological Association annual meeting, November, Washington, DC.

———. 1977. "The Management of Knowledge among the Kaulong." Paper presented at the Association for Social Anthropology in Oceania annual meeting, February, Monterey, CA.

———. 1978. "Saying It with Shells in Southwest New Britain." Paper presented at the American Anthropological Association annual meeting, November, Los Angeles, CA.

———. 1980. "Gender, Sexuality and Marriage: A Kaulong Model of Nature and Culture." In *Nature, Culture and Gender,* edited by Carol MacCormack and Marilyn Strathern, 119–42. Cambridge: Cambridge University Press.

———. 1982. "Production and Reproduction of Key Resources Among the Tiwi of North Australia." In *Resource Managers: North American and Australian Hunter-Gatherers,* edited by Nancy Williams and Eugene S. Hunn, 197–210. Boulder, CO: Westview Press.

———. 1983. "Siblings as Spouses: The Reproduction and Replacement of Kaulong Society." In *Siblingship in Oceania: Studies in the Meaning of Kin Relations,* edited by Mac Marshall, 275–305. Lanham, MD: University Press of America. ASAO Monograph No. 8. (Originally published in 1979 by University of Michigan Press, Ann Arbor)

———. 1985. "Pig's Teeth and Skull Cycles: Both Sides of the Face of Humanity." *American Ethnologist* 12 (2): 228–44.

———. 1987. "Gambling Is Hard Work: Card Playing in Tiwi Society." *Gambling With Cards for Money in Melanesia and Australia,* Special Issue, edited by Laura J. Zimmer. *Oceania* 58 (1): 6–21.

———. 1988. "The Tiwi Revisited: 1954–1987." In *The Tiwi of North Australia,* 3rd edition, edited by C. W. M. Hart, Arnold R. Pilling, and Jane C. Goodale, 127–46. New York: Holt, Rinehart and Winston.

———. 1994a. *Tiwi Wives: A Study of the Women of Melville Island, North Australia,* 2nd edition. Prospect Heights, IL: Waveland Press.

———. 1994b. "What Is Ethnography? Is It Real?" Distinguished lecture presented at the Association for Social Anthropology in Oceania annual meeting, February 10, San Diego, CA.

———. 1995. *To Sing With Pigs Is Human: Concepts of Person in Papua New Guinea.* Seattle: University of Washington Press.

———. 1996a. "Taramaguti Today: Changing Roles of Senior Tiwi Household Managers." *Women, Age and Power,* Special Issue, edited by Jeanette Dickerson-Putman. *Pacific Studies* 19 (4): 131–54.

——— (in collaboration with Ann Chowning). 1996b. *The Two-Party Line: Conversations in the Field.* Lanham, MD: Rowman & Littlefield.

———. 1999. "Tiwi." In *Cambridge Encyclopedia of Hunters and Gatherers,* edited by Richard B. Lee and Richard Daly, 353–57. London: Cambridge University Press.

———. 2003. "Understanding Relationships After Nearly Fifty Years Among the Tiwi of Melville Island, North Australia." Paper presented at the Association for Social Anthropology in Oceania annual meeting. March, Vancouver, BC.

———, and Jane Koss. 1971. "The Cultural Context of Creativity Among Tiwi." In *Anthropology and Art: Readings in Cross-Cultural Aesthetics,* edited by Charlotte M. Otten, 182–200. Austin: University of Texas Press.

Goodenough, Ward. 1949. "Premarital Freedom on Truk." *American Anthropologist* 51: 615–20.

Gordon, Deborah A. 1988. "Writing Culture, Writing Feminism: The Poetics and Politics of Experimental Ethnography." *Inscriptions* 3 (4): 8, 21.

———. 1995. "Conclusion: Culture Writing Women: Inscribing Feminist Anthropology." In *Women Writing Culture,* edited by Ruth Behar and Deborah A. Gordon, 429–41. Berkeley: University of California Press.

Goulet, J. G. 1998. *Ways of Knowing: Experience, Knowledge, and Power Among the DeneTha.* Vancouver: University of British Columbia Press.

Graburn, Nelson, ed. 1976. *Ethnic and Tourist Arts: Cultural Expressions from the Fourth World.* Berkeley: University of California Press.

Grau, Andree. 1983. "Dreaming, Dancing, Kinship: The Study of *Yoi*, the Dance of the Tiwi of Melville and Bathurst Islands, North Australia." Ph.D. thesis. Queen's University, Belfast.

Gsell, Francis Xavier. 1956. *The Bishop With 150 Wives: Fifty Years a Missionary.* Sydney: Angus and Robertson.

Hargrave, J. C. 1993. *The Best of Both Worlds: Aboriginal Health Then and Now.* Occasional Papers, No. 36. Darwin: State Library of the Northern Territory.

Harney, W. E., and A. P. Elkin. 1943. "Melville and Bathurst Islanders: A Short Description." *Oceania* 13: 228–34.

Harries-Jones, P. 1995. *A Recursive Vision: Ecological Understanding and Gregory Bateson.* Toronto: University of Toronto Press.

Hart, C. W. M. 1931. "Personal Names Among the Tiwi." *Oceania* 1: 280–90.

———, and A. R. Pilling. 1960. *The Tiwi of North Australia.* New York: Holt, Rinehart and Winston.

———, Arnold R. Pilling, and Jane C. Goodale. 1988. *The Tiwi of North Australia,* 3rd edition. New York: Holt, Rinehart and Winston.

Hatcher, Evelyn. 1972. *Footnotes,* 2nd edition. Minneapolis, MN: Intermittent Press.

Herdt, Gilbert. 1981. *Guardians of the Flutes.* New York: McGraw-Hill.

Herskovits, Melville. 1948. "Review of *The City of Women.*" *American Anthropologist* 50: 124.

Hiatt, L. R. 1996. *Arguments About Aborigines: Australia and the Evolution of Social Anthropology.* Cambridge: Cambridge University Press.

Holmes, Sandra. 1995. *The Goddess and the Moon Man: The Sacred Art of the Tiwi Aborigines.* Roseville, New South Wales: Craftsman House.

Hrdy, Sarah Blaffer. 1981. *The Woman That Never Evolved.* Cambridge, MA: Harvard University Press.

Hymes, Dell, ed. 1972. *Reinventing Anthropology.* New York: Random House.

Inhorn, M. C., and P. J. Brown. 1990. "The Anthropology of Infectious Disease." *Annual Review of Anthropology* 19: 89–117.

Jackson, Chantal. 2003. *Red Ochre.* Unpublished manuscript.

Jackson, Jean. 1986. "On Trying to Be an Amazon." In *Self, Sex, and Gender in Cross-Cultural Fieldwork,* edited by Tony L. Whitehead and Mary Ellen Conaway, 263–74. Urbana: University of Illinois Press.

Kaberry, P. M. 1939. *Aboriginal Woman, Sacred and Profane.* London: George Routledge and Sons.

Kahn, Miriam. 1986. *Always Hungry, Never Greedy: Food and the Expression of Gender in a Melanesian Society.* Cambridge: Cambridge University Press.

———. 1988. "'Men Are Taro' (They Cannot Be Rice): Political Aspects of Food Choices in Wamira, Papua New Guinea." In *Continuity and Change in Pacific Foodways,* edited by M. Kahn and L. Sexton, 41–57. Special issue. *Food and Foodways* 3 (1).

———. 1990. "Stone-Faced Ancestors: The Spatial Anchoring of Myth in Wamira, Papua New Guinea." *Ethnology* 29: 51–66.

———. 1996. "Your Place and Mine: Sharing Emotional Landscapes in Wamira, Papua New Guinea." In *Senses of Place,* edited by S. Feld and K. Basso, 167–96. Santa Fe, NM: Santa Fe School of American Research.

————. 2000. "Tahiti Intertwined: Ancestral Land, Tourist Postcard, and Nuclear Test Site." *American Anthropologist* 102 (1): 7–26.

————. 2003. "Tahiti: The Ripples of a Myth on the Shores of the Imagination." *History and Anthropology* 14 (4): 307–26.

————. 2004. "'Placing' Tahitian Identities: Both Rooted in Land and Enmeshed in Representations." In *Globalization and Culture: Change in the Pacific Islands*, edited by V. Lockwood, 285–306. New York: Prentice Hall.

————. 2006. "Postcards from Tahiti: Picturing France's Colonial Agendas, Yesterday and Today." Unpublished manuscript.

Kaplan, Martha. 1990. "Meaning, Agency and Colonial History: Navosavakadua and the Tuka Movement in Fiji." *American Ethnologist* 17: 3–22.

————. 1995. *Neither Cargo nor Cult. Ritual Politics and the Colonial Imagination in Fiji*. Durham, NC: Duke University Press.

Kasaipwalova, John. 1987. "Betel-Nut Is Bad Magic for Aeroplanes." In *Through Melanesian Eyes: An Anthology of Papua New Guinea Writing*, compiled by Ganga Powell, 69–77. Melbourne: McMillan.

Kasfir, Sydney. 1998. *Contemporary African Art*. New York: Thames & Hudson.

Keesing, Roger M. 1975. *Kin Groups and Social Structure*. New York: Holt, Rinehart and Winston.

————. 1994. "Theories of Culture Revisited." In *Assessing Cultural Anthropology*, edited by Robert Borofsky, 301–10. New York: McGraw-Hill.

Kilbride, Philip L., Jane C. Goodale, and Elizabeth R. Ameisen, eds. (in collaboration with Carolyn G. Friedman). 1990. *Encounters With American Ethnic Cultures*. Tuscaloosa: University of Alabama Press.

Kimmel, Michael S., and Michael A. Messner, eds. 2001. *Men's Lives*, 5th edition. Boston: Allyn and Bacon.

Knauft, Bruce M. 2002. *Exchanging the Past: A Rainforest World of Before and After*. Chicago: University of Chicago Press.

Kulick, Don, and Margaret Willson. 1995. *Taboo: Sex, Identity and Erotic Subjectivity in Anthropological Fieldwork*. London: Routledge.

Landes, Ruth. 1938. *Ojibwa Woman*. New York: Columbia University Press.

————. 1947. *The City of Women*. New York: Macmillan.

Langness, L. L. 1967. "Sexual Antagonism in the New Guinea Highlands: A Bena Bena Example." *Oceania* 37: 161–77.

Lawrence, Peter. 1964. *Road Belong Cargo*. Manchester: Manchester University Press.

Leacock, Eleanor. 1978. "Women's Status in Egalitarian Society: Implications for Social Evolution." *Current Anthropology* 19: 212.

Lefebvre, Henri. 1974. *La production de l'espace*. Paris: Editions Anthropos. (English translation by D. Nicholson-Smith published in 1991 by Blackwell, Oxford)

Lepowsky, Maria. 1993. *Fruit of the Motherland: Gender in an Egalitarian Society*. New York: Columbia University Press.

Levinas, Emmanuel. 1994. *Outside the Subject*, translated by M. Smith. Stanford, CA: Stanford University Press.

Lewis-Harris, Jacquelyn. 2004. *Not Without a Cost: Contemporary Papua New Guinea Art and Cultural Property Rights*, Special Issue. *Visual Anthropology* 17 (3–4).

———. 2006. "Gender, Location, and Tradition: A Comparison of Two Papua New Guinean Contemporary Artists." In *Exploring World Art*, edited by Eric Venbrux, Pamela Rosi, and Robert L. Welsch, 225–44. Long Grove, IL: Waveland Press.

Lieber, Michael D. 1990. "Lamarckian Definitions of Identity on Kapingamarangi and Pohnpei." In *Cultural Identity and Ethnicity in the Pacific*, edited by Jocelyn Linnekin and Lin Poyer, 71–101. Honolulu: University of Hawaii Press.

———. 1994. *More Than a Living: Fishing and the Social Order on a Polynesian Atoll*. Boulder, CO: Westview Press.

Lincoln, Bruce. 1994. *Authority: Construction and Corrosion*. Chicago: University of Chicago Press.

Lincoln, Louise. 1987. *Assemblage of Spirits: Idea and Image in New Ireland*. New York: George Braziller in association with the Minneapolis Institute of Art.

Lindstrom, Lamont. 1998. "Pasin Tumbuna: Culture and Nationalism in Papua New Guinea." In *From Beijing to Port Moresby: The Politics of National Identity in Cultural Politics*, edited by Virginia R. Domingues and David Y. H. Wu, 141–67. Amsterdam: Gordon and Breach.

Linton, Ralph, and Paul S. Wingert. 1946. *Arts of the South Seas*. New York: Museum of Modern Art/Simon and Schuster.

LiPuma, Edward. 2001. *Encompassing Others: The Magic of Modernity in Melanesia*. Ann Arbor: University of Michigan Press.

Lutkehaus, Nancy C. 1995. "Margaret Mead and the 'Rustling-of-the-Wind-in-the-Palm-Trees School.'" In *Women Writing Culture*, edited by Ruth Behar and Deborah A. Gordon, 186–206. Berkeley: University of California Press.

Lutz, Catherine. 1990. "Erasure of Women's Writings in Sociocultural Anthropology." *American Ethnologist* 17 (4): 611–27.

MacCormack, Carol. 1980. "Nature, Culture and Gender: A Critique." In *Nature, Culture and Gender*, edited by Carol MacCormack and Marilyn Strathern, 1–24. Cambridge: Cambridge University Press.

———, and Marilyn Strathern, eds. 1980. *Nature, Culture and Gender*. Cambridge: Cambridge University Press.

Macquet, Jacques. 1985. *The Aesthetic Experience: An Anthropologist Looks at the Visual Arts*. New Haven, CT: Yale University Press.

Malinowski, Bronislaw. 1922. *Argonauts of the Western Pacific*. New York: E. P. Dutton.

———. 1929. *The Sexual Life of Savages*. New York: Harcourt, Brace Jovanovich.

———. 1935. *Coral Gardens and Their Magic*. New York: Dover.

Maranda, Elli Kongas. 1971. "Theory and Practice of Riddle Analysis." *Journal of American Folklore* 84: 51–61.

Maranda, Pierre. 1972. *Introduction to Anthropology: A Self Guide*. Englewood Cliffs, NJ: Prentice-Hall.

Marcus, George, and Michael Fischer, eds. 1986. *Anthropology as Cultural Critique*. Chicago: University of Chicago Press.

———, and Fred Myers, eds. 1995. *The Traffic in Culture: Refiguring Art and Anthropology*. Berkeley: University of California Press.

Marshall, Mac, ed. 1983. *Siblingship in Oceania: Studies in the Meaning of Kin Relations*. ASAO Monograph No. 8. Lanham, MD: University Press of America. (Originally published in 1979 by the University of Michigan Press, Ann Arbor)

Maturana, H., and F. Varela. 1998. *The Tree of Knowledge: The Biological Roots of Human Understanding.* Boston: Shambala. (Originally published in 1992)

Maybury-Lewis, David. 1965. *The Savage and the Innocent.* Cleveland, OH: World Publishing.

Mead, Margaret. 1956. *New Lives for Old.* New York: Mentor Books/New American Library.

Meggitt, Mervyn J. 1964. "Male-Female Relationships in the Highlands of Australian New Guinea." In *New Guinea: The Central Highlands,* edited by J. B. Watson. Special publication of *American Anthropologist* 66 (4): Part 2: 204–24. Menasha, WI: American Anthropological Association.

———. 1968. "'Marriage Classes' and Demography in Central Australia." In *Man the Hunter,* edited by Richard B. Lee and Irven deVore, 176–84. Chicago: Aldine.

Merlan, Francesca. 1998. *Caging the Rainbow: Places, Politics, and Aborigines in a North Australian Town.* Honolulu: Hawaii University Press.

Meyer, J. P. 1995. *Oceanic Art* (2 volumes). Koln, Germany: Konemann Verlagsgesellschaft.

Morauta, Louise, and Dawn Ryan. 1982. "From Temporary to Permanent Townsmen: Migrants from the Malalaua District, Papua New Guinea." *Oceania* 53 (1): 39–55.

Morris, John. 2001. *The Tiwi: From Isolation to Cultural Change: A History of Encounters Between an Island People and Outside Forces.* Darwin: Northern Territory University Press.

Mullin, Molly H. 2002. *Culture in the Marketplace: Gender, Art, and Value in the American Southwest.* Durham, NC: Duke University Press.

Mulvaney, D. J., and J. H. Calaby. 1985. *"So Much That Is New": Baldwin Spencer 1860–1929, a Biography.* Carlton, Victoria: Melbourne University Press.

Murdock, G. P. 1949. *Social Structure.* New York: Macmillan.

Myers, Fred R. 1986. *Pintupi Country, Pintupi Self: Sentiment, Place, and Politics Among Western Desert Aborigines.* Washington, DC: Smithsonian Institute Press.

———. 1988. "Locating Ethnographic Practice: Romance, Reality and Politics in the Outback." *American Ethnologist* 15 (4): 609–24.

———. 1995a. "Representing Culture: The Production of Discourse(s) for Aboriginal Acrylic Paintings." In *The Traffic in Culture: Refiguring Art and Anthropology,* edited by George Marcus and Fred Myers, 55–95. Berkeley: University of California Press.

———. 1995b. "Re/Writing the Primitive: Art Criticism and the Circulation of Aboriginal Painting." In *Meaning in the Visual Arts: Views from the Outside,* A Centennial Commemoration of Erwin Panofsky (1892–1968), edited by Irving Lavin. Princeton, NJ: Institute of Advanced Study.

———. 1998. Discussant comments. Presented in a session entitled "Fieldwork, Ethnographic Realism and Reflexivity: The Legacy of Jane C. Goodale," co-organized by Laura Zimmer-Tamakoshi and Jeanette Dickerson-Putman, at the American Anthropological Association annual meeting. November, Philadelphia.

———. 2002. *Painting Culture: The Making of an Aboriginal High Art.* Durham, NC: Duke University Press.

———. 2006. "The Unsettled Business of Tradition, Indigenous Being, and Acrylic Painting." In *Exploring World Art*, edited by Eric Venbrux, Pamela Rosi, and Robert L. Welsch. Long Grove, IL: Waveland Press.

Napier, A. David. 2004. "Public Anthropology and the Fall of the House of Ushers." *Anthropology News* 45 (6): 6–7.

Narokobi, Bernard. 1980. *The Melanesian Way*. Boroko: Institute of Papua New Guinea Studies.

———. 1990. "Transformations in Art and Society." In *Luk Luk Gen: Contemporary Art from Papua New Guinea*, edited by Hugh Stevenson and Susan Cochrane Simons, 17–21. Townsville, Australia: Perc Tucker Gallery.

National Arts School of Papua New Guinea (NAS). 1977. *Kauage*. Exhibition of paintings. Boroko: National Arts School.

———. 1986. *Luk Luk Gen*. An exhibition of metal sculptures by Gickmai Kundun. Boroko: National Arts School.

Nijmeegs Volkenkundig Museum. 2002. *Mak Bilong Ol: Hedendaagse kunst uit Papua New Guinea*. Exhibition curated by Pamela Rosi with Jacquelyn Lewis-Harris. Nijmegen: Nijmegen Katholicke Universiteit.

Ortner, Sherry. 1973. "On Key Symbols." *American Anthropologist* 77: 1338–46.

———. 1995. "Resistance and the Problem of Ethnographic Refusal." *Comparative Studies in Society and History* 37 (1): 173–93.

Otto, Ton. 1997. *Social Practice and the Ethnographic Circle: Rethinking the "Ethnographer's Magic" in a Late Modern World*. Arbejdspapir, 1. Hojbjerg, Moesgard: Afdeling for Etnografi og Socialantropologi, Aarhus Universitet.

———, and Nicholas Thomas. 1997. *Narratives of Nation in the South Pacific*. Australia: Harwood.

Passaro, J. 1998. "Anthropologists Must Redefine the Boundaries of Fieldwork." *Chronicle of Higher Education*, September 18, p. B6.

Phillips, Ruth, and Christopher B. Steiner. 1999. *Unpacking Culture: Art and Commodity in Colonial and Postcolonial Worlds*. Berkeley: University of California Press.

Pilling, Arnold R. 1958. "Law and Feud in an Aboriginal Society of North Australia." Ph.D. thesis. Berkeley, University of California.

———. 1970. "Changes in Tiwi Language." In *Diprotodon to Detribalization: Studies of Change Among Australian Aborigines*, edited by A. R. Pilling and R. A. Waterman. East Lansing: Michigan State University Press.

Pomponio, Alice. 1990. "Seagulls Don't Fly into the Bush: Cultural Identity and the Negotiation of Development on Mandok Island, Papua New Guinea." In *Cultural Identity and Ethnicity in the Pacific*, edited by Jocelyn Linnekin and Lin Poyer, 42–69. Honolulu: University of Hawaii Press.

Poole, J. 1970. *Final Report to the Wenner-Gren Foundation: Field Work Among the Northern Baining, New Britain (1969–70)*, New York.

———. 1941. "Still Further Notes on a Snake Dance of the Baining." *Oceania* 13: 224–27.

Povinelli, E. 1995. "Do Rocks Listen? The Cultural Politics of Apprehending Australian Aboriginal Labor." *American Anthropologist* 97 (3): 505–18.

Powdermaker, Hortense. 1966. *Stranger and Friend: The Way of an Anthropologist*. New York: W. W. Norton.

Powell, Ganga, ed. 1987. *Through Melanesian Eyes: An Anthology of Papua New Guinea Writing*. Melbourne: McMillan.

Puruntatameri, Justin, et al. 2001. *Tiwi Plants and Animals: Aboriginal Flora and Fauna Knowledge from Bathurst and Melville Islands, Northern Australia*. Darwin: Parks and Wildlife Commission of the Northern Territory/Tiwi Land Council.

Pye, John. 1985. *The Tiwi Islands*. Darwin: Coleman's/Catholic Mission Headquarters.

Rascher, Matthaus. 1909. *Aus de Deutschen Sudsee: Miteillungen der Misionare vom Hieligsten Herzen Jesus: Band I: Baining, Land un Leut*. Munster: Druck and Verlag de Aschendorffachen Buchhandlung.

Read, P. 1997. "Eleven O'Clock on the Last Night of the Conference." *UTS Review* 3 (1): 142–59.

Read, W. 1931. "Notes on a Snake Dance of the Baining." *Oceania* 2: 232–36.

Reid, Gordon. 1990. *A Picnic With the Natives: European-Aboriginal Relations in the Northern Territory to 1910*. Melbourne: Melbourne University Press.

Reynolds, Henry. 1990. *The Other Side of the Frontier. Aboriginal Resistance to the European Invasion of Australia*. Ringwood, Victoria: Penguin.

Rose, Deborah Bird. 1991. *Hidden Histories: Black Stories from Victoria River Downs, Humbert River and Wave Hill Stations*. Canberra: Aboriginal Studies Press.

———. 1992. *Dingo Makes Us Human: Life and Land in an Australian Aboriginal Culture*. Cambridge: Cambridge University Press. (Reprinted in 2000)

———. 1993. "Worshipping Captain Cook." *Social Analysis* 34: 43–49.

———. 1996. *Nourishing Terrains: Australian Aboriginal Views of Landscape and Wilderness*. Canberra: Australian Heritage Commission. (Japanese translation published in 2003 by Heibonsha, Tokyo)

———. 1999. "Taking Notice." *Ecological Worldviews, Australian Perspectives*, Special Issue, edited by F. Mathews. *Worldviews: Environment, Culture, Religion* 3: 97–103.

———. 2002. *Country of the Heart: An Indigenous Australian Homeland*, with Sharon D'Amico, Nancy Daiyi, Kathy Deveraux, Margaret Daiyi, Linda Ford, and April Bright. Canberra: Aboriginal Studies Press.

Rose, F. G. G. 1960. *Classification of Kin, Age Structure and Marriage Amongst the Groote Eylandt Aborigines*. Berlin: Akademie Verlag.

Rosi, Pamela. 1991. "Papua New Guinea's New Parliament House: A Contested National Symbol." *Contemporary Pacific* 3 (2): 289–323.

———. 1994. *Bung Wantaim: The Role of the National Arts School in Creating National Culture and Identity in Papua New Guinea*. Ph.D. dissertation. Bryn Mawr College, Bryn Mawr, PA.

———. 1998a. *Nation-Making and Cultural Tensions: Contemporary Art from Papua New Guinea*. Exhibition catalogue. Boston: Pine Manor College.

———. 1998b. "Culture Creator or New *Bisnis* Man? Conflicts of Being a Contemporary Artist in Papua New Guinea." In *Modern Papua New Guinea*, edited by Laura Zimmer-Tamakoshi, 31–54. Kirksville, MO: Thomas Jefferson University Press.

———. 2002. "'National Treasures' or Rubbish Men? The Disputed Value of

Contemporary Papua New Guinea (PNG) Artists and Their Work." *Zeitschrift fur Ethnologie* 127: 2.

———. 2003. "The Contested Vision of Larry Santana." Paper delivered at the Pacific Arts symposium, June 23–26. Christchurch, New Zealand.

———. 2006. "The Disputed Value of Contemporary Papua New Guinean Artists and Their Work." In *Exploring World Art*, edited by Eric Venbrux, Pamela Rosi, and Robert L. Welsch, 246–69. Long Grove, IL: Waveland Press.

———, and Eric Venbrux, eds. 2003. "Introduction to Conceptualizing World Art Studies." Special Issue. *International Journal of Anthropology*, 18 (4): 191–209.

———. 2004. "Introduction to Confronting World Art." Special Issue. *Visual Anthropology* 17 (3–4): 217–28.

———, and Laura Zimmer-Tamakoshi. 1993. "Love and Marriage among the Educated Elite in Port Moresby." In *The Business of Marriage: Transformations in Oceanic Matrimony*, edited by Richard Marksbury, 175–204. Pittsburgh: University of Pittsburgh Press.

Rubinstein, Robert L. 1998. "Reflexive Anthropology as a Form of Moral Anthropology." Paper presented in a session entitled "Fieldwork, Ethnographic Realism and Reflexivity: The Legacy of Jane C. Goodale," co-organized by Laura Zimmer-Tamakoshi and Jeanette Dickerson-Putman, at the American Anthropological Association annual meeting. November, Philadelphia.

Rudmin, Floyd W. 2004. "Torture at Abu Ghraib, and the Telling Silence of Social Scientists." *Anthropology News* 45 (6): 9.

Salisbury, M. E., and Richard Salisbury. 1972. "The Rural-Oriented Strategy of Urban Adaptation: Siane Migrants in Port Moresby." In *The Anthropology of Urban Environments*, edited by T. Weaver and D. White, 49–68. Monograph No. 11. Washington, DC: Society for Applied Anthropology.

Salisbury, Richard F. 1962. *From Stone to Steel: Economic Consequences of Technological Change in New Guinea*. Melbourne: Cambridge University Press.

Sanjek, Roger, ed. 1990. *Fieldnotes: The Makings of Anthropology*. Ithaca, NY: Cornell University Press.

Schindlbeck, Markus. 1993. "Einfuhrung." In *Vom Kokos zu Plastik. Sudseekulturen im Wandel*, edited by Markus Schindlbeck. Berlin: Reimer.

Schneider, David. 1968. *American Kinship: A Cultural Account*. Englewood Cliffs, NJ: Prentice Hall.

Schulz, Roland. 2006. "Der Häuptling stirbt." *Süddeutsche Zeitung* 248, October 27, p. 11.

Scudder, Thayer, and Elizabeth Colson. 1982. "From Welfare to Development: A Conceptual Framework for the Analysis of Dislocated People." In *Involuntary Migration and Resettlement: Problems and Responses of Dislocated People*, edited by Art Hansen and Anthony Oliver-Smith, 267–87. Boulder, CO: Westview Press.

Searcy, Alfred. 1905. *In Northern Seas*. Adelaide: W. K. Thomas.

Seligman, C. G. 1932. "Anthropological Perspectives and Psychological Theory." *Journal of the Royal Anthropological Institute of Great Britain and Ireland* 62: 193–228.

Sexton, Lorraine. 1982. "Wok Meri: A Woman's Saving and Exchange System in Highland New Guinea." *Oceania* 54: 133–50.

———. 1987. "The Social Construction of Card Playing Among the Daulo." In

Gambling With Cards in Melanesia and Australia, Special Issue, edited by Laura Zimmer. *Oceania* 58 (1): 38–46.

Shestov, L. 1970. "Children and Stepchildren of Time: Spinoza in History." In *A Shestov Anthology,* edited by M. Martin, 215–43. Athens: Ohio University Press.

———. 1982. *Speculation and Revelation,* translated by B. Martin. Athens: Ohio University Press.

Shore, Bradd. 1996. *Culture in Mind: Cognition, Culture, and the Problem of Meaning.* New York: Oxford University Press.

———. 1999. "Strange Fate of Holism." *Anthropology News.* December. 40 (9): 4–5.

Slocum, Sally. 1975. "Woman the Gatherer: Male Bias in Anthropology." In *Toward an Anthropology of Women,* edited by Rayna R. Reiter, 36–50. New York: Monthly Review Press.

Smith, Michael French. 2002. *Village on the Edge: Changing Times in Papua New Guinea.* Honolulu: University of Hawaii Press.

Somare, Sir Michael. 1974. "Introduction." In *National Cultural Council Annual Report.* Boroko: N. C. D.

———. 1979. "Our Pride and Our Strength." In *The Arts of the People,* Special Issue. *Post Courier,* September 2.

Spencer, Walter Baldwin. 1914. *Native Tribes of the Northern Territory.* London: Macmillan.

———. 1928. *Wanderings in Wild Australia,* Volume 2. London: Macmillan.

Stephens, William. 1963. *The Family in Cross-Cultural Perspective.* New York: Holt, Rinehart and Winston.

Stewart, Pamela J., and Andrew Strathern. 2001. *Humors and Substances: Ideas of the Body in New Guinea.* Westport, CT: Bergin and Garvey.

Stoller, Paul. 1995. *Embodying Colonial Memories: Spirit Possession, Power and the Hauka in West Africa.* New York: Routledge.

———. 2006. "Circuits of African Art/Paths of Wood: Exploring an Anthropological Trail." In *Exploring World Art,* edited by Eric Venbrux, Pamela Rosi, and Robert L. Welsch, 87–110. Long Grove, IL: Waveland Press.

Strathern, Andrew. 1971. *The Rope of Moka: Big-Men and Ceremonial Exchange in Mount Hagen, New Guinea.* Cambridge: Cambridge University Press.

Strathern, Marilyn. 1972. *Women in Between: Female Roles in a Male World, Mount Hagen, New Guinea.* London: Seminar Press.

———. 1975. *No Money on Our Skins: Hagen Migrants in Port Moresby.* New Guinea Research Bulletin No. 61. Port Moresby and Canberra: Australian National University.

———. 1980. "No Nature, No Culture: The Hagen Case." In *Nature, Culture and Gender,* edited by Carol MacCormack and Marilyn Strathern, 174–222. Cambridge: Cambridge University Press.

———. 1987. *Dealing With Inequality: Analyzing Gender Relations in Melanesia and Beyond.* Cambridge: Cambridge University Press.

Sutton, Peter, ed. 1988. *Dreamings: The Art of Aboriginal Australia.* New York: George Braziller/Asia Society.

Swartz, Marc J. 1958. "Sexuality and Aggression on Romonum, Truk." *American Anthropologist* 60: 467–86.

Taussig, Michael. 1993. *Mimesis and Alterity: A Particular History of the Senses.* New York: Routledge.

Taylor, Vance. 1988. *Taim bipo: The Disappearing Traditions and Practices of Papua New Guinea Seen through the Eyes of Young Sogeri Artists.* Sogeri, Papua New Guinea: Expressive Arts Department of Sogeri National High School.

Thomas, Nicholas. 1991. *Entangled Objects: Exchange, Material Culture and Colonialism in the Pacific.* Cambridge, MA: Harvard University Press.

———. 1999. "The Case of the Misplaced Ponchos: Speculations Concerning the History of Cloth in Polynesia." *Journal of Material Culture* 4: 5–20.

Thomas, Philip. 1999. "No Substance, No Kinship? Procreation, Performativity, and Temanambondro Parent-Child Relations." In *Conceiving Persons: Ethnographies of Procreation, Fertility, and Growth,* edited by Peter Loizos and Patrick Heady, 19–45. London: Athlone Press.

Thurston, Lucy C. 1882. *The Life and Times of Mrs. Lucy C. Thurston, Wife of Rev. Asa Thurston, Pioneer Missionary to the Sandwich Islands.* Ann Arbor, MI: S. C. Andrews.

Trawick, Margaret. 1992. *Notes on Love in a Tamil Family.* Berkeley: University of California Press. (Originally published in 1990.)

Tumulty, Amanda Georgia. 1994. "Gender, Fieldwork and the Construction of Knowledge: An Anthropology of Anthropologists." Senior project, Division of Social Studies, Bard College, Annandale-on-Hudson, NY.

Turnbull, C. 1990. "Liminality: A Synthesis of Subjective and Objective Experience." In *By Means of Performance: Intercultural Studies of Theatre and Ritual,* edited by R. Schechner and W. Appel, 50–81. Cambridge: Cambridge University Press.

Turner, Terence. 1971. "Transformation, Hierarchy, and Transcendence." In *Secular Ritual,* S. F. and B.M. Moore, ed. Amsterdam, Netherlands: van Gorcum.

Turner, Victor. 1969. *The Ritual Process: Structure and Anti-Structure.* Chicago: Aldine.

———. 1967. *The Forest of Symbols.* Ithaca: Cornell University Press.

———. 1975. *Schism and Continuity in an African Society: A Study of Ndembu Village Life.* Manchester, England: University of Manchester Press, on behalf of the Rhodes-Livingstone Institute.

Van Allen, Judith. 1976. "'Aba Riots' or Igbo 'Women's War'? Ideology, Stratification, and the Invisibility of Women." In *Women in Africa: Studies in Social and Economic Change,* edited by Nancy J. Hafkin and Edna G. Bay, 59–85. Stanford, CA: Stanford University Press.

Van Gennep, Arnold. 1960. *The Rites of Passage,* translated by M. B. Vizedon and G. L. Caffee. Chicago: University of Chicago Press.

Venbrux, Eric. 1993. "Les politiques de l'emotion dans le rituel funeraire des Tiwi d'Australie." *L'Ethnographie* 89: 61–77.

———. 1995. *A Death in the Tiwi Islands: Conflict, Ritual and Social Life in an Australian Aboriginal Community.* Cambridge: Cambridge University Press.

———. 2000. "Cross with the Totem Pole: Tiwi Material Culture in Missionary Discourse and Practice." In *Anthropology and the Missionary Endeavour,* edited by Ad Borsboom and Jean Kommers. Saarbrucken: Verlag für Entwicklungspolitik.

———. 2001a. "On the Pre-Museum History of Baldwin Spencer's Collection of

Tiwi Artefacts." In *Academic Anthropology and the Museum*, edited by Mary Bouquet. New Directions in Anthropology, 13. Oxford: Berghahn.

———. 2001b. "Nieuwe Perspectives in Het Denken Over Inheemse Volken." In *Over de Grenzen van Het Weten*, edited by Erik Kerstel and Herman Veenhof. Amsterdam: Koninklijke Nederlandse Akademic van Wetenschappen.

———. 2002a. "The Craft of the Spider Woman." In *Pacific Art, Persistence, Chance and Meaning*, edited by Anita Herle et al., 324–36. Honolulu: University of Hawaii Press.

———. 2002b. "The Postcolonial Virtue of Aboriginal Art." *Zeitschrift für Ethnologie* 127: 2.

———. 2003. "'Wild and Barbaric Manners': The Exotic Encountered in a Dutch Account of Australian Aborigines in 1705." *Nederlands Kunsthistorisch Jaarboek/Netherlands Yearbook for the History of Art* (NKJ) 53: 161–80.

———. 2006. "The Postcolonial Virtue of Aboriginal Art from Bathurst and Melville Islands." In *Exploring World Art*, edited by Eric Venbrux, Pamela Rosi, and Robert L. Welsch, 201–23. Long Grove, IL: Waveland Press.

———, Pamela Sheffield Rosi, and Robert L. Welsch, eds. 2006. *Exploring World Art*. Long Grove, IL: Waveland Press.

Warry, Wayne. 1986. "Kafaina: Female Wealth and Power in Chimbu, Papua New Guinea." *Oceania* 57: 4–21.

Watson, James B. 1970. "Society as Organized Flow." *Southwestern Journal of Anthropology* 26: 107–24.

———. 1990. "Other People Do Other Things: Lamarckian Identities in Kainantu Subdistrict, Papua New Guinea." In *Cultural Identity and Ethnicity in the Pacific*, edited by Jocelyn Linnekin and Lin Poyer, 17–41. Honolulu: University of Hawaii Press.

Weiner, Annette. 1976. *Women of Value, Men of Renown: New Perspectives in Trobriand Exchange*. Austin: University of Texas Press.

———. 1983. "From Words to Objects to Magic: Hard Words and the Boundaries of Social Interaction." *Man* (N.S.) 18: 690–709.

———. 1993. "Culture and Our Discontents." Presidential address. American Anthropological Association annual meeting, November, Washington, DC. Revised version published in 1995 as "Culture and Our Discontents." *American Anthropologist* 97 (1): 14–40.

Whitehead, Tony Larry. 1986. "Breakdown, Resolution, and Coherence: The Fieldwork Experiences of a Big, Brown, Pretty-Talking Man in a West Indian Community." In *Self, Sex, and Gender in Cross-Cultural Fieldwork*, edited by Tony Larry Whitehead and Mary Ellen Conaway, 213–39. Urbana: University of Illinois Press.

———, and Mary Ellen Conaway, eds. 1986. *Self, Sex, and Gender in Cross-Cultural Fieldwork*. Urbana: University of Illinois Press.

Wilmsen E. 1989. *A Land Filled With Flies: A Political Economy of the Kalahari*. Chicago: University of Chicago Press.

Wolf, Margery. 1972. *Women and the Family in Rural Taiwan*. Stanford, CA: Stanford University Press.

Yengoyan, Aram A. 1968. "Demographic and Ecological Influences on Aboriginal Australian Marriage Sections." In *Man the Hunter*, edited by Richard B. Lee and Irven deVore, 185–99. Chicago: Aldine.

Zimmer, Laura J. 1979. *Man in the Middle: Melanesian Man as Transactor and Mediator: Making Oneself and Society in the Context of Interregional Exchange.* Master's thesis, Bryn Mawr College, Bryn Mawr, PA.

———. 1983. "Rural-Urban Relations and the Impact of Urban Remittances on the Rural Community." *Research in Melanesia* 7 (1–2): 12–34. Port Moresby: University of Papua New Guinea.

———. 1984. "Pigs, Money, Migrants or Men? Identity Crisis in the Highlands of Papua New Guinea." Paper presented at the American Anthropological Association annual meeting. December, Denver, CO.

———. 1985. *The Losing Game: Exchange, Migration, and Inequality Among the Gende People of Papua New Guinea.* Ph.D. dissertation, Bryn Mawr College, Bryn Mawr, PA.

———. 1986. "Card Playing Among the Gende: A System for Keeping Money and Social Relationships Alive." *Oceania* 56: 245–63.

———. 1987a. "Introduction." *Gambling With Cards in Melanesia and Australia,* Special Issue, edited by Laura J. Zimmer. *Oceania* 58 (1): 1–5.

———. 1987b. "Playing at Being Men." *Gambling With Cards in Melanesia and Australia,* Special Issue, edited by Laura J. Zimmer. *Oceania* 58 (1) 22–37.

———. 1988a. "Development for Whom?" In *Jimi Valley 1987 Rapid Rural Appraisal Report,* edited by James Joughin and Brian Thistleton, 75–79. Department of Agriculture and Livestock, Port Moresby: Government Printers.

———. 1988b. "Land, Society, and Change." In *Jimi Valley 1987 Rapid Rural Appraisal Report,* edited by James Joughin and Brian Thistleton, 18–22. Department of Agriculture and Livestock, Port Moresby: Government Printers.

———. 1990a. "Conflict and Violence in Gende Society: Older Persons as Victims, Trouble-Makers, and Perpetrators." In *Domestic Violence in Oceania,* Special Issue, edited by Dorothy A. Counts. *Pacific Studies* 13 (3): 205–24.

———. 1990b. "When Tomorrow Comes: Future Opportunities and Current Investment Patterns in an Area of High Outmigration." In *Migration and Development in the South Pacific,* edited by John Connell, 82–96. Pacific Research Monograph No. 24. Canberra: National Centre for Development Studies, Australian National University.

Zimmer-Tamakoshi, Laura. 1992. "Constraints on Women and Development in Urban Papua New Guinea." Paper prepared for the Association for Social Anthropology in Oceania meeting. March.

———. 1993a. "Bachelors, Spinsters, and '*Pamuk Meris.*'" In *The Business of Marriage: Transformations in Oceanic Matrimony,* edited by Rick Marksbury, 83–104. Pittsburgh: University of Pittsburgh Press.

———. 1993b. "Nationalism and Sexuality in Papua New Guinea." *Pacific Studies* 16 (4): 61–97.

———. 1995. "Passion, Poetry, and Cultural Politics in the South Pacific." In *Politics of Culture in the Pacific Islands,* Special Issue, edited by Richard Feinberg and Laura Zimmer-Tamakoshi. *Ethnology* 34 (2): 113–27.

———. 1996a. *The Anthropologist in the Field.* Retrieved from http: //www .melanesia.org/fieldwork/tamakoshi/

———. 1996b. "The Women at Kobum Spice Company: Tensions in a Local Age Stratification System and the Undermining of Local Development." *Pacific Studies* 19 (4): 71–98.

————. 1997a. "Empowered Women." In *Social Organization and Cultural Aesthetics: Essays in Honor of William H. Davenport,* edited by William W. Donner and James G. Flanagan, 45–60. Lanham, MD: University Press of America.

————. 1997b. "Everyone (or No One) a Winner: Gende Compensation Ethics and Practices." In *Compensation for Resource Development in Papua New Guinea,* edited by Susan Toft, 66–83. Papua New Guinea Law Reform Commission Monograph No. 6. Port Moresby: Law Reform Commission and Resource Management in Asia and Pacific; Canberra: Research School of Pacific and Asian Studies, Australian National University.

————. 1997c. "Moga-Omoi's Daughters." *South Pacific Journal of Philosophy and Culture* 2: 1–20.

————. 1997d. "The Last Big Man: Development and Men's Discontents in the Papua New Guinea Highlands." *Oceania* 68 (2): 107–22.

————. 1997e. "When Land Has a Price: Ancestral Gerrymandering and the Resolution of Land Conflicts at Kurumbukare." In *Rights to Land and Resources in Papua New Guinea: Changing and Conflicting Views,* Special Issue, edited by Paula Brown and Anton Ploeg. *Anthropological Forum* 7 (4): 649–66.

————. 1997f. "Wild Pigs and Dog Men: Rape and Domestic Violence as Women's Issues in Papua New Guinea." In *Gender in Cross-Cultural Perspective,* edited by C. Brettell and C. Sargent, 538–53. New York: Prentice Hall.

————. 1998. "Women in Town: Housewives, Homemakers, and Household Managers." In *Modern Papua New Guinea,* edited by Laura Zimmer-Tamakoshi, 195–210. Kirksville, MO: Thomas Jefferson University Press.

————. 2000. The Anthropology of Gender. Online course. Bell and Howell.

————. 2001a. "Development and Ancestral Gerrymandering: David Schneider in Papua New Guinea." In *The Cultural Analysis of Kinship: The Legacy of David Schneider and Its Implications for Anthropological Relativism,* edited by Richard Feinberg and Martin Ottenheimer, 187–203. Urbana: University of Illinois Press.

————. 2001b. "Papua New Guinea." In *Countries and Their Cultures,* Volume 3, edited by Carol Ember and Melvin Ember, 1727–40. New York: Macmillan Library Reference.

————. 2004. "Rape and Other Sexual Aggression." *The Encyclopedia of Sex and Gender: Men and Women in the World's Cultures,* Volume 1, edited by Carol Ember and Melvin Ember, 230–43. New York: Kluwer.

————. 2006. "Uncertain Futures, Uncertain Pasts." Paper presented in a working session entitled "Mine Closure in the Pacific: Past Experiences and Anticipated Futures," co-organized by Dan Jorgensen and Glenn Banks, at the Association for Social Anthropology in Oceania annual meeting. February, San Diego, CA.

CONTRIBUTORS

JOY A. BILHARZ (Bryn Mawr Ph.D., 1987) is a professor of anthropology at the State University of New York at Fredonia. She has examined the long-term effects of forced relocation on the Seneca Indians of the Allegany Reservation as well as the effects of female participation in the electoral politics of the Seneca Nation. She has done applied research in the United States and Canada for the U.S. National Park Service, serving as project director and principal investigator on the Mohawk Valley Battlefield Ethnography Project (Parts I and II) documenting the connections of native peoples to historic events in the eighteenth and nineteenth centuries in central New York, especially the participation of Indian warriors in the Battle of Oriskany, in *The Allegany Senecas and Kinzua Dam: Forced Relocation through Two Generations* (1998) and "L'heritage de Kinzua: La reconquete du pouvoir chez les femmes senecas" (with Thomas S. Abler) in *Recherches amerindiennes au Quebec* 29 (2): 51–62 (1999).

JEANETTE DICKERSON-PUTMAN (Bryn Mawr Ph.D., 1986) is an associate professor and chair of the department of anthropology at Indiana University–Indianapolis. She conducted research in the Eastern Highlands Province of Papua New Guinea in 1983–84 that explored how age and gender stratification influenced women's participation in local, regional, and national development. In 1987–88, she joined a cross-cultural aging project and undertook a study of the participation of the elderly in a small town in County Wicklow, Republic of Ireland. Most recently (1994, 2002, and 2004), she conducted research on the French Polynesia island of Raivavae where she is involved in a long-term study of the effects of environmental change and globalization on island life.

MICHÈLE DOMINY is a professor of anthropology and vice president and dean of the college at Bard College, Annandale-on-Hudson. She received her B.A. from Byrn Mawr College in 1975. Jane Goodale instructed her in kinship and social organization, Oceanic ethnography, and supervised her honors thesis. She earned her Ph.D. (1983) in anthropology from Cornell University with areas of specialization in social anthropology and women's studies. The National Science Foundation, Wenner Gren, and the National Endowment for the Humanities have supported her research. She published *Calling the Station Home: Place and Identity in New Zealand's High Country* (Rowman & Littlefield) in 2001, and has published articles in *American Ethnologist, Anthropological Forum, Anthropology Today, Cultural Anthropology, Current Anthropology, Journal of Cultural Geographies, Landscape Review, Pacific Studies, Signs,* and Association for Social Anthropology in Oceania (ASAO)–edited volumes. She is a former board member and chair of ASAO and former ASAO monograph series editor. She recently served on the *American Anthropologist* editorial board.

WILLIAM W. DONNER, as an undergraduate at Haverford College in 1969, took Introduction to Anthropology at Bryn Mawr College from Jane Goodale. He became a major in anthropology at Bryn Mawr and did an undergraduate honors thesis with Jane. He received his Ph.D. in anthropology from the University of Pennsylvania (Jane was a member of his dissertation committee). He has done long-term research among the Sikaiana people of the Solomon Islands in 1980–83, 1987, and 1993. More recently, he has done research on Pennsylvania German culture and language. He has published articles in *Man* (journal of the Royal Anthropological Society), *Ethnology, Pacific Studies, Journal of the Polynesian Society, Sociological Inquiry, Pennsylvania Magazine of Biography and History,* and *Der Reggeboge* (journal of the Pennsylvania German Society), among other journals.

JANE FAJANS is an associate professor of anthropology at Cornell University. She has worked with the Baining of East New Britain, Papua New Guinea. She was an undergraduate at Bryn Mawr College where she first became interested in Melanesia through her studies with Jane Goodale. She received her B.A. from Bryn Mawr in 1971 and her Ph.D. from Stanford University. She is the author of *They Make Themselves: Work and Play Among the Baining of Papua New Guinea* and editor of *Exchanging Products: Producing Exchange,* Oceania Monograph 43. She has written on emotion and personhood and has an article on "Autonomy and Relatedness" that is forthcoming in *Critique of Anthropology.* She is currently beginning research on regional foods and regional identity in Brazil and Portugal.

MIRIAM KAHN (Bryn Mawr Ph.D., 1980) is a professor and chair of anthropology at the University of Washington, Seattle. She conducted research in Papua New Guinea in 1976–78 and 1981–82 and in French Polynesia in 1994, 1995, 1996, and 2001. She is the author of *Always Hungry, Never Greedy: Food and the Expression of Gender in a Melanesian Society* (Cambridge University Press, 1986) and coauthor (with Erin Younger) of *Pacific Voices: Keeping Our Cultures Alive* (University of Washington Press, 2005). She is currently completing a book on the politics of place in French Polynesia.

MICHAEL D. LIEBER is a professor of anthropology at the University of Illinois at Chicago. He has conducted field research with the western Shoshone of central Nevada; with African American men in Pittsburgh, Reno, and Seattle; and with the Kapingamarangi people on Kapingamarangi atoll and Pohnpei Island in Micronesia since 1965, and has done evaluation research on university–community collaboration with the University of Illinois at Chicago, Loyola University, University of Chicago, and their partners in communities on the south and west sides of Chicago. He was a visiting professor at Bryn Mawr College in 1985. He is the author of *More Than a Living: Fishing and the Social Order on a Polynesian Atoll* (1994).

DEBORAH BIRD ROSE is a senior fellow in the Centre for Research and Environmental Studies, Institute of Advanced Studies, at the Australian National University, and a fellow of the Academy of Social Sciences in Australia. She writes widely in the fields of anthropology, history, philosophy, and religious studies. She is the author of prize-winning books, and has most recently published *Reports from a Wild Country: Ethics for Decolonisation* (UNSW Press, 2004). She has worked with Aboriginal people in their claims to land and in other decolonizing contexts. Her work in both scholarly and practical arenas is focused on the convergence of social and ecological justice in cross-cultural domains.

PAMELA SHEFFIELD ROSI (Bryn Mawr Ph.D., 1994) teaches in the Anthropology Department at Bridgewater State College, Massachusetts. Her research focuses on the contemporary arts of Papua New Guinea (PNG) and the contested contributions of art to emergent national PNG culture and identity. In addition to articles and book chapters, she has also curated exhibitions of contemporary PNG art in several academic venues in the United States and, in 2003, at the Nijmeegs Volkenkundig

Museum at the University of Nijmegen, the Netherlands. In 2003 and 2004, she coedited with Eric Venbrux (Radboud University Nijmegen) "Introduction to Conceptualizing World Art Studies," which appeared in the *International Journal of Anthropology* 18 (4), and "Confronting World Art," a special issue of *Visual Anthropology* 17(3–4). She is presently coediting with Robert Welsch (Dartmouth College) and Eric Venbrux (Radboud University) *Exploring World Art* (Waveland Press, 2006).

ERIC VENBRUX is a professor of anthropology at Radboud University in Nijmegen, the Netherlands. He has worked with the Tiwi from Bathurst and Melville Islands, Australia, since 1988. Jane Goodale gave him the most helpful advice before he went to the Tiwi. Jane then had been principal lecturer in Darwin for a year; she filled the position that Eric's supervisor Ad Borsboom was prevented from taking by the Australian authorities. At Bryn Mawr, Longina Jakubowska, the wife of Eric's other professor (Anton Blok), happened to replace Jane. Eric is indebted to Jane for the invaluable support and inspiration she so generously gave him, and also later on in obtaining a research fellowship of the Royal Netherlands Academy of Arts and Sciences and the subsequent research into Tiwi art history. From this emerged an interest in world art, leading to a collaborative project with Pamela Rosi, whose innovative work on contemporary Papua New Guinea art had been encouraged by Jane. Having studied under Anton Blok, Eric also specialized in the field of European ethnology. He conducted fieldwork in Switzerland and the Netherlands, and worked in the Department of European Ethnology and Folklore at the Meertens Institute in Amsterdam. He is combining his interest in narratives, material culture, and ritual—topics on which he has published extensively—in a new project on innovation in death rites, which aims to gain a better understanding of ritual change. He is the author of *A Death in the Tiwi Islands: Conflict, Ritual and Social Life in an Australian Aboriginal Community* (Cambridge University Press, 1995). In 2007, he coedited with Pierre Lemonnier "Hertz revisité: Objects et changements dans les rituels funéraires," a special issue of the Journal de la Société des Océanistes 124 (1).

LAURA ZIMMER-TAMAKOSHI (Bryn Mawr Ph.D., 1985) has worked in Papua New Guinea since her 1982–83 dissertation research with the Gende people, returning often as fieldworker, consultant, and university professor (1986–90, 1994,1995, 2000, and 2007). Her interests include development, inequality, violence against women, the politics of culture and sexuality, and the Internet as a teaching tool. Notable works and professional roles include *The Anthropologist in the Field*, www.ianth. org/fieldwork/tamakoshil/ (1996–present), her edited volume *Modern Papua New Guinea* (1998), her roles as the first visual media review editor for *Pacific Studies* (1996–2001) and board member (1999–2001) and chair of Association for Social Anthropology in Oceania (ASAO) (1999–2000), and her cross-cultural overview of "Rape and Other Sexual Aggression" in the *Encyclopedia of Sex and Gender* (edited by Carol and Melvin Ember, 2004). Now retired from teaching, Laura has taught at West Chester University, the University of Papua New Guinea, Bryn Mawr College, the University of Pennsylvania, and, most recently, as an associate professor of anthropology at Truman State University in Missouri (1991–2001). She is currently a research associate at Bryn Mawr College and engaged in research (including fieldwork in Papua New Guinea and research at the State, Society and Governance in Melanesia Programme at Australian National University) on "Troubled Masculinities in Melanesia" and the impact of two big mines on Gende gender and intergenerational relations.

INDEX

cross-cultural and human friendship,
91, 93; every action is, 82, 88; failure to
be fully human, 116; the human component, 80
Huntsman, Judith, 6, 16, 25; brother-sister
relations, 63; pig lunch, 138; Tokelau
data, 44
Hymes, Dell, 15

imagined communities, 101
indigenous: anthropology, 19; collaboration with indigenous peoples, 19; land
and environmental issues, 22
Inhorn, M. C. and P. J. Brown, 170
Institute of Applied Social and Economic
Research, 66. *See also* National Research Institute
intercultural space, 4, 168, 170
intergenerational conflict, 72
Internationl Congress of Anthropological
and Ethnological Sciences, 146
intersubjectivity, 120
*Introduction to Anthropology: A Self
Guide* (Maranda), 44, 78–79, 83, 133
invention of culture, 16
Iroquois Nations, 146

Jackson, Chantal, 8
Jackson, Jean, 59
Jamparipari (Tiwi spirit), 171, 179–83 pas-
sim, 186n31
Jimi, 73
Johnson, Asa, 28
Johnson, Pauline, 147
Joseph, Rebecca, 146
Journal of International Anthropology, 96

Kaberry, Phyllis M., 32, 58
Kahn, Miriam, 4, 5, 7, 8, 52, 81, 84, 86,
106, 111
Kapingamarangi, 5, 126
Kaplan, Martha, 48
Kasaipwalova, John, 97
Kasfir, Sydney, 95
Kauage (PNG artist), 99
Kaulong, 5, 44, 221; comparisons with
Tiwi, 8, 39; cultural models, 9; ideas of
personhood, 81; "skull exchange is the
thread," 49
Keesing, Roger M., 1, 47–48
Kerbo/Korupu, 169, 171–79 passim,
183n8, 184n14; Jane's Tiwi great-grand-
father, 172
Kilbride, Philip L., vii, 7, 29, 31, 40, 41,
217
Kimberley mountains, 32

Kimmel, Michael S. and Michael A. Messner, 58
kinship: ancestral gerrymandering, 72;
systems, 214
Kinzua Dam Reseroir, 140, 141
Kluckholn, Clyde, 29, 46
Knauft, Bruce, 106
knowledge in Oceania: ASAO sessions,
126; Kapingamarangi and Kaulong
knowledge systems compared, 126–29;
relation between knowledge and personhood, 130
Kobum Spice Company: short-lived Gende
development, 69
Kroeber, Alfred, 29–30, 31
Kulama yam ceremony, 100, 168, 170,
172, 176–179, 182–83, 219–20; kulama
yam a key symbol, 170, 177
Kulick, Don and Margaret Willson, 59
Kundun, Gickmai (PNG sculptor), 105
Kurumbukare (Ramu Nickel mine site),
72, 73

Laguna, Frederica de, vii, 2, 10, 125, 214;
style sheet for taking notes in anthro-
pology/dialectical notebooks, 39–40, 45
Lamarckian identity, 129, 130; Kap-
ingamarangi and Kainantu, 131; Pom-
ponio contrasts between Siassi and
Tairora, 131
Landes, Ruth, 18
Langness, L. L., 62
Lawrence, Peter, 16
Leach, Edmund, 50
Leacock, Eleanor: marginalization of Ruth
Landes' *Ojibwa Woman,* 19
Leahy, Joe, 71
Lefebvre, Henri, 86
Lepowsky, Maria, 1
Levinas, Emmanuel, 119–20
Levi-Strauss, Claude, 44; nature/culture
distinction, 46
Lewis-Harris, Jacquelyn, 102
Lieber, Michael, 5, 6, 7, 93, 122, 130; co-
founder of ASAO, 126
*The Life and Times of Mrs. Lucy C.
Thurston, Wife of Rev. Asa Thurston,
Pioneer Missionary to the Sandwich
Islands* (Thurston), 27
"The Limitations of the Comparative
Method of Anthropology" (Boas), 24
Lincoln, Bruce, 164
Lincoln, Louise, 106
Lindstrom, Lamont, 73, 97
Linnekin, Jocelyn, 129
Linton, Ralph and Paul S. Wingert, 93

The University of Illinois Press
is a founding member of the
Association of American University Presses.

Composed in 9.5/12.5 Trump Mediaeval
by Jim Proefrock
at the University of Illinois Press.
Manufactured by Sheridan Books, Inc.

University of Illinois Press
1325 South Oak Street
Champaign, IL 61820-6903
www.press.uillinois.edu